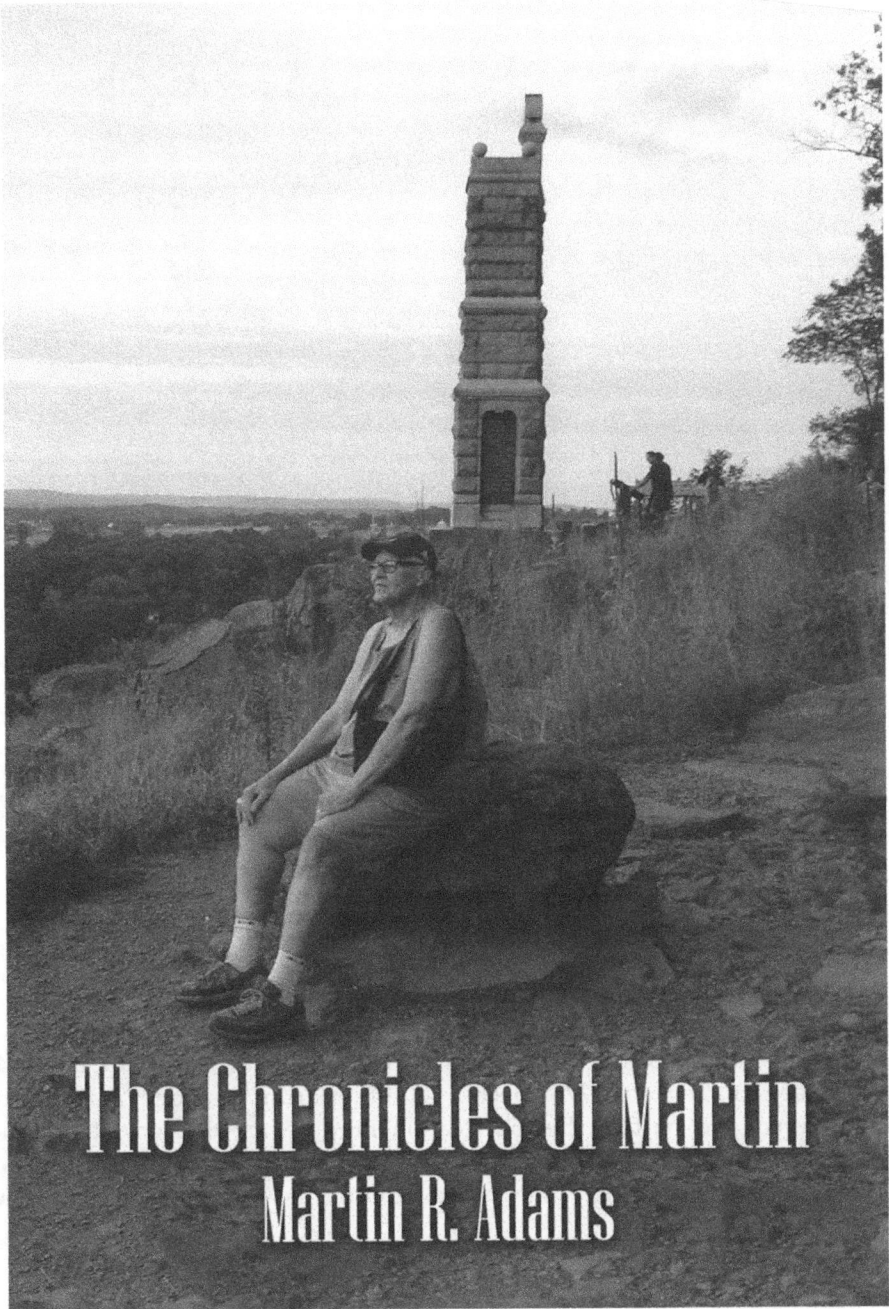

The Chronicles of Martin
Martin R. Adams

Cover Photo:

A late afternoon visit to Little Round Top; Martin looks out over the Gettysburg Battlefield.

Photo by M.H. Adams

"The Chronicles of Martin," by Martin R. Adams.
ISBN: 978-1-62137-464-0 (Softcover); 978-1-62137-465-7 (eBook).

Library of Congress Control Number: 2014933467

Manufactured in the United States of America.

TABLE OF CONTENTS

DEDICATION

The memories, thoughts and ideas contained in this work are dedicated to my two children and step-daughter and to their children ---- and to any others desiring to learn about my journey, experiences and beliefs.

To Sallie Lesue, Samuel Mason and Heather Ellen and to my grandchildren:

Martin Albert, Anna Sage, Jack King, Daniel Scott and William David.

INSPIRATION

Born in the flesh January 27,1936,I lived a natural life until being reborn in the Spirit by the Grace of God through Jesus Christ, April 14, 1974.Twenty years later May 28,1994, on the occasion of marrying the love of my life, Margery Temple Hughes, God began His work of Redemption and Sanctification in me, which continues to this day. It's no coincidence that my determination to no longer consume alcohol of any kind began then. Now I have accumulated twenty years of sobriety.

God has seen fit to bless my life in many ways, including the gift of children and their children; reasonable mental and physical health; great friends; and enough material substance to live reasonably well. Praising God and thanking Him for His grace and mercies, my life with Margery in Jesus Christ has made all the difference. She has been and is His answer to the prayers of my life.

Margery is the very essence of the ideal wife described beautifully by King Lemuel in the Book of Proverbs, Chapter 31, verses 10 – 31..... "She is far more precious than jewels...the heart of her husband trusts in her, and he will have no lack of gain...she does him good and not harm, all the days of her life...she rises while it is still night and provides food for her household...she girds herself with strength...she opens her hand to the poor and reaches out to the needy...she makes garments and sells them...she opens her mouth with wisdom, and kindness is on her tongue...her husband says 'many women have done excellently, but you surpass them all'...charm is deceitful, and beauty is vain, but a woman who fears the Lord is to be praised"...

ACKNOWLEDGMENTS

Help. Technical Help. Understanding the interface between my computer and my mind. I am thankful for the help and support of two specific people. First, Anna Cronberg of Brazos Valley Computers for technical assistance. Second, the efforts of Carroll Hedrick, Copy Corner in College Station, in providing formatting and fine tuning to make this book possible.

PROLOGUE

You are about to begin a journey with me down my particular road in life. I want my children, grandchildren and others to read, understand and perhaps reread my story, learning more about me and hopefully about themselves, life in the fast lane, and the miracle of God's love and grace. This work consists of three parts----BOOK ONE, My Beginnings, is my life's story. BOOK TWO tells you about my drinking life as an alcoholic, and my recovery. BOOK THREE is a collection of Essays I have written over the years.

BOOK ONE discusses three distinctly different parts of my life---1) Before I knew Jesus Christ as my Lord and Savior---2) After He became my Lord and Savior---3) Then Redemption and Sanctification, moving me to a closer, more intimate relationship with Him.

The first part of my life spanned about 38 years. It was marked by successes, sometimes confusion, occasional heartaches, and some unfulfilled dreams. It was characterized by self-striving and after my considerable successes, failure.

The second part covered about 20 years, after I came to know Jesus Christ as my Lord and Savior. I continued living in the world, occasionally drinking to excess, sometimes womanizing, and striving harder than ever to achieve my goals. I still wanted badly to have my own way. Some would say this part of my life exemplifies " carnal Christianity". Others would question whether I had met Jesus Christ at all twenty years earlier. Regardless, I absolutely knew in my heart and believed totally that if I died, I would be in heaven-- in the arms of Jesus Christ. The old question about whether one can lose his salvation was settled in my heart. I had never committed that unpardonable sin as I understand it, declaring overtly or covertly that I reject and renounce Jesus Christ as my Savior. I was satisfied knowing I was saved for all eternity, certain beyond all doubt that Jesus Christ was and is my Savior.

Twenty years passed before events in my life conspired for the Lord to begin the process of Sanctification, in which I was drawn into a much deeper relationship with Christ Jesus than I had ever known or imagined. Sometimes I have to pinch myself to realize I'm that person Christ changed.

No, I haven't emoted into Mr. Goody Two Shoes by any means. But my entire outlook has been changed by the hands of God during the past twenty years. I sometimes wonder if this Martin would succeed again today as a businessman in the cutthroat world in which I've lived. The short answer is "yes", because I am led by the Lord whether into success or failure. God changed my desires when I got out of His way.

Finally I wanted Him to have His way with me. I wanted to walk so close to Him that I would KNOW His will for me. I knew alcohol had stood between me and my desire for that fuller richer fellowship with Him. I wearied of analyzing everything to death and just finally decided to rest in His will for me.

Joy and contentment generally characterize my life, joy beyond anything I knew during those first 58 years. I don't want to disobey the Lord. Sins of the flesh no longer please or fulfill me. In fact I want to avoid committing sin, looking daily to the Lord to help me.

Thank you for letting me share my story with you. It's a long personal journey, from my provincial upbringings ultimately to my life with Christ Jesus. I think many who walk in the ways of the world, eventually coming out the other end, will identify with my experiences. This is meant to be a source of encouragement to you. If sometimes it seems to you like all is lost and there is no way out, my story is for you.

During the last 20 years, I've written many essays covering a variety of topics. Many are spiritual, some are philosophical, and some are simply my analytical way of looking at things. I've collected those I believe you'll enjoy into BOOK THREE---ESSAYS. Please read them slowly and thoughtfully-- maybe only one or two at a time. Think about what you've read afterwards. Maybe some light will shine on things you may have wondered about. Reread them, and see if they help with riddles in your life.

Martin R. Adams, September, 2013

College Station, Texas

"And we know that in all things God works for the good of those who love him, who have been called according to his purpose."

Romans 8:28 (NRSV)

BOOK ONE:
MY BEGINNINGS

MY CHILDHOOD

S he never let him forget that he missed the blessed event of my birth.....

It was a cold snowy day in East Texas that January 27 morning in 1936. He was making his way back to Longview after delivering a prisoner to authorities in Dallas and he was caught in a snowstorm.

Her best friend, one of my namesakes, Rachel Owens, comforted her that morning at Markham McCree Hospital in Longview, while Dr. W. P. Farrar delivered me. I was an 8 pound 11 ounce 'bouncing baby boy,' and Dr. Farrar immediately christened me "Right Tackle for the Longview High School Lobos." Of course, I don't remember the events of that morning; all I know is the lore that I was told over the years.

I was named Martin in honor of my dad's mentor Martin Hayes, the Gregg County Sheriff and my dad's old boss, and Ray for Rachel, my mom's best friend and my dad's stand-in at the birth. They would have named me Sunni, if I'd been a girl. In light of this, they hung the nickname, Sonny, on me. I absolutely hated this moniker, finally leaving it behind in favor of Martin when I started school. My mom and dad were exceptions, never calling me by my proper name. They both insisted on calling me Sonny all the way to life's end!

I inherited physical traits from both parents, nothing unusual about that. Like it or not, many physical traits pass on from generation to generation. Over time, some disappear through breeding. I got my 6-foot 4-inch height from my dad, who was the same height.

His must have come from his father, Wylie, because his mother, my Grandma, was a short, dumpy little thing. I also inherited dad's dark eyes and a tendency toward darker skin tone, especially brought out by exposure to direct sunlight. My dad had trim, muscular legs and a chest so thick a special setup was needed for his annual chest x-rays.

I, unfortunately, inherited my mother's tendency for a large belly, bottom and legs. These were difficult characteristics for me to deal with in organized sports like football and baseball. I was simply too slow, too bottom heavy and clumsy to become a viable footballer or baseballer. How I wanted it to be different! Unfortunately, I also got my mom's bad feet, bunionated and hammertoed, causing me grief in adult life, requiring considerable surgeries. Mother, in turn, inherited these unfortunate traits from her mother Zona's side of the house. I will always regret passing on bad feet to my dear daughter, but mercifully my son was spared. Balding by my twenty first birthday was another characteristic of mother's family, and showed up prominently in her brother Everett, my uncle.

Hopefully I inherited a good brain from both parents.

Dad was the newly minted Chief of Police in Longview, Texas, our prosperous hometown in East Texas. Mother helped make ends meet working as a long distance telephone operator for Southwestern Bell Telephone Company. She worked in that capacity for forty years, retiring in the mid 1960's as a pensioner.

All together, I suppose we had a strange household. My dad's mother, Sarah, and my mother's mother, Zona, both lived with us under one small roof. My parents employed a live-in, Virginia (Ginna) to take care of me in exchange for room and board. She was attending school, planning to become a nurse. It must have been terribly cramped in that small two bedroom house with only a single bathroom and a living room converted to sleeping space for Virginia. The two grandmothers shared a room. My mom, dad and I bunked in the same bedroom.

It was 1936, and America still struggled with the ravages of the Great Depression. There was no money to be had anywhere, and just about everyone had a hard time making ends meet. But the big oil boom had propelled East Texas into the limelight as one of the few bright spots in the nation. Hoards of people rushed to East Texas, living in tents and any other kind of shelter they could find, just to get a play in the oilfield. Some adventurers like the Hunts, Murchinsons and a few others had hit a bonanza, so many others hoped to hit it rich too.

Somehow our modest kitchen met the needs of our six-person family. It had an ice box, really and truly, keeping things cool with a 25 pound block of ice dad loaded in every day. I have no recollection of whose job it was to empty the water collected from the melted ice. The kitchen had a four burner gas stove with an oven. Meals were taken around an enamel kitchen table. We must have eaten in shifts, the grandmothers waiting their turn on the back porch where they could enjoy dipping snuff and shelling fresh peas. My dad kept them supplied with "toothbrushes", twigs from a sweet gum tree with the ends frayed.
I fondly remember Lou the red rooster, always perched on the back of

my chair at mealtimes, no kidding. One day Lou didn't show up for dinner. They all said the "Appetite" had gotten Lou. In my childhood mind I thought Appetite was some kind of cruel ogre that ate innocent chickens and maybe even little children.

It was hot as blazes in the little house on Park Street. We never heard of home air conditioning in 1939, and comforted ourselves with several whirring electric fans around the house. They did little more than beat the fetid air around. The grandmothers fluttered old straw fans, blotting sweat with hand towels. Soon we would have the luxury of an attic fan, drawing air from the outside through open windows up through a large grill vent in the ceiling then expelling the air back outside. Sometimes mother sprinkled beds at night to put a little moisture on the sheets while the outside air was sucked in through the windows letting evaporative cooling do its magic. Crazy as this might sound in modern times, it gave us respite from the torrid Texas heat of the day when temperatures could exceed 100° for weeks at a time.

One hot afternoon, I dreamed a large black sedan was flying down Park Street about treetop high. It spread an unbelievably foul odor in its wake. All these years later I distinctly recall the dream. Soon the car was out of sight, but the obnoxious smell remained. I awoke wringing wet with sweat, naked as a little picked chicken. I decided to sneak out the front door while no one was looking and check out this strange thing, wondering if it was real. Dirt streets were topped with a heavy coating of oil-- there wasn't much in the way of concrete or asphalt in residential areas. Thinking I was really getting away with something, I stepped barefooted and naked onto the black oil surface. I didn't realize the street was like a hot plate in the blazing sun and the gooy semi-melted oil would stick to the bottoms of my feet like blazing glue. Mother had been taking all this in, watching from the front door. She laughed as she carried me in to soak my burned little feet in kerosene, dissolving the goo, then drying me off lovingly. The black gumbo was gone. She said the foul odor I smelled was indeed real and had come from a neighbor's kitchen where they were pickling cucumbers. It wasn't from the mysterious flying black car.

Park Street ran North and South for a quarter of a mile, parallel to and alongside the city park, thus the name Park Street. I was endlessly fascinated by the big road graders and oil spray trucks plying their way up and down our street once or twice a year. I loved the smell of oil sprayed down on the plowed up road so it could be worked in with the big fork and grader blade. I thought those big machines going up and down the street were about the coolest things imaginable, hoping someday I might be driving big machines like those. I was equally attracted to the large grotesque looking street sweeping machines that made their way around the city in the middle of the night, headlights shining like two eyes in the dark. I thought they had a neat smell too, but then again I've always been told my sense of what smells good is unique. I guess I've always been a little weird in my likes and dislikes.

Old Mr. Woodall's house was next door. He was an old time fiddler, hosting dances most Saturday nights to the tunes ground out by his little band. He charged a quarter (two bits) per head, and no booze was allowed. Mr. Woodall was the paternal head of the Woodall clan scattered throughout the area. There must have been nothing in his wardrobe but old faded blue overalls, a long sleeved khaki shirt and a floppy old sweat stained brown felt hat that had seen better times. He was a kindly old gentleman who said few words and walked or took the bus everywhere he went.

Directly across the street from our house was the commodious home of Mr. and Mrs. Pete Campbell. The size and style of the Campbell's place definitely was a misfit in our modest neighborhood. Mr. Campbell had been successful in the East Texas oil business. They enjoyed the luxury of a live-in yard man (Tom--no last name) and a full-time live-in maid cook and housekeeper, Nanny. The Campbells were in their 60's and, with no grandchildren of their own, they literally took me in. My guess is they had owned much of the property up and down the street and had sold it off bit by bit. Their house had beautiful hardwood floors adorned with fine Oriental rugs. I enjoyed playing on the Orientals as Nanny pushed the vacuum cleaner around. I was fascinated by its sound and how it sucked up everything in its path.

Old Tom lived above the Campbells' garage in a small apartment. He used the stairs outside the garage to get to and from his place. The Campbells' big black Chrysler dominated the garage below. Mrs. Campbell was the sole driver, as Mr. Pete was chronically ill and usually bedridden.

A goldfish pond, shaped like a giant's footprint, was the centerpiece of the back yard. The sides and top were natural East Texas porous red stone, smelling peculiarly metallic, like iron ore. Stones like these were plentiful in East Texas and often used to build facades and porticos.

They always emitted a characteristic metallic smell. A large willow spread its shade over the pond. This was really a great spot for me on hot summer afternoons as Tom worked nearby, keeping an eye on me. One afternoon I leaped into the pond and was startled, suddenly imagining killer goldfish were nibbling my legs. I jumped out screaming at the top of my lungs that I had been attacked by a swarm of goldfish. Tom, Nanny and Mrs. Campbell rushed to my rescue and, relieved, had a big laugh, wiping the tears from my eyes. Those vicious goldfish bites, while preposterous, won me a dish of Nanny's delicious homemade ice cream. I must have decided that afternoon that the stunt of "crying wolf" can bring rewards I hadn't counted on.

Martin Hayes, the oil rich straight arrow Sheriff of Gregg County, owned our house and other houses in Longview. He rented the Park Street house to his protégé, my dad, for a pittance. By 1939, he began prodding my dad to stop paying rent and invest in a home. Mr. Hayes wanted my parents to buy a house he owned in the same neighborhood, one street over, on Harrison Street. Finally dad relented, agreeing to a price of $3000, believing it to be a better fit for the family. Mr. Hayes held the mortgage and gave my dad liberal terms. The $3000 price was a little more than a year's wages for our family. Buying 235 Harrison St. was a huge step, as they had always "thought poor", while in fact they might have actually been considered middle class, at the lower end of the spectrum.

Harrison Street ran north and south two miles, parallel to Park Street a block over. Both ends of Harrison were totally black neighborhoods. In between, along the length of Harrison, was strictly blue collar. Everything was segregated then — schools, city playgrounds, public restrooms and drinking fountains. Blacks rode in the rear of buses, and in upstairs balconies at movie theaters. Prudent white movie goers always sat towards the rear, underneath the upstairs black seating to avoid being hit by unsavory missiles from above. Integrated sports hadn't been thought of, and black-white boy-girl relationships were unimaginable except among the "trashiest of people."

Our neighborhood was home to several police officers who worked for my dad. I never understood why so many of them clustered in the Harrison-Park Street area, but they did. Like shoe stores clustering near one another in a city, police officers in Longview seemed to do the same thing. Buster and Zellie Calloway, Marvin and Irene Woodall, Mr. And Mrs. Spiller, Glen Bean, and others. Mr. And Mrs. Spivey

Eubanks Sr. lived next door in a large house. The Eubanks family were house painters and wall paperers. Sons Richard and David, their wives and children all were neighbors. The brothers worked for their dad. Our neighborhood was definitely considered one of Longview's safest, with my dad holding down the fort.

Lots of foot traffic traveled Harrison Street, mostly black, traipsing from one end to the other. Harrison Street to the south dead ended into Nelson Street, the length of which was known as "Niggertown". It's horrible to remember that term was widely used in reference to people of color. Nelson Street was a big draw for blacks-- there were grocery stores, cafés, barbershops, hair salons, churches--just about everything needed by the segregated black community. The once famous East Texas Cotton Club where Billy Eckstein and Fatha Hines once appeared was at the heart of Nelson Street.

Clyde Whitfield, an adult white man, walked back and forth the length of Harrison Street every day, constantly clenching and unclenching his fists as he walked, turning his head from side to side with a toothless grin. He never spoke, yet he was absolutely frightening to us kids. I'm sure he was harmless, but "you could never be sure what someone like that might do". The floppy brimmed hat and red suspenders holding up old faded baggy pants made him even stranger looking. Mother was sure she knew the source of Clyde's problem, and by telling me about it she hoped I wouldn't do what Clyde purportedly did---he "played with himself when he was a little boy, and became that way. He will never be normal." That scared me out of my wits and made me want to "be a good boy" in spite of my budding awareness of the opposite sex.

Nelson Street was a lively source of business for the Police Department on Saturday nights, as there were fights, shootings, stabbings, drunkenness and general rabble rousing. Once in a while there were killings. But on Sunday mornings the churches along Nelson Street were packed to the rafters all day long, and picnics covered church grounds, as congregations visited and prepared to return to evening service.

The Missouri Pacific Railroad tracks ran alongside and parallel to Nelson Street, before reaching the depot near downtown. MOPAC, as it was known, connects San Antonio and the southern corridor of Texas with St. Louis, Missouri to the north by way of Longview. Our town was an important rail cross road because the East-West line, Texas Pacific, also came through Longview making our town important enough to justify a roundhouse and major repair shop. Two passenger trains passed North and South, East and West, four in all every day. I often rode my Western Flyer bike down Harrison Street to Nelson, even though it was on the edge of taboo territory. It was a thrill to watch the mighty locomotives pass. Engineers always waved and blasted out a loud honk. During the war, giant steam locomotives pulled long strings of black passenger cars on these tracks. Some of the trains pulled by the steam giants were called Sunshine Specials, and were rumored to hit speeds of 80 or 90 mph on long straightaways in West Texas.

Soon after the war ended, the giant steam locomotives were replaced by fancy blue and cream colored diesel engines, called Texas Eagles, each with a large silver eagle adorning their noses. The sights and sounds of these magnificent machines blew me away whenever I saw them, and engineers always blasted the air horn, waving as they passed. I loved the speedy, sleek looking diesel streamliners, but it just didn't seem right that they continued to pull a string of the same old black passenger cars. Once in a while, a shiny new car that matched the fancy blue and cream locomotive showed up. I was thrilled at the thought that some afternoon I might see an entire matching set of locomotive and cars speeding by. I didn't realize it was all just a matter of economics, having nothing to do with aesthetics.

Mother and dad knew how I was really excited by the new breed of streamlined diesel locomotives. They got me a Lionel electric train set for Christmas, complete with switches, lights, transformer, the whole works. It was styled after New York Central's Century Limited, running from New York City west. The Limited was actually powered by a streamlined high speed steam locomotive, not a diesel engine, but that didn't matter to me. It was one of my favorite toys of all time, and I played with it for hours on end. But my introduction to the train was marred by having to lie uncomfortably on the living room floor, on my stomach, to operate it. I couldn't sit on my butt because I had suffered second degree burns on my rear the night before, Christmas Eve. I accidentally sat atop a hot gas stove warming myself after a bath. I had to lie on my stomach the rest of the Holidays. I never had to be warned again about touching hot stoves.

My dad blew me away when out of nowhere one morning he invited me to ride with him to Dallas on the new Texas Eagle to attend the State Fair of Texas. Visits to Longview's rail yards, roundhouse and repair shops had already boosted the grandeur of railroading in my mind, and I fantasized that someday I would sit at the throttle of a streamliner like the Eagle. I was awed by the powerful roar of its diesels and blasts from its big air horns—oooowah, oooowah---so different from the toooot, toooot, toooot coming from steam locomotives.

I hardly slept the night before our trip. It was early October, the sky was blue and the morning air was crisp. The Eagle was scheduled to depart in the early morning, and mother served us a good breakfast, sending us on our way to a great adventure. As always, my dad looked like a million bucks in suit, tie and Stetson. I was thrilled to be on that train with him, even if I was disappointed that all the passenger cars were of the old black vintage. Once inside, I was surprised our car was very clean and comfortable. As the Eagle rolled out of the station, I imagined it sprouting wings as if to fly.

Along the way we met an oncoming Eagle traveling at high speed as was our Eagle—whoosh--our car swayed from the sudden burst of air pressure between the trains. Experiencing such power gave me a thrill!

After an hour or so, I started getting sick at my stomach, probably because I had gotten so excited. I tossed up breakfast. Dad was very comforting and, once in Dallas, we took a taxi to the Medical Arts Building downtown to get help. Soon a doctor looked me over, gave me a sedative and sent us on our way to enjoy the fair. I was touched that day by my dad's tenderness, thoughtfulness and how this gentle giant had taken care of me. It felt really nice.

We had a fabulous day at the fair, generally steering clear of the enormous midway with its exciting rides, except for bumper cars which were safe for my sensitive tummy. I rode a couple of times and had a blast, ramming as many cars as I could. The highlight of the day was taking in a Jimmy Durante show with Harry James and his big band.

We rode the late Eagle home, pooped but joyful. I got to be with my dad up close seeing through that impenetrable veil that often covered him as the chief law enforcer in our town. It was one of the best days ever with him, just the two of us out on an adventure. The only other experiences that came close were our times together in the woods.

By the time we moved to 235 Harrison Street, mother's mom had passed but we still had Grandma with us. I was four and had outgrown my babysitter Ginna. My parents hired Annesta Myles to look after me and keep house. My mom helped Ginna move on to nursing school in Dallas, training at Parkland Hospital.(After the war, she married Tex Braun, a war veteran turned rancher, and became a successful nurse in New Braunfels,Texas).

But it was an odd setup in our house—at least I always felt funny about it—I didn't know anybody else whose home ran like ours. Grandma's room was the choicest in the house, up front with windows on the side and front, a door to the front porch and a doorway to the living room. A short hallway connected Grandma's room to a back bedroom, intersected in the middle by another short hallway to the one bathroom in the house. Closets were few—many houses had only one or two good ones. Grandma's room had the best closet in the house and a smaller one was in the back bedroom. Our bathroom included a small closet. I don't know how we made it all work, but we did. Behind the back bedroom was a screened porch. It was also adjacent to our kitchen. We had a decent sized dining room adjoining the kitchen, and the living room up front adjoined the dining room and Grandma's bedroom.

Now the odd thing was how we used space. With Grandma up front, my mom and I shared the back bedroom. She had a double bed, and my little bed was next to the two windows. Dad slept on the back screened porch. In winter a rolling tarp dropped over his window screens and in summer, the tarp was up. Fresh air rushed in through screens and windows, drawn by the attic fan. Our dining room was used for meals when we had guests. At other times, dad often studied law enforcement materials and lessons from Texas A&M at the dining table. We usually took meals at a small table in the kitchen. Grandma rarely ate with us--she prepared a bowl of oatmeal at four o'clock every afternoon, which was supper for her. Hobbling to her bedroom, cane in hand, she studied her old family Bible before going to bed with the birds.

An RCA console radio sat in a corner of our dining room, with a pair of rocking chairs nearby. Most evenings dad and I listened to our favorite radio shows including Gabriel Heater, H.V. Keltenborn or Walter Winchell reporting the latest from the war in Europe and the Pacific. Occasionally we'd tune in a "short wave" channel that beamed

17

broadcasts all the way from Europe...we never got Japanese broadcasts. More than once, we picked up speeches coming out of Nazi Germany, maybe even the rants of Adolph Hitler, but of course we didn't understand German.

Then we'd tune in Dagwood and Blondie, Fibber McGee and Molly, Twenty Mule Team Borax's Death Valley Days which often carried a scary supernatural story, or my favorite show, Amos and Andy with Shorty the Barber struggling to get past severe stuttering—the Shorty character especially brought us lots of laughs. Then there was scary "Inner Sanctum" with its trademark creaking door slamming closed...this created such a frightening aura I was glad my dad was there to protect me!

We had to rely on our imaginations, since there was no such thing as television screens to convey the stories.

Summers were really hot, the only air conditioning was in a few stores downtown and in our two movie theaters. Shopping malls hadn't been invented. We used oscillating table fans which really didn't cool--about all they did was stir up hot air. The whirring sound made you hope a little bit of cooling was happening. When I was five an attic fan was installed. This thing was a marvelous improvement over the old oscillating fans. It sucked air through the windows then up and into the attic, expelling it back outside. So strong air movement through the house could be like a virtual hurricane blowing through the windows. Often before bedtime, mother would make the rounds sprinkling the sheets on each bed with a stoppered bottle sprinkler. The cooling effect of the airflow through the windows was wonderful. You could slip between cool sheets and drop off into dreamland, even on warm nights. You had to be sure windows were open when the attic fan was running because its strong suction could strip wallpaper right off the wall.

My mom used a hot weather trick to squeeze into her tight fitting girdle--first chilling it in the icebox, then sliding it on over her talcum powdered torso.

We eventually graduated to an electric "Frigidaire", as refrigerators were commonly called. The electric was sheer magic, making ice cubes in trays. My dad no longer had to stop by the icehouse every day on his way home, tying a 25 pound block of ice on the front bumper. The icehouse was central to everyone's life. They had a local monopoly on the magic of freezing water. Everyone had a "food locker" at the icehouse. The summer's harvest of fruits, vegetables and meats could be frozen and stored. We literally ate out of our lock box through the winter, supplementing these goods with home canned fruits and vegetables. Most of our meat and much of our produce came from my aunt and uncle's farm at Omen, forty miles away.

Our ice house was a virtual cornucopia of wildlife every fall, as all the hunters hung their deer and other large game carcasses in a special freezer vault before processing. Strolling through the vault, examining legal tags along the way, oohing and aahing at who had shot what and where, was great fun. Local hunters kept taxidermists busy every fall and winter, mounting heads of prized animals and creating rugs from their hides. One of the biggest thrills of my young life came when my first deer hung among other trophy kills in that cold vault—a magnificent eight pointer from deep in the woods of East Texas.

Kids found relief in the city natatorium (swimming pool) afternoons during the summer heat. We were in the water until supper time or later and sometimes grabbed dinner at the soda stand. Mr. Stamper, the park superintendent, made delicious ooey-gooey grilled cheese sandwiches in a waffle iron contraption. The sandwich, a bag of chips, and an RC Cola, all for a quarter, and you were in business. Maybe a Moon Pie for dessert. Not the most nutritious dinner, but it filled the bill. Then back into the water for more cool fun as the sun went down. We'd made it through another hot summer day in relative comfort.

Saturday was off limits for us "white kids" at the city pool. It was the only time available for "colored kids" to enjoy cooling off in the big pool. They could swim until late Saturday afternoon, and then the pool was drained, washed down and refilled overnight. Locker rooms were off limits to them. Sunday afternoon after church, we "white folks" were ready to go again, and the pool would fill with shrieking, happy kids.

Saturday afternoons with the pool unavailable to us, we sat in in the air-conditioned comfort of the Rembert or Arlyne movie houses, taking in "shoot-'em-ups" starring Gene Autry, Roy Rogers, Hopalong Cassidy and others and catching up on our favorite serials like The Green Hornet. It cost the grand sum of ten cents to get in and a nickel for a big bag of greasy, buttered popcorn that squeaked when chewed.

Wartime in America saw the kids in our neighborhood throw our lot in with our brave fighting men -- digging trenches and caves and building forts to make our war games as realistic as possible. Sometimes our battles would last for several days, as we'd be crawling around fox holes, hiding out in treetops and trying to surprise the make believe enemy, inevitably the "Germans or Japs". Our weapons for the most part were homemade "rubber guns". We made various sizes and shapes, carving them from pieces of wood scrap. Our ammunition was bands of stretchy natural rubber snipped from rubber inner tubes. Automobile tires were held up by these inflated natural rubber tubes. Salvaging them was a very important part of scavenging, as stretchy natural rubber could be put to many uses. The band of rubber was looped over the end of the barrel and stretched back to the rear of the gun and pinned. When the trigger was squeezed the band released and flew like a missile to its target. If you got hit just right on your bare back or chest it would register a good sting and could even leave a welt.

We organized patrols to stalk out our neighborhoods, searching for suspicious looking spies. I don't know what we'd have done if we ever came across a real one. Still, our war games made excellent fodder for a bunch of kids trying to do their part for Uncle Sam during the long Second World War. Wartime Texas ran rife with rumors that Nazi U-Boats had landed spies along our Gulf Coast, and we were on the lookout in our neck of the woods.

Longview was the wartime home of Harmon General Hospital and an incarceration facility for German Prisoners of War (POW's). It wasn't unusual to see a band of gray uniformed POW's, under military guard, making the rounds in downtown Longview. A few liked the town so much they decided to stay on after the war. My mom regularly visited American boys undergoing rehabilitation at Harmon. She grew especially fond of a young Army Capitan, Shelby White, who had been seriously injured when the glider he was piloting, loaded with troops, crashed in Germany. Shelby and his wife, Dena, grew up in South Texas. They hit it off great with my mom and dad, becoming frequent guests for Sunday dinner at our house. Shelby couldn't get enough of my mother's fried chicken, mashed potatoes and cream gravy or her incredible pot roast. I sat captivated by Shelby's stories about the fierce war in Europe. His fascinating tales just added to the wartime sentiment felt by all the kids in our neighborhood. Shelby White landed a great job in law enforcement after the war as the chief immigration officer for Texas' border with Mexico, based in San Antonio.

We made most of the things we played with every day, including coasters and scooters, rubber guns, periscopes which, crafted out of shoe boxes, mirrors a little glue and some ingenuity, could be used to stealthily look around corners and over fences, undetected. We also developed skills in the art of building scooters. For the most part, parents didn't have money to buy such toys from Sears or a local store, even if they were available. Metal was scarce during the war, and scrap collection was an important part of the homefront's efforts to help win the war. We needed to be creative and resourceful to have many of the kinds of things kids now take for granted. We built scooter frames from scraps of wood scavenged from shipping crates. We cannibalized wheel sets from roller skates, bolting four or more to the bottom of a wood frame. A vertical piece, bolted to the horizontal riding board, provided a strut to which we fashioned a wooden cross piece at the top that served as the handle bar. We found that a nice long hill at the north end of Harrison Street was great for coasting, the downside being the necessity to hike back up the long hill to start all over again.

We discovered that kite string stretched taut over a couple of hundred yards between two cans, one can attached to each end, gave us a sort of walkie-talkie, not anything like as good as a real one. But it passed for a decent homemade toy.

I was the master kite builder in our neighborhood. We learned to make and fly a variety of designs and sizes. A nearby open field was our airport. Kite string and glue were easy to come by. Moms' old bed sheets made excellent kite tail for ballast. We had to be a little creative to come up with other materials. Using a sharp Xacto knife, we slitted bamboo poles to get sticks. Archie Tubbs, our nearby grocer, kept us supplied with brown butcher paper, just the right thickness and weight. We painted colorful designs to dress up the brown paper. We flew at night sometimes when there was a good, steady wind, with a small pocket flashlight dangling beneath the kite. My favorite was a seven foot tall two-sticker which required a gale wind to get it off the ground and maintain flight.

East Texans speak with their own strange dialect. In fact, Texas is so immense and multi-cultural that visitors can tell the difference in how the English language is spoken from one part of the State to another. But for sure, East Texans have a dialect all their own. I grew up thinking "barbed wire" was actually and more correctly "bob wire". That in the past tense, we "clamb trees". That "well I swan" was about

21

as declarative as my mother could get. That "winders" was the proper word instead of "windows". That "well I'll be John Brown" was almost like swearing. Many called the old Sabine River a "ruver". Some of us even thought a "chest of drawers" was more properly called a "chester drawers". My dad called someone a "scannel", more properly a scoundrel, meaning a really bad dude. "Shet the door" instead of shut it. One of my mom's favorites was "well fiddle de-de"." "Fixin' to do this or that" is woven throughout the East Texan's lingo, meaning "I am starting or I am preparing to do something". I grew up hearing bicycles called "wheels". The list of colloquialisms is long, these being only a few examples.

 I give my high school English teacher, Miss Ruby Phenix, credit for having the patience and persistence to correct us and to prepare me for college level English and grammar. Any good writing and speaking skills I may have resulted in large part from Miss Phenix' excellent coaching and training.

The outbreak of that dreaded disease polio, infantile paralysis, spread across America like the Plague. The public pool was off-limits to us for almost two years, as it was believed that public swimming pools were a source of contagion. Ultimately and thankfully, Salk vaccine freed us from this terrible scourge. The nationwide polio scare and epidemic led to the March of Dimes held annually across America. Proceeds helped fund research in prevention of diseases, such as polio. I don't know how it was done in other cities, but the approach in Longview might have been unique. Dimes, thin ten cent pieces, were placed touching each other in a row along the length of downtown city sidewalks. For example, a contributor might find four dimes in his pocket change, placing them in line, extending the existing line by four dimes. A line of dimes stretched all around downtown Longview's sidewalks, becoming our city's contribution to that year's March of Dimes. These events were on Saturday mornings when shoppers were plentiful, coins jingled in pockets while Lions Club, Kiwanians and other groups policed the long line of dimes. The sight of all these dimes was unforgettable.

Dad strung outdoor lights in our backyard, removed the grass and smoothed out an area for neighborhood washer tossing events, helping everyone pass the time on warm evenings. The game of Washers is played the same way as Horseshoes, but instead of stakes driven into the ground at each end, the player tosses two inch washers trying to sink them into a two + inch hole at the opposite end. Dad was a skilled tosser and taught me his underhand tossing motion, similar to pitching horseshoes. Mr. Eubanks, Mr. Rose and other neighbors joined dad and me for games. Everybody knew the games were on when they saw the lights aglow in our back yard. Washers, the "red neck" equivalent of horseshoes, is fun and challenging. Rules and scorekeeping is much the same as horseshoes.

Dad enjoyed tossing baseball with me after "supper", as cooling shade crept across our back yard. As he prepared to "toss", I lifted my new Rawlings first base claw-style glove on my left hand. Baseball was my dad's favorite game, and he threw a mean knuckle ball, seams hardly moving as it streaked across sixty feet and stung into my glove. He had an unusual delivery I can best describe as an overhand "push". In spite of his awkward looking form, his knucklers were blistering. Too bad he never pitched a real game with his wicked knuckle ball.

ALBERT, MY FATHER

H e was born September 15, 1899, near Kilgore in East Texas to Wiley and Sarah Adams.........

They had been post bellum tenant farmers in Georgia. They looked for a new life in Oklahoma, and then Texas after the great Civil War had destroyed much of the Southland. Subsisting off the land, growing most of what they ate, money was scarce if there was any at all. Albert was one of twelve children, born in the middle of the clan. In many families, a child was given only a single name, thus Albert Adams was the whole story.

Life was extremely hard for the Adams', as it was for all tenant farmers. Formal education for many children stopped at third or fourth grade because they were needed to help farm, just to make ends meet. Girls helped run the house; cooked on a wood stove; washed clothes outdoors in a cast iron pot over a wood fire; scrubbed them on a rubbing board; wrung them out by hand and hung them on line to dry in the sun; made clothing and quilts for the family; and performed all the other things necessary for everyday living.

While life was no bowl of cherries, the family survived. They even enjoyed special events now and then. The occasional family trip into Kilgore on horse-drawn buckboard was a special treat. Everyone got to visit a few friends during these outings and see the sights, such as a circus, minstrel show, sideshow or church supper. Just a few pennies could buy plenty of chocolate or licorice sticks. Christmas usually brought an apple and orange in stockings for each child and not much more.

My dad was a physically imposing man who stood out in a crowd all his life. Albert grew up a 6'4", 200 pound, handsome muscular brute, strong as an ox. His high cheek bones, black hair, and dark features harkened back to Cherokee roots on his mother's side. Sarah, his mother, was one-fourth Cherokee. Some of her relatives claimed that she was fully one-half Cherokee—there wasn't full agreement on her genetics even among those who knew her best.

Albert's demeanor was stern and strong. His dark, piercing eyes could cut a hole right through a person. He was very bright, and self-educated. He read extensively about world and national events to keep informed. He grew to become a man of few words, and when he spoke you listened.
Albert was a student of wood lore and wildlife. He grew up hunting in

the Sabine River bottom of East Texas, helping put meat on the family table. His quarry was squirrels, rabbits, occasional deer, dove and quail. He hunted with a single shot .22 rifle or a 12 gauge shotgun. Every round or shell had to count for a piece of game, leading him to become a marksman. Throughout his life, his happiest times came when he was deep in the woods of East Texas, observing wild life and hunting. He had no use for hunting dogs, depending instead on his own keen senses and stealth. He could sit on a log for several hours at a time, hardly moving, blending in perfectly with the forest around him.

He carried himself with pride and strength. Seeing him walk along a city street, you'd be impressed. "There goes a man who is somebody," you might say. He was straight as an arrow physically, and morally there wasn't a dishonest bone in his substantial body.

Albert was neat as a pin in dress and manner--everything was in the right place, always tasteful. His business suits were made locally by tailor Louis Ricci. He tried to afford a new Ricci suit every year or two. His suits included a vest and two pairs of trousers for long lasting wear. He wore black size 12 Nunn Bush shoes and black silk stockings held up with elastic supporters. His shoes were fitted with special insoles crafted by Dr. Park to ease pain in his badly fallen arches. Shirts were white, hand starched and ironed, with French cuffs. Ties were in good taste, in soft colors. He wore blocked Stetson hats, brims snapped down in front. A handsome 21 jewel gold watch keeping perfect time rode in his vest pocket, fobbed gold chain latched in the top buttonhole. His necktie was adorned with a one carat diamond stick pin. This beautiful gem had to be sacrificed to pay for teeth extractions and upper and lower dental plates. After shedding a few tears, my parents soon replaced it with a less conspicuous small diamond, set in a gold horse shoe tie pin.

Most days he dressed in his sharp, navy blue Police Chief's uniform which was more formal than today's. It resembled "dress military". But if the occasion warranted, he wore a Ricci business suit, looking great. Dad nearly always dressed in a suit and hat when we took in a night baseball game or wrestling match at Mattie's Palm Isle. I guess neatness and formality were just part of his persona.

He shaved using a straight edge razor, avoiding the new type safety razor with replaceable blades. He sharpened the straight edge on a leather strop hanging from a bathroom wall. I watched with awe as he whirled his brush, whipping up a thick head of lather in a shaving mug. The thick lather looked like whipped cream, good enough to eat. After coating his face and the strop with lather, he whetted the straight edge back and forth on the strop and tested its sharpness.

Shaving with a sharp straight edge was no joking matter. He held the open razor just so as he carefully raked the sharp instrument over his lathered face and neck. Often I played grown-up, daubing my little cheeks with lather, shaving right along with him using a harmless comb as my make believe razor. True to Indian genetics, dad had little body hair except for the black pate and generous dark facial stubble.

Showers in homes were rare. Everybody bathed in clawfooted enamel tubs, certainly a big improvement over the once a week scrubbing in outdoor washtubs filled with tepid water. My dad had a peculiar way of bathing. After scrubbing his face, neck and torso, he stood in the tub scrubbing the rest of his body, then sat in the water to rinse off. After draining the bathwater, you had to vigorously scrub the tub with Babbo to remove all the scum and dirt so the tub would be ready for the next user.

Dad was gifted with a sixth sense about people and personalities. He could look right into the soul of a person and know a lot about him, a talent which probably saved his life more than once. Townspeople trusted him explicitly, knowing he was truthful almost to a fault. Bad guys feared him for good reason. He educated himself throughout life by reading widely, compensating for limited formal schooling that ended at grade three.

As a young man, he was accustomed to very hard physical labor. He once worked in the roundhouse for the Texas & Pacific Railroad Company on a repair crew. This was hot, filthy, physically exhausting work. From time to time he worked as a rough neck on one of Uncle Everett's oil drilling rigs. He worked at various sawmill jobs, loading giant logs on the runner at the Kelly Plow Works in Longview.

He was scarred from childhood labors on the farm. While splitting logs with a sharp axe, the blade slipped and sliced through the top of his left shoe, splitting the big toe and nail right down the center. The nail never grew back together, remaining split the rest of his life. Protruding edges of the big toe nail needed trimming and filing from time to time.
You might care to learn a few things about Albert not generally known,

even by friends. He had a terrific "ear" for music. No, he didn't read sheet music and couldn't tell you the difference between a sharp and a flat. But he chorded beautifully on guitar, a favorite solo piece being what he called "Spanish Fandango". It was a beautiful piece with chords, runs, transitions and scales. His attempts to teach guitar to me were futile, the best I could manage being a few chords. He sang with a rich, deep, but untrained bass, but his solos were strictly private affairs inside his car. He never joined a choir or singing group, yet he would go out of his way to attend a concert by the Stamps Quartet gospel singers. He was good with a fiddle, and played square dances with three other string players, including mandolin, banjo and guitar, to earn extra money during his 20's and early 30's.His string band had all the weekend work they wanted.

I've wondered if the "musical ear" ran in my dad's family. Several brothers played guitar, including Floyd, who tried in vain to teach me to chord. I dreaded those sessions with Uncle Floyd. He always came by unannounced with his guitar, insisting I'd strum along with him on mine. Dad's youngest sister Ellie was a reasonable fiddler. If there were musical genes in Dad's family, they didn't make it into my gene pool. Maybe one of my children or grandchildren will be more fortunate. Don't get me wrong----I love to listen to music of all kinds, my two favorites being classical and country/western.

In his 30's and 40's, dad worked out at Smith's Gym in Longview, one of the only facilities in East Texas. Richard Smith was Longview's version of the Strong Man. He moonlighted at the gym while holding down a regular job. His gym, on East Whaley Street, was Spartan by today's standards but adequate, with lots of dumbbells, wall mounted exercise contraptions, and punching bags. Mr. Smith occasionally performed amazing feats of strength in downtown Longview, once pulling a heavy city fire truck along downtown Main Street by a rope clenched between his teeth. My dad liked and admired Richard Smith, and enjoyed working out at Smith's Gym.

He was a proud member of the Knights of Pythias local lodge, wearing his white gold signet ring to the grave. This was the only organization, except church and state law enforcement associations, getting his involvement.

My dad was solitudinous, comfortable with who he was, content in his own skin.
Looking carefully, you could spot several small scars on his throat. He was

viciously attacked by a large dog at a county fair when he was seven. His life was saved only because older brother Jim saw the attack and quickly pulled the beast from his little brother's throat. Fortunately no permanent damage was done other than giving him a lifelong fear of all dogs. Only with great reluctance did he permit me to have a dog when I was five years old. It was a harmless little Fox Terrier I named Skippy. But some cruel person fed him a meal of glass shards ground into hamburger. Little Skippy was in misery until dad could come home and put him down. He hated having to do this, knowing how losing Skippy hurt me. By the way, it's no coincidence that older brother Jim who had saved dad from the vicious attack was the only member of the Adams clan with whom dad bonded. They were occasional hunting partners for years.

Dad got into law enforcement as a deputy in the Gregg County Sheriff's Department in the 1920s. His hard work, presence, strength, intelligence, and sense of fairness together with his acuity with firearms caught the attention of Sheriff Martin Hayes.

The big oil boom brought fortune seekers into East Texas from all over the world, much like gold prospectors poured into California in 1849. People lived in tents or any other kind of shelter they could find. Local resources were stretched beyond their limits, and crime was rampant. Young deputy Albert Adams and partner, an older deputy fondly called "Uncle" Charlie Davis, scooted around East Texas in a shiny black Ford sedan. They searched out bootleggers, pimps, burglars, killers and all manner of criminals. Dad told many unforgettable stories about their adventures enforcing the law in the wiles of Gregg County. One of my favorites involves his six-shooter, a handsome nickel plated .38 caliber Smith & Wesson. In mint condition, it fires as well today as it did seventy years ago.

Dad hated unfairness of any kind, even though enforcing the law sometimes brought him into conflict with his moral convictions and sense of fairplay. It seems the county court ordered that a particular farm be confiscated because of nonpayment of taxes. Apparently a seesaw battle had gone on for some time, and the court finally ruled. It fell my dad's lot to deliver the eviction notice and oversee the confiscation. He and Uncle Charlie drove to the rural farmhouse, finding the entire family sitting somber faced on the front porch as they arrived. Dad got out of the car with the written court order in hand, his partner keeping watch from the parked car. It particularly troubled Dad that the family was black, knowing them to be hard working, and like many farmers, falling on hard times. He absolutely hated doing what had to be done. As he neared the front porch, one of the men got up from his chair and went into the house. Dad's survival instincts that paid off for him so many times quickly kicked in. He and Charlie were about to become easy targets for a massacre.

At that moment a mockingbird, the official state bird of Texas, lit on a fence post thirty paces away from where he stood. Dad slowly turned to face the bird, drew his shiny six-gun from its holster, took aim at the Mockingbird and literally shot its head off, the carcass falling to the ground. One by one, every family member got up and went into the house, heads shaking. They wanted no part of this young lawman's handgun. Though serving the warrant troubled him, he did so without further incident. Dad always said, "I couldn't have made that shot again in a hundred years". I never believed that because I'd seen him hit bottles, cans and other targets on the fly. He was awfully good with that S & W, and his expertise was respected far and wide.

There were many other examples of his fair and equitable treatment of all citizens under the law in his jurisdiction. During the war, he and his force of police officers were especially on guard for activities which might indicate the presence of spies and saboteurs in proximity to the huge oilfields nearby. These fields, supplying oil essential for America's war efforts, attracted the enemy's attention. Pressures were exerted by some to impound and in some cases deport American citizens of Japanese descent. Dad stood up for those in good standing in the community, blunting efforts in East Texas to implement draconian policies implemented elsewhere. To him, the key was citizens "in good standing". He knew who was and wasn't.

Dad enjoyed a reputation for removing warts and other blemishes. He was thought to use some secret magical scheme, rooted in Cherokee Indian lore. I never knew what he did or how he did it, and he couldn't or wouldn't tell me. But I saw the results with my own eyes. He simply looked at the wart or blemish while gently touching it, and then instructed the person, "Go away now and don't think about it anymore". These "patients" usually reported the thing gone after a couple of weeks. How did he do this magic? Who knows. He never revealed the secret, taking it to his grave.

Albert's honor and honesty were simple and pure, learned the hard way by experience. In his late teen years, he single-handedly saved his mother and father from financial ruin. They had borrowed from a local bank in

Oklahoma, as was the practice of the day, to put in the season's crops. In turn, the bank would be repaid out of proceeds from the sale of corn, cotton and other produce. This was all well and good if the crops came in, but if there was failure, the farmer defaulted and could be financially ruined.

The dreaded crop failure happened that year to the Adams', resulting from little rain, torrid heat and poor planning. The already poor Adams family would have to default on the loan, losing everything they owned, which wasn't very much anyway. Albert was not going to let this to happen to his parents if he could help it. I don't know where his brothers and sisters were, but he took on the entire load himself. He helped them get relocated to a place near Kilgore in East Texas, near other relatives. He made a deal with the bank to lend him money to put in next season's crops. Indeed, his crops yielded enough to pay off his parent's debt as well as his new debt. With what little was left, he relocated himself to East Texas, near family.

Struggling to make good on the indebtedness, he was almost sucked into the vortex of a rampaging tornado as it moved across an open field. The twister roared closer and closer, and he laid flat on the ground clutching the base of a small sampling for dear life. As the funnel roared overhead, he saw up inside its twisting circumference, lightning flashing from one side to the other. He went on to successfully make the crop.

He earned extra money for food and other necessities in Oklahoma by riding and breaking in horses. He always had a special knack with them--horses seemed to trust him, knowing he was gentle. Before long, he'd have the wildest unridden stallion eating corn and oats out of his hand. Much later in life, after his law enforcement days were over, he loved riding his big roan, appropriately named Red, through the woods of East Texas.

For 15 years after leaving law enforcement, he was in charge of security for a subsidiary of Eastman Kodak, opening large new petrochemical manufacturing facilities near Longview. He patrolled the extensive forested properties Eastman acquired near the Sabine River, riding his big roan. A newfound peace came over him which was a joy to see. He was no longer a target for criminals on the run. Our telephone stopped ringing in the middle of the night to tell him about some emergency. He was able to keep regular hours, actually having days off work each weekend. He and my mother started getting along much better than I could remember.
He left behind an up to date, well-functioning Police Department in the

City of Longview, with a trained, experienced officer force. His special course work from Texas A&M in criminal law and forensics paid off, as he put new practices and techniques to work training his officers. He installed a state of the art radio system, opening a whole new era in police communications. The innovations Albert Adams brought to law enforcement without a doubt saved lives and enhanced the effectiveness of anticrime activities in Longview and East Texas. I take great joy that our daughter (my stepdaughter) now owns and daily uses the dining table which doubled as his work table at home where my dad studied and prepared for the examinations in the courses he took at A&M. It's remarkable in this day and age to look back on Albert Adams' tenure, knowing there was no corruption or appearance of corruption, that he and his officers served their city honestly and fairly.

It was a new day for my dad after leaving the Longview Police Department. For the first time in my memory, he and my mom were doing things together, attending church regularly, socializing with neighbors and attending picnics and other functions sponsored by Eastman. Dad was a faithful member of the Business Men's Bible Class. Many of his old buddies were in that class--men who had known each other for a lifetime, so there could be no guile between them. They met in the church chapel every Sunday morning, and each man more or less "owned his special seat." I sometimes attended the class with my dad when I came to visit, and it was always a wonderful thing to experience. Even some of his hunting buddies were members.

He and my mother retired in 1965, buying a modest home on Fox Lane in Longview. It turns out it was in a neighborhood where several old friends and neighbors had relocated from the Harrison and Park Street area. Their new place was a great spot for my children to visit during summer vacations. Sometimes they spent the entire summer there, playing with friends in the daytime, going to movies, riding bicycles, eating ice cream, swimming and enjoying their grandmother's home cooking.

The final chapter in my dad's life was April 1976. He was suddenly stricken by a massive heart attack, and he died before the ambulance could get him to the hospital. It happened so suddenly he didn't know what hit him. There had been no warning signs.

My mother handled his death courageously, just as she had lived her entire life. His funeral was impressive, held fittingly in the church chapel where his Sunday School class met. It was an open casket funeral, and he looked like his distinguished self. The eulogy was given by his Sunday School teacher Ken Mann who was dearly beloved by all the men in his class. A large number of Blacks and Hispanics attended, paying their last respects, a testimony to his fair treatment of the entire community irrespective of race and ethnicity. The trip to the cemetery resembled a military funeral. The entire uniformed police force turned out, taking up stations at intersections en route to the cemetery. He was buried wearing the white gold insignia Knights of Pythias ring on his right hand, having been a member of this old conservative society for many years. The presence of his hunting buddies, including George Hibbin, was a tender and special touch for his farewell.

My dad was a simple man, with simple values, of modest means, and deep intelligence and wisdom. He was, as they say in Texas, "Honest as the day is long." Though he might not have realized it, I always believed his strongest suit was teaching. Teaching was a big part of his life — training his subordinates in all aspects of their jobs, mentoring them to be better people, teaching me to love and respect the great outdoors, training me to respect but know how to use firearms, and teaching me to drive cars and other vehicles safely, understanding danger. He loved his God and the Lord Jesus Christ and is with them today. He had a greater influence on me than any other person, and I cherish the fact that I will be with him again in Heaven. My dad was truly "a man's man", and I am proud to be his son.

With great love, I look back on all the 'gifts' my dad gave me. He taught me many valuable lessons. And so, as a postscript to this chapter, I should like to pass these 'gifts' along to you. I call them, "Albert's Life Lessons."

Lesson 1

Firearms are wonderful tools. Used carelessly, they can and will kill you or someone else. Safe use of firearms of any kind must always be your goal, Never, never, never point a firearm at anyone. Always treat a firearm as if it is loaded. Keep all firearms in mint condition, wiping down metal and wood after the firearm is handled. Be sure the barrel is swabbed clean and that there are no residues of powder or metal left behind.

Lesson 2

Be prepared for anything you can imagine happening while driving your car. Wrecks happen unexpectedly and rapidly. Drive 'defensively.' Avoid any temptation to become 'offensive' on the road. Like a firearm, a car is a wonderful thing when used safely and properly. When driving in traffic, give other drivers wide berth – all the room they want. Don't force your way in just because you have the right-of-way. Crowding, being crowded or demanding your right-of-way is a sure fire formula for having a collision. Keep your car in safe, reliable condition.......do all the maintenance! Remember, "oil changes are the lifeline of the car's engine."

Lesson 3

Outdoors.....the woods, nature and wildlife....are among God's best gifts to us. Spend time loving and enjoying these glorious gifts. Don't shoot animals in the wild frivolously. Hunt with intent and enjoy meals prepared with your quarry.

Lesson 4

Be a conservative politically in your thinking. Don't get caught in empty promises and illusions that politicians create. Row your own boat...don't expect the government to bail you out. Make your way and expect others, who are able, to do likewise. Make allowance for those among us who cannot.

Lesson 5

Be honest, even if the truth hurts.

Lesson 6

Few things can beat a good meal of fried catfish and hushpuppies, washed down with sweet iced tea! Or a platter of my mother's pan fried squirrels, with biscuits and cream gravy.

LETA, MY MOTHER

S he was named Corrie Leta by parents Zona and Fayette Wilkinson of Troop, Texas.....

She was born on March 30, 1902, the youngest of three girls and one boy. Zona was a Francis before her marriage to Mr. Wilkinson about 1880. Leta was born at home, as were all Zona's children. Leta was close to all of her family, but she absolutely adored her big brother, Robert Everett. The family traced its history back to two Wilkinson brothers from Ireland, arriving in North Carolina in the late 1700's or early 1800's.

If my mother ever had a fault, and she must have, I never knew it. She was the essence of goodness, fairness and purity. A devout follower of Jesus Christ, she was one of those people who came to know the Lord without having to face upheaval or crisis in her life. She grew up knowing Jesus as her Lord and Savior from her earliest memories. She was sharp of mind and wit. If the situation warranted, she could be tough as nails, yet gentle as a lamb at the same time. She gave all of herself; she endured much, and never complained, even when complaining was justified.

She came by her toughness honestly, having seen toughness practiced at home on their modest farm. For example, when Leta was ten years old, her mother had such severe problems with her teeth that it was necessary to extract all of them. Hand-in-hand, she and Zona walked the two miles to what passed as a dentist's office in Troop. There, in that office with little anesthesia, all of Zona's teeth were pulled in one sitting. Afterwards, Zona and young Leta returned home, hand-in-hand, in what must have been an agonizing walk. There is sometimes a fine line between toughness and stoicism, and I've often wondered which had the upper hand in the example of Zona and the dentist.

Life was far from easy on the family's little hard scrabble farm outside Troop. Yet all four children went through and graduated from Troop High School where Leta was an honor student. She and her sisters learned to cook on a wood stove, and over the years she perfected her culinary skills becoming one of the best cooks in East Texas. She and her sisters did weekly washes for the family, outdoors in iron cauldrons over open fires. Having no faucet or running water to fill the pots, it was necessary to draw water from a deep well by the bucket full. After fresh water rinsing and wringing by hand, everything was hung on lines to air dry in the sun. Fresh air dried cottons and linens smell heavenly, as I can attest from my childhood. Dry items were pressed using irons heated on the wood stove. She and her sisters were proficient in all household skills required to live as well as possible in rural Texas.

After graduating from Troop High School in 1919, Leta went to work for the Bell Telephone Company as an understudy telephone operator in the two-person Troop office. The first telephone lines were going up in rural Texas, and phones were a novelty. A typical phone set up consisted of wall-mounted wooden box about eye level with a swiveled adjustable microphone in front, protruding toward the user. A receiver, wired into the system, was held by the user to one ear. A small hand crank on the side of the box was turned to get the attention of an operator at the central switchboard. When the operator came on line, you might chat about the weather or the latest town gossip before giving her a two-digit number, or simpler still, a name you wanted to reach.

Most telephone lines were "party lines", having five or six homes connected to the same line. You could easily eavesdrop on your neighbor's conversations, if you were the nosy type. There was no such thing as telephone privacy.

As it turned out, the switchboard office was in the front parlor of Alma and John Shore's Troop home. The Shores, like many in rural America, earned a fee from the phone company for use of their home. Alma was a paid employee as well, senior to young Leta who was learning the ropes under her guidance. The Shore home perched on a little hill at the head of Main Street, overlooking the village of Troop. John Shore's butcher shop was a block away on Main Street. The Shores had one child, son John T., an enlisted man in the wartime Navy. Leta of course had no idea that Alma's brother, Albert, existed, and someday would be her husband.

She and Albert met accidentally one morning as she was strolling up Main Street to the telephone office. Albert and older brother Jim were in serious conversation in front of the local pharmacy as Leta walked by. Word was that upon hearing Albert, a total stranger, say something off-color, she stopped and took umbrage at him. Alma heard about the incident, immediately identifying the parties involved, deciding to introduce them properly. The rest is history.

It's interesting to note that my father's brother, Jim, and my mother's sister, Clara, married and had two children, Dorothy and Jimmie Beth, who therefore were my "double first cousins". I don't know many with double first cousins, but this degree of kinship must lie pretty high up the food chain. I believe they, in turn, would be "first cousins" to my children and "second cousins" to theirs.

Leta stuck with the telephone company through several reorganizations and evolutions, retiring finally in 1965 after more than forty years of service. While much of the work might have seemed menial during those four decades, she brought her smile, happy spirit and intelligence to work every day. Climbing the ladder or seeking advancement held no attraction for her. She was content with her lot, doing her own thing, putting all her earnings with dad's into the family till, which she budgeted and managed.

After several telephone company reorganizations, Leta joined the AFL/CIO Labor Union, insisting this was the only way employees could protect themselves from abuse by management. She was an ardent union member, going out on strike when called upon, walking picket lines with union sign in hand, and excoriating so-called "scabs", employees who crossed picket lines to work as they refused to join the strike. She was conservative in almost every other way. Dad, a total conservative, was as unalterably opposed to unions as mom was pro union. Organized labor and labor unions were usually avoided in discussions at home.

I became aware of her demanding work schedule after we moved to Harrison Street when I was three. Her shift hours were appalling to my young self, wanting his mother to be at home in the evening ---three to six p.m., an hour for dinner, then seven to eleven at night.

We didn't own a family car during the war years. Dad drove a 1941 Plymouth police car he parked in our driveway at night. A police car couldn't possibly serve a family's needs. The Plymouth was white with red flashing siren on top, Police Chief stenciled on both doors. Mother got by using the city bus, stopping at a street corner a few steps from our house. Dad usually came for her about 2:30 in the afternoon, driving her downtown for her 3:00 shift. She had dinner in the lounge with other operators, usually a sandwich and soda. Dad and I had dinner at home, enjoying good things she left for us --- meatloaf, fried chicken, fresh homemade biscuits, or one of her creative casseroles.

36

After our favorite evening radio programs, I was in bed by eight "with the chickens". My small bed was alongside the double window in my mother's bedroom. Dad always passed through in his pajamas, seersucker robe and slippers, and we both said the same refrain every night, "Good night, sleep tight, remember I love you".

My sleep was fitful until mom came home. I worried about her, afraid something might happen to her. There wasn't any logical reason for me to worry this way, I just did. I wasn't alone in the house by any means, with dad in the room next to me, grandma up front. I just missed her, wanting her to be home like moms in "normal" families. Soon I'd hear dad snoring, thinking I could quietly slip to the telephone in the hall, contacting my mother to be sure she was ok. I would ask the operator to please connect me to Mrs. Adams on the long distance board. Just hearing my mom's voice comforted me. If my silly calls were annoying she didn't show it. After her calm reassurance, I could sneak back to bed, knowing she'd be home before long.

My child's mind couldn't understand the heavy demands on each of my parents. I just felt "my needs came first and should take precedence over anything else". Both were doing their part providing for the family, and both were serving important wartime needs on the home front---dad, Police Chief, exempt from military service because of his job---mom, handling a heavy load of long distance and overseas calls, many pertaining to oil supplies from the huge oilfield nearby. Oil to meet allied forces requirements in Europe came from this East Texas field. Mom was adept at getting long distance and overseas calls through, many relating to oil production and the war effort. East Texas was rumored to be a hotbed of German agents and saboteurs, entering the mainland from Axis submarines off the Texas Gulf Coast. Helping prevent any enemy action aimed at oil production and rail shipment through Longview's large network came under my dad's purview together with the FBI.

Explaining to me the seriousness of their work did nothing to assuage my insecurities. I was hurting and found comfort several times talking with my cousin Virginia who was more like a big sister than my cousin. My parents were simply doing the best they could with a tough situation, and couldn't do much to change things.

About 11:30 I'd hear a city bus stop in front of our house letting mother off, and would know she was home, soon to be in her bed. But first, she'd make her way to the kitchen for a quick late-night snack. On occasion, seeing a cockroach skittering across the floor, she made lots of noise swatting the thing. Pest control outfits were unheard of. Everyone did their own thing to control infestations of roaches, ants, mice, gophers and other pests, prevalent in Texas.

Next morning after breakfast, I was off to preschool at Mrs. Denton's place across town, driven by dad in his police car. Being driven around in a police car made me feel odd, out of place. Sometimes I felt like I didn't belong, that my life was different from other kids my age. I was sometimes teased by older boys, getting into a scuffle or fist fight to defend my honor. I was becoming a pretty insecure little kid, thinking everyone had it in for me.

I was almost sure I would be forgotten or even abandoned, that no one would come pick me up. I was anxious after other kids had been picked up and I was still waiting. Finally, the car would show up and I'd run for it with all my might. My parents never gave me any reason to feel this way. I knew I was dearly loved by them both. Certainly they wouldn't leave me stranded. If this happened today instead of seven decades ago, I'd be a candidate for therapy to help me get past my insecurities, but treatments taken for granted now were unheard of when I was a child. Life in those days was pretty simple---you either "go on" or you "go under". Talks with Cousin Virginia from time to time in which I cried on her shoulder were more helpful than anything else, and I always felt indebted to her for being my Big Sister.

I'm happy to admit I've seen therapists from time to time as an adult, dealing with insecurities left over from childhood. Therapists opened windows on the nature and depth of my insecurities, helping me to deal with them more effectively. I learned that while some issues had little basis in logic, my parents perhaps should have handled things differently, impacting me less. Imagined fears to a child can be as vivid and impactful as the real thing, and if not dealt with may be deep and long lasting. I can't say enough good things about outstanding therapists who have helped me, especially Dr. Harold Kaplan in Vienna, Virginia. I'm afraid fear and stigma still prevent too many from getting vital help they need to live a happier and better more complete life. More on this later, but excessive drinking at times in my life was my futile attempt to compensate for insecurities---a form of "self-medication".

By ten, I was a chubby little kid with kinky curly brown hair who didn't much like himself. I unfortunately saw myself having a half empty glass instead of one half full. I loved playing sports and was ok, but not athletically gifted like some of the kids. I tended to be a little clumsy and wasn't very fast. We almost always had a game of stickball, baseball or football going on in our neighborhood, and I loved every minute, especially when I was up to bat. But comparing my performance against some of the other kids, I definitely came up short. I participated anyway in organized team sports at school in spite of my deficiencies.

I came to realize I had a different gift from many other kids. I was smart, analytical, loved to study and learn. I especially liked math and science, anathemas to most kids. Yet, I needed to come to grips with not being particularly gifted with the whole package---intelligence plus athleticism. I didn't really know anyone else who was blessed with both. I had to reconcile that being a big, strong kid didn't necessarily equate to becoming a good athlete. I could try and try, only to find I still had the same body type with its inherent limitations. I think what I must have coveted most about athletes was the public acclaim and adoration they received, thinking such accolades might go far in assuaging my insecurities. I thought recognition on the field of play would make me feel like I belonged, that I was actually OK. That kind of thing wasn't to come to me. I'd have to settle for "something else"--- academic achievement. Later in life, developing a passion and adeptness for snow skiing, this all-consuming activity became my sport of choice and thoroughly filled this inner need.

Grades mattered to me a lot. I'm sure it helped that both my parents fully expected me to do well in my studies. I didn't dare insult them or myself by bringing home a poor grade. I observed that making top grades earned the greatest kudos from my parents. I liked how it felt when they were proud of me. Academic achievement, not athletic prowess, earned me their attaboys. Neither parent ever attended a sporting event in which I was a participant. But I sure got rave reviews bringing home good grades.

Late one night, the stress of trying to balance the demands of work and home caught up with my mom. After the phone rang, dad told me to get up and dress, we had to go to mother. Her supervisor, Mrs. Dowdy, called to say mother was very sick and crying uncontrollably. We found her lying on a sofa in the employee lounge, sobbing. A few minutes later, she was able to walk with us to dad's car. It was a quiet ride home, nothing was said. I was on the back seat, worried sick about her. She slept through the night, exhausted from her ordeal. Our family physician came, looked her over and prescribed medication. I had no idea what Dr. Farrar meant when he pronounced she had experienced a "nervous breakdown". It sounded very ominous to me. There were no smiles in the room when he somberly gave his diagnosis. He ordered quiet and rest for about six weeks. She was not to return to work during that time. On one hand, that had been the scariest experience of my life. But I was overjoyed that, sick though she might be, I'd have my mom at home to myself "where she belonged"!

With time off work (without pay) and lots of rest, she regained her strength and composure, finally returning to work. Nights with her at home for six weeks were wonderful. I was sad she returned to those same old horrible shift hours—3 to 6 and7 to 11. I vowed to myself I'd be a better boy from then on. I'd be better behaved and would help out more around the house. Dad pitched in, doing more of the necessities with his mother. All of us tried to make life a little easier for mom. I turned over a new leaf, not calling her at work late at night. I don't think she ever mentioned those late night calls to dad.

With almost any ailment I described, my mother applied one of two remedies---obviously designed to see if I was faking it----a strong dose of paregoric mixed with orange juice; or just as bad, castor oil and orange juice. Both tasted so horrible if I wasn't sick before, I'd surely be nauseated and vomiting after. Orange juice didn't make it taste any better, in fact making the concoction even worse. The threat of a "litmus test" showed her whether I was actually sick. And if all else failed, the faithful enema was threatened. I didn't miss many days of school, having a near perfect attendance record.

Life at home improved enormously after the war's end in 1945, followed by grandma's passing soon after. A new spirit of freedom and victory swept across the land---you could feel it in the air, everywhere you went. The heavy strain my parents had been under seemed to lift. I was saddened by grandma's departure, because I loved her and enjoyed her company as far back as I could remember. But it's an ill wind that blows no good. The stress of providing her daily care was gone, bringing precious relief especially to mom. War's end meant automobiles again were available. Purchasing a new Chevrolet sedan completely changed the life of our family. Mom would be able to drive to work, come home for dinner with dad and me, returning to finish her shift.

At the age of nine, I had the first room of my own. When I closed that door, the rest of the world disappeared. With windows on two sides, my own entrance onto the front porch, and plenty of wall space for pictures and gadgets, the room was "this boy's dream". The closet was an added bonus, with space for clothes, toys and paraphernalia I used in making things.

A table across two side windows made an ideal spot for my rudimentary chemistry lab, with Bunsen burner, and assorted racks of test tubes. Another table provided a place for my microscope and glass slides for studying bugs, leaves and other small things. Mom put a study desk, lamp and two bookcases along a windowless wall, ideal for my modest collection of story books, atlases and several reference books and encyclopedias. I had space for building electronic gadgets, mostly battery operated flashing signal lights and fascinating little crystal radios. There was plenty of room on the floor for building kites during our windy springs known as "kite flying season".

Life at our house became very good for the first time I could remember. I took enormous joy in my new room, keeping it neat, orderly and clean. Night was now a special time for me, listening to faraway places on the crystal radio I made, stations like KVOO Tulsa, WOAI San Antonio or WFAA Dallas. Mom kept me supplied with spare parts such as earphones, plugs and wire. Though scrapped by the telephone company, they still had plenty of life for my uses.

Fast forward to much later in my life because I want to give you a very clear picture of my mother, and I want you to understand the kind of person she was. In 1976, she rescued me and my children after my twenty year marriage collapsed. I was responsible for providing a home for two teenagers, a son and daughter. They were well beyond needing a nanny, but to provide the secure, supportive home they deserved was a daunting task staring me in the face. It absolutely had to be done--I had to find a way. This experience gave me empathy for women suddenly finding themselves divorced with children to raise.

While my marriage was breaking up, my precious dad suffered a sudden massive heart attack, dying almost immediately. This was a huge blow to my mom and me. I got to Texas as quickly as possible to be with her, paying my last respects to dad. After his funeral and interment, mom wanted to talk seriously with me over dinner about her future. She demonstrated in spades that "Wilkinson Toughness" running in her genes. Knowing my predicament, she came to a decision prayerfully to sell her home immediately, then move1500 miles to a place she'd never been to help make a home for my two kids, herself and me. This would require an enormous leap of faith for anyone in their mid-70's, basically beginning life anew. In fact, it would take a huge leap for one much younger than she.

My mother's trust in God was simple, and her faith total. She was a Romans 8:28 believer through and through, trusting wholeheartedly that "All things work together for the good of those that love the Lord and are called according to His purposes." She had unswerving faith that God called her to minister to my family through those troubled times. She totally trusted that God, as her Rock, would help her overcome physical limitations, especially rheumatic knees and feet, to be God's Angel in our home. I agreed, realizing there was no one else who could come in, lovingly take over, and provide continuity to the two children and me. They loved her dearly and had spent lots of time with her and my dad since the day each was born. Her low key, unassuming manner always wore well with them during their summer visits.

Her bold offer stunned me---to think she'd uproot from home, friends, church where she'd spent a lifetime was more than I would ever dare ask or hope for. I hadn't realized that I was about to be privy to one of God's miracles, that often God does things in ways we least expect. All this was happening as my very own life was in upheaval---the breakup of my twenty year marriage, the sudden death of my precious dad, the major responsibility for rearing two early teenagers pretty much alone, and an extremely important and demanding job I loved. I might have to leave it unless I could come up with reliable help at home. I was still new to "God's World", not yet fully understanding God's miraculous handiwork first in saving me, then drawing me half way across America to begin a new life in Washington, D.C. where I knew no one, to make a wholly new beginning. And now all this. God was literally roaring into my life with His mighty presence!

I accepted her offer, tearfully and thankfully, knowing what it would mean to my children and me and what it would require of her. Since selling our large home in a really nice neighborhood, I had bought a townhouse near school, thinking it would work best for the children and me, if we had to go it alone. Even before dad's death, I had thought seriously about moving back near my parents in Texas to help with my children. It weighed heavily on me that Mother's offer to come to us would not have been possible if my dad hadn't passed. This would mean my two children, my mom and I all would have a stable home at this crucial time in all our lives. And for a real bonus, I would be able to continue my important work in Washington. Over four decades later, I am still awed by this set of events in which all my whole family experienced, up close and personal, God's amazing handiwork!

Mother cleared out everything in Longview and said her goodbyes. Then accompanied by her good friend Sue (my wife's mother), she drove to Washington. They braved a major snow storm across Tennessee, riding it out for two days in a motel. Upon reaching our home, she moved in and began to function as our female head of the house. Navigating up and down in a three level townhouse wasn't easy for her, but in her strong, unique way she took over the reins of running the house. Quickly learning her way around, she did most of our grocery shopping and prepared family meals. She did laundry every week on the basement level, reading and napping until the laundry was done, avoiding trips up and down stairs. With God at her side, she moved into her new life almost seamlessly. Both kids adored and respected her, glad to be close to her.

Soon while visiting our nearby Post Office, she and a total stranger struck up a conversation waiting in line to buy postage stamps. Mary Jo (MJ) Jones and her husband Homer were natives of a small town in southern Arkansas, not far from Longview's northeastern corner of Texas. Mother and MJ "spoke the same language", had the same drawl, knew many of the same places, especially around Dallas and Shreveport. MJ's mother, Lena, lived with them and was about my mom's age. (Are you beginning to get the remarkable picture of how God works in the lives of those who love Him and according to Romans 8:28 are called unto His purposes). She urged mother to attend their church the next Sunday, meet Lena and join them for lunch after church at the only Texas style cafeteria in the Washington area. By the way, it's no coincidence that the church was the same denomination in which mother spent her entire life in Texas, Southern Baptist.

Lena and mother became "best friends" in a world strange to both. Mother found a church home and Sunday School for her age group, attending regularly. She and Lena planned two or three outings a week, stopping for lunch along the way. What could have been gloom and doom in mother's life was changed by the Grace of God, whom she trusted, into a new life, rich with joy, love, family and friendship. God, in His abundant mercy, provided a new way for me and my children to deal with circumstances beyond our control, enriching our lives with the special unassuming touch of my precious mother.

In 1976, I bought a small second home in Stowe, Vermont, the "Ski Capital of the East". It gave my kids and me a base from which we went out to ski, our favorite family pastime. For mother, that little place was a "destination of love". She especially loved cold, snowy days when she held down the fort at home while the rest of us spent the day skiing at Mount Mansfield. We always knew she'd have a hot stew of some kind and fresh homemade bread waiting by a warm fire for her hungry skiers. She loved those days when the snow came hard and fast, as she watched the panorama through a large picture window, as she kept warm and toasty inside.

I can't imagine anyone else coming into our circumstances circa 1976 so seamlessly as she, daily lighting our lives with her totally loving and giving spirit. She had instant acceptance from both children because they knew, loved and respected her. She exceeded everyone's hopes and expectations in all she did. At the same time, she made a new life for herself in the church and with friends God led her to. Mother's entire life was testimony to trusting God, living and doing for others quietly, usually without recognition.

After five years, she decided to move to her own small apartment in a retirement village near our home. Ten years later, God called her home to her reward in Heaven where my dad waited. I look forward to sharing eternity with them in God's Heavenly Kingdom. My mother, Corrie Leta Wilkinson Adams, was as near perfection as I can imagine this side of Heaven. She lives indelibly in the lives of my family and everyone she touched.

The only other person I've ever known like this is the wife God graciously gave me in 1994, Margery. She comes out of a cut of cloth similar to my mother in terms of her wisdom, intelligence, strength, generosity and love of God and country.

MY GRANDMOTHER, SARAH ADAMS (Grandma)

S arah Chamness Adams was born near Columbus, Georgia in 1861, just as the Civil War between the States was breaking out, ostensibly over the issue of slavery...

She died in 1948 following complications of throat and mouth cancer. It's no coincidence that she was a heavy snuff dipper most of her life.

She lived with my mother, my father and me until I was nine, when she moved to a daughter's home after she was found to have cancer. From time to time, she spent a few days or weeks with one of her other children. A constant stream of family visitors called on her at our house. Occasionally, they brought along a gift for the house such as a bushel of potatoes or other fresh produce. Though it was but a pittance in the scheme of things, I'm sure my parents appreciated these favors as Grandma was totally dependent on them. My grandfather, Wiley, had passed many years before.

Grandma was one-fourth Cherokee Indian, and she looked every bit the squaw, with high cheek bones and other telltale features. Some relatives insisted she was fully half Cherokee. Of all her children, my father, Albert, most reflected this Indian heritage.

Sarah and Wiley had twelve children in all, seven girls and five boys. All were born at home, the old-fashioned way. I can't imagine the daily challenge of feeding, clothing and housing a family of this size on a subsistence farm.

All were given single names, as was the tradition in much of the South. I've always found the array of names of the twelve fascinating....see what you think :

> Tane
> Dora
> Lola
> Mary
> Alma
> Kate
> Ellie
> Frank
> Jim

Albert
Jep
Floyd

I've listed each gender in order of the ages, as best I can remember, oldest at the top to youngest at the bottom. I came into contact with all of them during my childhood, one way or another. Tane, Dora, Lola and Mary lived in Oklahoma, so we saw them only occasionally when they visited Texas. All the others were Texas residents.

My dad was close to only one of the clan, Jim, an older brother who once saved young Albert from being torn apart by a vicious dog attack. Jim often hunted deer and other game with Dad.

After the war, when my parents bought a new Chevy 4-door Sedan, dad also bought a second car from sister Dora....her mint condition 1938 black 2-door Dodge Coupe. He used the old car mostly for driving to and from his hunting place on the Sabine. Aunt Dora drove it down from Tulsa and took the train back.

Sarah, Wiley and their children moved away from Georgia sometime between 1890 and 1900, headed for Oklahoma, near Tulsa. I don't know whether it had anything to do with the Trail of Tears, the westward relocation of the Cherokee Nation by the US government. I always believed it was more than a coincidence that the Adams' family left Georgia for a new life in Oklahoma, with its large Indian population. I regret not finding out more while I had the opportunity during her life with us.

Let this be an object lesson to you, dear reader... learn all you can about your heritage while those who know it best are living. Many specifics about how and when the family moved from Georgia to Oklahoma then on to Texas are unclear to me. How I now wish I'd asked more questions about this period when those who could have illuminated me were still living.

She and her husband Wiley were in pursuit of a better life for their family when they moved to a strange new place to start over with a totally new beginning. They sharecropped a farm outside Tulsa, a meager subsistence at best. Wild game, when it could be found, was about the only source of meat.

Farming conditions became desperate in Oklahoma and across the plains. Little rain fell and winds blew constantly, parching the land so badly it became known as the Dust Bowl. Crop failures were rampant and subsistence farmers like the Adams' were in dire straits, some near starvation. This transplanted family wondered what they had gotten into by leaving Georgia.

They heard conditions were better in East Texas. After crop and financial failures in Oklahoma, they headed south to settle near Kilgore as tenant farmers. Sarah bore twelve children, ten in Texas, two in Oklahoma. The oldest was Frank, the youngest Ellie. My dad Albert was in the middle.

Although the East Texas weather for farming was better than Oklahoma, it was still far from ideal. The family suffered yet another crop failure, owing considerable money to a lending bank. My dad took it upon himself to bail them out. Almost singlehandedly, he farmed, made a crop, broke wild horses and cowboyed, earning enough to pay off his parents' indebtedness.

Older brother, Jim, was the Chief Detective in Tyler, Texas. Albert and Jim respected each other, often comparing notes on criminal cases. They sometimes hunted deer together with a group of friends during the fall season.

Grandma was a proverbial font of tales about the old South, spanning the early to mid-1800's through the 1860's and the great Civil War. Connecting with her let me experience firsthand through her eyes and mine over more than 150 years of life in America. She happily shared many stories with me when I was a child.

During my elementary school years, I'd usually make a bee line for grandma's room after getting home, sitting at her feet to hear a story. I had my favorites among her litany, and requested some of them many times. Dad kept her supplied with "toothbrushes" for dipping snuff. He made these from twigs of a sweet gum tree out back, flaying out an end of a three inch long twig. She moistened the flayed end, dipped it into her brown glass snuff bottle and held the saturated brush between her lower gum and cheek as she spoke. Her spittoon, a large empty coffee can, was within easy reach, near her rocking chair.

Grandma dressed in the old style--ankle length dresses made by one of her daughters, with apron tied in back. In cooler weather she wore a "smock" over dress and apron. Everything in her ensemble was homemade, from scratch.

Every morning she twisted her long hair into a neat, tight bun behind her head. She walked with a cane that thump-thumped as she tottered about the house. Dad usually brought her a "hot toddy" to get her started for the day, a potent mixture of whiskey and black coffee.

She ate alone in the kitchen promptly at four thirty every afternoon, always the same meal — a large bowl of oatmeal with butter, milk and sugar. She never seemed to tire of this monotonous fare. She ate apples, oranges and pears throughout the day. Oatmeal and fruits made up most of her diet. She was especially fond of dried apples. The rest of the day she kept to herself in her front bedroom, sitting in her rocking chair, catnapping and reading her Bible. By seven at night, she'd be in bed. If nature called at night, she used her bedside chamber pot, affectionately called the "slop jar". During my mother's morning rounds, she emptied and cleaned it for the next night. Except for occasional visits by family members, she lived a sedentary life, quiet and alone.

I had no idea at the time how unique it was to be able to sit at her feet and be in touch with more than a century and a half of history--- from her memory of ancestors from the early 1800's through to my childhood in the 1930's and 40's--- first hand. Many things she told me were handed down from one or two generations back.

America was more innocent back then, feeling its way in an older, wiser world. Every activity we now take for granted, and things we took for granted even in my childhood, did not exist. There was no radio, telephone, television, cars, airplanes, movie theaters, and only rudimentary medical treatments. Those treatments that were available well might have been fatal. She grew up in an era before surgeons knew much about germs infections and viruses. In fact, post amputation infection and disease claimed more lives in the great Civil War than anything else.

Few Americans strayed more than fifty miles from their roots, except of course in wartime when they got a chance to see the world. Dangerous bacteria were a pestilence and medicine was in the Dark Ages. Superstition and folklore abounded in many communities. Through my grandmother, I was teleported back in time to this old world, and I got to experience it firsthand with her. That old world was like night and day compared to the "modern" world we lived in during the 1930's and 40's.

Some of her tales etched strong impressions on my young mind. So much so that I asked her many times again to tell me the story about "this or that." She always obliged. I especially loved afternoons with her when the weather was bad, setting a spellbinding mood.

I heard the story of her father's gruesome death after the Battle of Peach Tree Street in Atlanta during the Civil War. Both his legs were blown off at the knee by a cannon ball. He was removed by medics, given available treatment and somehow managed to survive a ride home to Columbus, Georgia. Grandma described his sufferings in the last hours of his life, as she sat near, holding his hand. She watched as he breathed his last. A little girl had just lost her father. She, her mother and family survived after his death with the help of family members who were in close proximity during the long war.

The tale of the "talking cat" was one of my perennial favorites. She described mid-1870s Georgia when nearby relatives often took evening meals together. The kitchen, or cook house, was separate from the main house where bedrooms dining room and living quarters were located. This provided a margin of safety from fire hazards if the cookhouse went up in flames. Meals were prepared on a wood burning cook stove and stews in a pot swung over an open fire. After supper, the women and girls cleaned up in the cook house as menfolk lounged in the main house, smoking and talking.

One particular night, a stray cat no one recognized showed up in the cook house. The ladies had finished cleanup and were sitting around talking and smoking corn cob pipes. Grandma was among them. Two sisters in the group were named Emma and Maggie. The strange stray cat looked Emma straight in the eyes and meowed as clear as a bell, in a falsetto tone, E-M-M-A...E-M-M-A..., then turning to the other sister in the same falsetto, M-A-G....M-A-G. The ladies were stunned as this mysterious cat hopped out the open door and was gone. A few minutes later, Uncle Jake, a gnarly old Civil War veteran came in. The girls excitedly told him the story about the talking cat. Jake responded, "If that cat comes back tomorrow night, I'll catch it and cut off its tail."

As if on cue, Tabby made its appearance the following night after dinner and performed the same séance. Jake was ready, grabbing the cat before it disappeared, quickly lopping off its tail with his pocket knife. Then he put the cat out the door, letting it go. Jake said, "Now girls, if that cat comes back tomorrow night I'll cut off one of its ears". The same thing happened the next night, and Jake promptly removed an ear. To this, Jake added, "Now girls, if that cat comes back tomorrow night I'll cut off its other ear". This he did, after hearing the strange looking bobbed tail cat with one ear cry, E-M-M-A and M-A-G. Uncle Jake then told the girls, " With no ears and no tail it won't ever be back". And that was so, thus ending one of grandma's strange tales from the old South.

Grandma had many more stories in her repertoire. I can't remember them all, but wish I could. Suffice it to say, her tales kept this child wide eyed and rapt many an afternoon. She was truly old world in dress, manner, thought and speech. She called my friends and me "little scholars" instead of kids or children. She described fat babies as being "fleshy", supposedly a healthy sign. If you said, "How are you today, grandma". She would reply "tolable" meaning, of course, tolerable.

Another of her remarkable stories was about the "flying chairs". It seems one afternoon the family was working in a field, all but one sister. The sister suddenly appeared running and screaming that everyone had to come to the house quickly to see what was happening. As they approached the house, there were loud bumps, clatters and noises, like pieces of wood banging together. Approaching a window they saw chairs flying in the air all over the room, slamming into each other. Then suddenly, the chairs settled down and landed upright on the floor, all in their proper places.

Were her stories merely made up, to entertain her inquisitive grandson? I'll never know for sure. But I can say that every time she told a story, there was no deviation. It was always the same. She claimed her stories were the honest truth. Suffice it to say, true or not, she spent many afternoons regaling me with her mysterious tales, and I loved her dearly.

When grandma passed in 1948, I was twelve and really sad to lose her. But it's an ill wind that blows no good. I inherited her bedroom for my own after she moved away under a daughter's care. For the first time in my life I had my own private bedroom and I was overjoyed. I would have places to keep all my toys and stuff I loved. I took great pride in the room that my dear, mysterious grandma lived in, respecting her space now that it was my own. I even inherited her bed. My parents set me up with a desk and chair where I could study. They got a book case for me with enough shelves for all my books, World Books, Encyclopedias and my collection of books I enjoyed reading for pleasure. I put a work bench near the bedroom's two side windows for building model airplanes and kites. My chemistry set rested on a bench nearby. I had a passion for making stink bombs that my mother was not so crazy about. I got enormous joy out of hand carving rocket ships, making propellant charges using gunpowder and launching them into the sky as my friends and I stood and gaped.

I've strayed from completing my story about grandma. A strange thing happened one day after I had lived in her room for about a year. The mounted head of my first big buck hung proudly on the wall above my desk and chair. Coming in one afternoon to study, I took one look at the desk and realized that a black stripe about four inches long and half an inch wide marked the left side of the desk top. Realizing it was a burn, I was annoyed and upset, because there was not any logical explanation for this. My parents knew nothing about it. Then I wondered if somehow grandma had sent me a message that she was still around, looking in on me. If so, it would certainly fit right in with her old-world stories, her unique ways and superstitions.

ROBERT EVERETT WILKINSON, MY UNCLE

"U ncle" was my favorite relative and my role model. Next to my dad, he was the most important guy to me.

Robert Everett Wilkinson was my mother's only brother, eight years her senior. She called him "Brother" all her life. He and my dad, aside from being in-laws, were best friends. I wanted to be just like him to the point that I would plant my own little feet in his footprints, as I walked behind him in a plowed field.

Uncle married into money---Fannie Mae Wilson was the only daughter of East Texas land magnate, Jasper Wilson of Omen, Texas. The Wilsons were not showy, living simply but comfortably amid their thousands of farmland acres. To me, my aunt was always just "Auntie"--not Aunt Fannie Mae, just as "Uncle" was never Uncle Everett. They were pretty much my second parents, and I knew if anything ever happened to my mom and dad, I would live with them. I had many aunts and uncles as well as cousins on my dad's side of the family, but they just didn't count like these two.

Uncle and Auntie had only one child, a daughter Jacqueline Virginia. She was ten years older than I, and was effectively my big sister, as I was her little brother. Her first name was never used, only Virginia, or more familiarly, Ginny.

The Wilsons gave substantial homes and farms to each of their two sons and daughter. Auntie and Uncle were given the old original pre-Civil War home at Omen with its associated acreage. This was where the Wilsons had originally lived and raised their children. It was a stately home in the old Southern tradition, with columns in front and a porch around almost the entire house. Lolling around on the front porch swing was a special delight for me

The big house had two levels, the second strictly for storing old family relics and pieces of furniture. The ceilings were very high throughout the house, nine or ten feet or more. This made the stairway between the first and second floors seem long, dark and mysterious to me. To discourage me from wandering upstairs, meddling where I shouldn't, Auntie made it clear that "Raw Head and Bloody Bones lives up there and he doesn't like little children". For sure, there wasn't a problem keeping me away from upstairs where I didn't belong.

Though upstairs was off limits, I reveled in being free to roam around the four hundred acres surrounding the house as I grew older. There were barns, pastures, forests and ponds (in Texas they are called tanks). There were fields of cotton, corn, grain and groves of peaches, pears and apples. In addition, Uncle ran a herd of a hundred or more cattle.

The farm was managed day in and day out by old Doc. His family, descended from Ante Bellum times in East Texas, had lived at this place for generations. This was the only home they knew. Doc and his boys handled the cattle, plowed and maintained the fields, cut hay, picked fruits, vegetables and cotton, and provided all physical labor required. A grandson Robert, a preschooler about my age, was my steady playmate. Our favorite activity was throwing dry corncobs at each other in one of the barns.

Something always needed doing around the place. If nothing else was going on, the thousands of feet of barbed wire fence could be inspected and fixed as needed. I was assigned to this chore when Uncle thought I was old enough to be responsible.

Hogs, chickens and beef cattle provided abundant meat and eggs for everyone on the farm. From time to time, especially during the War years, milk cows were kept and provided plenty of fresh raw milk, cream and butter. When operated full up, the farm provided virtually a self-sufficient life for Auntie, Uncle and all the farm hands. Electric power and rural telephone service were the predominant outside purchases.

Every fall, tasks turned to slaughtering, butchering and preparing beef, chicken and pork, fruits and vegetables for the freezers. Uncle and my dad were always heavily involved, as both our families drew from this bounty. Summers were spent harvesting the crops of all kinds, canning and hauling cotton to be ginned.

When I was ten, Auntie and Uncle provided a gentle mare for me to ride, complete with saddle, reins and bit, and all the fixings. Her name was Maudie. I was free to ride Maudie all over the farm. Doc taught me to curry, saddle, feed and care for her. When Uncle asked me to check out fences around the farm and its pastures, Maudie was my transportation. This was an altogether joyful chore, and I was expected to make simple repairs, reporting any bigger problems back to Doc.

Doc plowed behind a team of mules, the old fashioned way. I often followed behind him barefooted, traipsing through the warm fresh broken sod. Uncle decided to upgrade the plowing and bought a new Ford Ferguson tractor. He bought a Farmall for smaller jobs. Old Doc didn't take to this new equipment, continuing to use his trusty team of mules. Soon I was learning to drive the Farmall, doing a few simple chores like mowing hay.

Once I asked Doc his age. He didn't know exactly, but carried in a silver dollar which bore the date of his birth, 1879. Doc didn't have much "book learning" as they say, but he was blessed with abundant common sense and a flair for getting things done, including mechanical jobs. He was a gentle soul, as was all his family. I loved them all dearly. Auntie took care of all their medical needs, whether it necessitated pulling teeth, treating bad colds and flu, or childbirth---she arranged and paid for everything. She and Uncle were as good to them as anyone could possibly be. They were basically part of the family.

Uncle generally earned his living drilling oil wells under contract. He oversaw as many as three rigs, operating simultaneously. He and my aunt would be away from Omen for several months at a time when he was drilling. Being a "tool pusher" who hired rig crews including roughnecks and drillers, he ran these large machines day and night until the well was brought in. He was responsible for everything that happened on the drilling site. Often I got to go with him for a day at the rig, getting early exposure to lots of oil patch lingo. I saw crews go "fishing" for lost drill bits, manage drilling "mud", pull cores aligning them in long wooden troughs so Uncle could inspect them. I watched as wireline logs were run, with Uncle examining the squiggly lines looking for pay zones. I took it all in as wells were cased and valving and production hardware installed. At an early age I fell in love with the pungent but sweet smell of freshly produced crude oil.

Uncle was outstanding with all kinds of machinery. For example, he rigged up a cotton gin at the farm, pulling the engine and transmission out of an old Buick automobile and using its power to drive a system of belts to operate the gin. Homespun, but it worked.

Uncle was a veteran of World War 1. He had enlisted at the age of twenty and served his entire stint at Wright Field, Dayton, Ohio. He was responsible for maintaining and repairing Curtiss and other biwinged aircraft of the World War One era. There he developed formidable mechanical skills that served him well throughout his life. Fortuitously, I served three years at the same base four decades later as an Air Force officer. My daughter was born at the Base Hospital.

Uncle, like most men in his trade was fair, intelligent, an outstanding manager of men and equipment. Yet he was rough and tough. He had a burly build; he was six feet tall and stocky, a Wilkinson family trait. H−e t−a−l−k−e−d r−e−a−l s−l−o−w, with a deep Texas drawl. But his mind ran like lightning, ahead of the game. His hands were rough like sandpaper, callused from hard manual work.

I must share a loving memory of Uncle from my perspective as a three-year-old. He hoisted me up on his shoulders as we stood watching the huge "steam shovel" scoop out red earth to make way for an underpass near the railroad depot in Longview. These huge machines were also called drag lines because of the heavy gauge cables controlling the movement of the giant shovel. Today machines are known as front end loaders, pond hogs, and a variety of other names. Technology has advanced to the point that steel cables are mostly reserved for really heavy duty tasks, like strip mining, dredging and major building construction. Almost everything now is done by the magic of hydraulics. I still remember the sweet smell of East Texas clay as it was scooped out that morning more than 70 years ago. As I sat on his shoulders, Uncle patiently explained what was going on step-by-step, and he answered many questions asked by his three-year-old nephew. I grew up loving the sight and sound of big, powerful machinery and the sweet smell of oil, sprayed on Harrison Street in Longview. I've been told more than once my sensory likes and dislikes are a little strange.

Uncle passed away during my sophomore year at Texas A&M, suffering from severe, chronic high blood pressure. I had one last visit with him in the hospital in Tyler just before he passed, suffering immensely as he went. He was only in his mid-60's.

ROBERT MCCLURE, MY COUSIN

I had to be somewhere safe, secure and "homey" after school.

That's where my cousin, Bobby, came in. He was involved in my "life after school" from the time I was five until I was a second grader. It's remarkable that Bobby, a teenager, put up with his kid cousin as well as he did.

Cousin Bobby, dad's nephew, was the only child of dad's youngest sister Ellie. The McClures lived near downtown Longview. Aunt Ellie was a frail little thing, rolling her cigarettes with a fascinating small hand operated contraption. It chunked out a perfect roll of tobacco in tissue thin cigarette paper with every crank of a lever. The tobacco link to cancer hadn't come front and center, and practically everyone smoked including medical doctors. "I'd Walk A Mile For A Camel" and "LSMFT" (Lucky Strike Means Fine Tobacco) slogans were everywhere. Aunt Ellie's cigarette roller was in fact provided by Lucky Strike as an inducement to buy their tobacco.

Miss Jodie McClure, Robert the Senior's sister, lived next door. Miss Jodie was a legend in Longview, having taught first grade seemingly forever. Practically everyone had been a student of Miss Jodie at one time or another, no matter their age. She was strict but fair, an outstanding teacher whom youngsters were fortunate to experience. Miss Jodie never married, teaching until she was ancient.

Many afternoons I was dropped off at the McClure house after kindergarten or elementary school. This arrangement had been orchestrated by my mom, to be sure I was in good hands after school until someone could come drive me home. I sometimes wished I could go straight home after school like other kids, but must admit exposure to this fascinating and ingenious cousin, nine years older than I, usually more than made up for missing out on playtime with neighborhood friends or listening to more of Grandma's mysterious tales.

Bobby's part of the house was a menagerie of fascinating things he built. Frugal with his earnings from delivering newspapers early every morning, he was able to accumulate a wide variety of interesting things to build. Model airplanes of every kind hung from his bedroom ceiling, all of which he built from model kits. Many could accommodate powerful little Olson engines.

The smell of glue, oils and model airplane dope filled the air. To make one of these planes required steady hands, good eyes and the ability to carefully follow a schematic diagram. The first step was to carefully cut strips from a sheet of balsa wood, according to a detailed diagram. This required using a razor sharp Xacto knife and steady hands. Straight pins then conformed the balsa strips to perfectly fit a diagram, and all joints were then glued together. The fuselage, wings and tail subassemblies were built in this manner. When everything was dry, the pins were pulled out, leaving behind a rigid subassembly. These, glued properly together, formed the airframe. Next, thin sturdy paper was glued on, covering all surfaces, to form the airplane's skin. Finally a dope was brushed on the surfaces, becoming rigid after drying and curing. Insignias such as stars, targets, or swastikas were glued on, and voilà you had an airplane that could fly once the engine was installed.

There were twenty or more completed planes hanging from the ceiling in Bobby's room, some I had "helped build". We often flew them in a city park, Bobby at the ground end of two long control wires, affixed to a simple hand held C shaped handle grip clutched tightly. The plane sped round and round in a great circle, swooping and looping, with Bobby at the controls. Manipulating this handle pulled one wire or the other, causing the control surfaces to change so that the plane climbed, dived or looped as it hurtled through the air. The powerful, noisy little Olson engine did the trick, spinning a wooden propeller. Occasionally we'd have a crash, demolishing the entire package. A time or two the control wires broke, and the plane flew off to goodness knows where. We always tried to chase it down and recover the plane. Though the airframe usually was damaged, we really wanted to recover the valuable little engine to reuse it in another plane.

The screened back porch outside Bobby's bedroom was his magical workshop. He had built a large stand up workbench for making and testing model airplanes and anything else he decided to work on. At one end of the bench, engines were mounted and tested before they were installed in an airplane. The sound was earsplitting when engines were put through their paces, but no one seemed to mind. They just knew that Bobby was at work in his shop.

He once built a small steam engine powered by aviation fuel. The little generator turned a shaft connected to a generator, making electric power. I learned from Bobby that AC and DC power were different. It just made sense to me that rotating coils of wire through a magnetic field generated an alternating current, unlike the steady DC current from storage batteries we used to fire up an Olsen engine.

Bobby's engine test stand was equipped with a scale to measure the thrust an engine developed. He worked like a mad scientist in his lab, not wanting Aunt Ellie or anyone else to interrupt. Bobby didn't sit me down and teach me about thrust, lift, drag or power. I learned from just being around as he worked. He was too busy to explain things, expecting me to follow what was going on and ask only intelligent questions. I was forever fascinated by the control surfaces, how they changed the attitude of an airplane in flight---rear flaps down, tail up, nose points down in a dive---flaps up, the opposite happens and you climb---one up and one down, the plane rolls--- pretty soon you'd get the idea. Vertical rudder left pushes the tail right and nose left, so the plane turns left....reversing this turns the plane right....all elementary lessons in aerodynamics.

Bobby was a born daredevil as well as a skilled model builder. He took flying lessons at the small Kilgore airport, learning to fly a single wing Piper Cub. At the county fair, Bobby always rode the dizzying "flying boot", looping over and over until he spent all his money. Ordinary people would be tossing up their cookies after just one or two trips on the flying boot. Bobby never did--- he reveled in it. I realize that Bobby himself paid for everything he did, including college. His parents weren't in a position to help him much. I suppose this is one reason I've always admired Bobby.

Bobby regaled me with many other gizmos and contraptions. We went together on my first airplane ride at the grand opening of the new Gregg County Airport when the war came to an end. Rides in a shiny new DC3 Goony Bird were five dollars apiece for a 45 minute trip over East Texas. This plane was the starship of Trans Texas Airlines connecting Longview to Dallas and other cities. The Goony was the standard in airline travel with plush seating. It was so much fun I came back for a second ride the next day. I've been in love with airplanes and what makes them fly ever since. I never developed a hankering to be a pilot, being more into the technical side of things.

Bobby McClure was my childhood science maven. I credit him for instilling in me an insatiable curiosity about how and why things work. Building on this foundation, I had the good fortune to study under really outstanding teachers in high school and college. They challenged and motivated me to learn more, to ask more probing questions, and to study throughout my life.

Cousin Bobby ultimately became a medical doctor, starting out at Kilgore College, then East Texas State in Commerce, finishing up at the University of Texas Medical School. After contracting tuberculosis while in college, he took a term off before continuing, deciding on anesthesiology as his major.

Bobby married Joan Straun, whose father owned a pharmacy in Longview. The McClures' established a medical practice in Houston, and Bobby became a prominent anesthesiologist. Bobby found a welcome home in hospital operating rooms filled with sophisticated devices.

Poor Aunt Ellie died of alcoholism. She was so very sweet, but just couldn't put the bottle down....it eventually killed her.

DOWN IN THE RIVER BOTTOM

In many places it's called a "river valley". Where I come from it is called the "river bottom".

The Sabine River establishes the border between Texas and Louisiana, flowing from the northeastern most part of Texas into the Gulf of Mexico two hundred miles to the South. The Sabine is one of the major tributaries in the State of Texas. The Sabine River bottom was an endless source of adventure, joy and excitement, a magical place for us all, kids and adults alike. Our camp was very near Longview, only half an hour away. This was a special spot for me from the age of five on. The bottom was rife with wild life of all kinds--- creeping things, running things, growling things, climbing things and many kinds of crawling things.

Two separate areas were available to us---my dad's 300 acre hunting lease, and further down the way the father of my schoolmate, Frank, owned a 2000 acre plot. Both were heavily wooded and bounded by the Sabine River. Crude camp sites and tarpaper shacks, suitable for sleeping, and outdoor grated pits for cooking were at each. We had makeshift outdoor tables for preparing and eating meals. Our dads didn't have to worry much about us, knowing exactly where we were, what we were doing and how to find us. They trusted us with firearms, content knowing we had been well trained in their safe and proper use. We had literally grown up around firearms, as they were an inceptive part of our culture.

My favorite time of year was the fall hunting season in September through most of December. The crisp morning air carried the hypnotic fragrance of decaying leaves on the forest floor. Leaves moist with morning dew allowed a skillful woodsman to move about stealthily and silently. These same leaves are a mixed blessing, because when dry leaves are walked on they crackle like magpies. Might as well broadcast on a loudspeaker to forewarn wildlife, "Here I come"! One learns early to tread softly when looking for wildlife---after all, you are in their habitat, it's where they live every day. A skilled woodsman like my dad could carefully move through the woods on a cushion of leaves without a sound. He expected me to follow him through the forest with the same skill, and my lessons started early in life.

My friends and I spent much time in the woods, becoming reasonably good stalkers, hunters and wilderness campers. We were in the woods most weekends in the fall and winter, weather permitting, camping, cooking over an open fire, and just enjoying each other and the experience of being out in the woods together. A soft down-filled olive drab sleeping bag was always with me. It was more like a duvet than a sleeping bag when totally unzipped, covering a sleeping surface. Zipped, it was a warm, soft cozy bag where I often slept on a soft mattress of dry pine needles. At home, I slept in the bag most winter nights, not turning down my bed. The sleeping bag and my trusty .22 long rifle Remington or my 30-30 Winchester were my most prized possessions and were always with me.

I can't begin to count the many good times my dad and I had there. He started me shooting when I was four with a simple Red Ryder B-B gun, then at five with a Benjamin pump air rifle shooting B-B's at a blistering speed. I was always under his close supervision when shooting. He was an extremely able teacher and mentor, and I loved opportunities to go shooting with him. Often he brought his nickel plated S & W handgun and got in some practice of his own. These occasions were my very best times with my dad while he was Chief. Otherwise being around him was not always fun because he was so somber.

When I turned seven years old, dad promoted me up to a semi-automatic Remington 22 caliber Speedmaster rifle, holding 10 rounds of long rifle ammo, loaded through a slot in the stock. It was a beautiful firearm, streamlined, sleek and wonderful to shoot. Again, dad closely supervised all aspects of my handling this firearm, always with greater emphasis on safety than anything else including marksmanship. He drilled into my head early on that a gun of any kind is dangerous and potentially deadly. To bring his point home, I once got spanked for pointing my empty Red Ryder B-B gun in his direction. He brought home the point that there was absolutely no excuse for carelessness or sloppiness with a gun--it was inexcusable and there was zero tolerance for error.

By age eight, dad introduced me to several hunting techniques including "still hunting", hunting from a stand on the ground or in a tree, and stalking. I learned to skin and dress a squirrel or rabbit by age ten, and I had become a fairly decent shot with both the Benjamin and the Remington. We never took game of any kind wastefully, always preparing it for the table.

Please bear with me as I tell you a story about an afternoon adventure with my dad, long ago, down in the river bottom. He and I went to his hunting place on a fall afternoon in late October, before the November deer season to scout out a couple of spots where we might get a deer. I was about eight at the time. Dad told me we were going to sit for a spell in an area rumored to be frequented by a giant buck called "Old Blue." The dark hue of his heavy winter coat, seen through hazy afternoon light, looked blue. Old Blue was rumored to have an enormous rack of antlers.

Dad preferred sitting on a log or stump off the ground instead of a tree blind. But this method of hunting means you must be doubly cautious, avoiding any abrupt movements like scratching your nose or fluttering your hands. Dad explained that the deer's vision is so sharp as to detect any careless or sudden movement, like the flick of a hand. He taught me to move any part of my body in slow motion, avoiding detection. Sitting still was a tall order for a kid of seven or eight. Yet I was excited and almost ecstatic at the very thought of getting a glimpse of any deer in the woods, much less the fabled old stag. Blue had survived many hunting seasons and had come out on top of scrapes with other bucks to earn his spot as "Alpha Buck" in the forest.

We sat as still as possible on opposite ends of a brushy fallen tree while late afternoon light streamed through the autumn leaves above and illuminated the carpet of fallen leaves across the forest floor. It was an incandescent sight, a spectacle of orange, green and gold.

Then we saw him about a hundred yards away. He appeared suddenly, out of nowhere, the way deer often do. He must have gotten a whiff of our scent, because he walked around in a circle, nose in the air, snorting as he went, pawing the ground with large cloven hooves. The big stag was remarkable and sure enough he was very dark, and almost appeared to be "blue". He was accompanied by fifteen other deer, some with racks, but mostly females. They put on a show, parading about for fifteen or twenty minutes, snorting and pawing the ground. I would've been frightened if I'd been there alone. Suddenly, the herd broke and ran in all different directions through the woods. Blue quickly disappeared, and a large doe ran straight for us, jumping the log between dad and me in a single bound. She sailed over the log near enough for me to touch!

There was nothing left to do but get up, slip out of the woods to the car and drive away, grinning from ear to ear. We were filled with delight over the spectacle we had been privileged to witness that afternoon, and filled with hope for good luck in the upcoming hunting season.

That adventure many years ago was the precursor to a rite of passage. It brought me to bagging my first big stag, near that same spot in the woods.

The fall afternoon in 1947 was glorious, crisp and cool . My schoolmate hunting partner Jere and I finished our lunch sandwiches and chips with my dad and his hunting buddy that day, Dee McHaney. Our spirits were high in this first week of fall deer season. Nobody in dad's usual hunting group had gotten a shot, but signs were all over the place. Large, cloven hoof prints spread wide under the weight of a big one. Fresh rubs on many saplings and hoof scrapes here and there on the ground meant bucks were staking out their mating territories. These were obvious signs that rutting was underway. With weather cooperating, we just needed patience and a little luck. Lots of does had been seen, but so far no bucks. This time of year, these guys are skittish with only one thing in mind--- mating. With necks swollen and antlers shining, every buck is preened, hoping to find the right female which by his definition is a doe in estrus, ready to mate.

Jere and I left camp at one o'clock to resume the day's hunt. Jere went one direction to his favorite spot and I went another. My favorite spot was near the place dad and I had seen Old Blue and his tribe of deer several years before. The sight and sound of that big deer snorting and pawing the ground drew me back to the same place again and again. I didn't have any great illusions that I might be lucky enough to bag Old Blue, yet this remained my favorite hang out in the woods. Failing to take a buck in the two previous hunting seasons when dad had permitted me to sit alone at my own spot, I was anxious to prove my mettle. I was almost twelve, and had become proficient with my 30-30 Winchester rifle, the result of dad's excellent mentoring. I was a pretty decent shot by the time he let me hunt on my own, I knew my way around the woods, and I understood the importance of stealth.

Dad taught me to always walk facing into the wind to prevent my scent from invading the area in front of me. The wind was light, more like a gentle breeze. Still, I was careful to face into the wind as I slipped carefully through the woods to my spot. My movements were slow and silent, the way my dad moved through the woods.

63

When I was well on my way to my spot, the crack of a high-powered rifle echoed through the woods. Then a second crack. I knew the shots didn't come from anyone in our party, as the sound was from the wrong direction. Frozen, I held my Winchester in a ready position, stock to my shoulder, not knowing what to expect. Within half a minute about 50 yards to my left a large buck crashed through a thicket of brush into my clear sight. I couldn't believe my eyes! Someone had obviously shot at him, and he was on-the-run. I had always heard about the phenomena called "buck fever" whereby you would develop the shakes so badly that you couldn't draw a bead, causing you to miss. I wasn't about to let this happen and somehow forced myself to stay calm.

As he drew broadside, antlers flashing in the afternoon light, I took careful aim as dad had always taught me, just behind his front leg aiming for the heart, and shot the first round. I was shocked that he kept going in a steady trot--either I had missed entirely or failed to hit a vital spot. Quickly I cranked the Winchester's lever, took aim and fired again. He didn't drop. He continued trotting, quickly getting away from me as he headed for a thicket just ahead. I no longer had a broadside view as he was beginning to look at me through his rear view mirror. Now, seventy yards away and trotting at an angle, the third shot hit him, causing him to stagger. Still he didn't drop, and I began feeling panicky. I hadn't realized how fast I could operate that 30-30, cranking the lever, ejecting the spent cartridge while slamming a new round into the chamber. At the fourth shot he stumbled and dropped. Approaching cautiously, gun ready to fire, I had to be sure he was dead. Otherwise you can find yourself on the wrong end of sharply pointed antlers and sharp hooves.

The big deer was dead. The third shot hit his rump, and number four hit him in the neck finishing the job. Jere, hearing my rapid fire, had started coming my direction. We stood for a minute admiring my beautiful first deer. This was to be my rite of passage to becoming a full-blown young hunter. He was quite a prize for a twelve year old, sporting a sturdy eight point rack, swollen neck typical of rutting bucks and a sleek, powerful body. He certainly wasn't the old fabled blue deer, but I couldn't have been prouder. Weighing in at 180 pounds, he was a load to get out of the woods and back to camp. We managed it, swinging him under a strong ten foot long pole on our shoulders, one of us in front the other following, with hooves tied together.

Dad and the others back in camp beamed as we strung up the big buck to do the necessary things to prepare the venison, including removing entrails, genitals and musks. We tied him on the fender of dad's car and returned to town, taking a victory lap around the square before depositing him at the icehouse for processing.

The proud head of that first buck taken long ago adorns my office and remains one of my most cherished possessions. It's been with me everywhere I've ever lived, as has my faithful old 30-30 Winchester. The old Winchester still has a special place of honor in our home. The cozy bedside rug provided by the big buck's hide is long gone, but for years it brought me joy whenever I stepped on it, always remembering that fall day long ago deep in the river bottom. Mounted head and rug graced the front bedroom at 235 Harrison along with my Winchester. These trophies were fine additions to the books and bookcases and other items I cherished in grandma's old room, now mine.

The venison was mouthwatering. Mother had a special way of preparing it so that its tenderness and flavor was more like a very young deer. Old timers used to say a year for each point, but I never believed that. They would say my buck was an eight year old. I believe it's more a function of habitat and diet. I've been blessed to hunt extensively in my life for deer and other game, and I've harvested my share. Yet no hunting adventure or success has ever quite lived up to that splendid fall day nearly seven decades ago, down in the river bottom with my dad, his pal Dee and my friend Jere.

SCHOOL

I earned good marks in high school, even though I didn't do as well as I hoped playing the national sport of Texas, football.

I wasn't fast enough in spite of my strength, and I was clumsy. I fell short of Dr. Farrar's optimistic athletic christening at my birth. I excelled in math and science and loved those subjects, though I didn't particularly care for biology and life sciences. Induction into the National Honor Society was one of my best achievements in High School. Another was finishing in the top ten percent of my graduating class with a three year 94 average.

A high school math teacher, Mr. C.C. Turner, was not only gifted but generous with his time, sometimes coaching a small group of us after hours and during a weekend. He introduced us to many of the finer points of math, and stimulated me to want to learn more. I was not so gifted in English but had the good fortune to have Miss Ruby Phenix as an instructor. She was very creative in her approach, sometimes having us write essays about an object we could see and describe, such as an orange or apple. She too worked extra hours with a group of us.

Having decided against studying to become a medical doctor, I wanted to do something that would take me further in math and science. It was fortuitous that Eastman had broken ground, building a huge petrochemical complex to convert gases from the East Texas fields to a variety of products. Dad arranged for me to meet with a top Eastman engineer, who helped me understand and ferret through options for college studies. I glommed onto chemical engineering, because this field of study incorporated under one umbrella, all of my main interests.

It was settled---I wanted to attend Texas A&M and become a chemical engineer.

Texas A&M, a.k.a. "Aggieland", was, is and will always be a cornerstone in my life. My Alma Mater helped shape me into what I am, in ways that are beyond my comprehension. A&M has always been a special place that provided what is called "the other education". That is the education that derives from the experience of living and working together as students in this unique tradition filled institution.

There's an apt old saying about A&M that comes to mind---"Outside looking in, you can't understand it. Inside looking out, you can't explain it." It is true that "Once you are an Aggie, you are always an Aggie".

Two possessions mean more to me than all others---my wedding band and my big, gold Aggie ring. Both are worn on my left hand ring finger, because I am married to both---Margery and Texas A&M. As the wedding band symbolizes the unbroken, eternal nature of my wedding vows, the uniquely designed Aggie ring is the highest symbol of everything A&M stands for.

An interesting side note about my Aggie ring--- I recovered it from a six foot depth of churning ocean at a beach in Tahiti after a large wave knocked it off my hand as I was body surfing. Searching frantically, I found it when luckily I stepped on it, chest deep in the ocean. What do you think the odds were for that?

It's been said "Football is the religion at A&M, and Kyle Field is the cathedral". I can attest that over my five and a half decades as an Aggie, there is simply no place on earth like Kyle Field and Aggieland on game days in the fall of the year. In the old days, we had 30-40,000 raucous fans in the stadium---now it's 90,000 and will be well over 103,000 when the rebuilt Kyle Field opens for business in 2015.The new Kyle will be the largest venue in Texas and the third largest in the country. No other sports venue in the nation will surpass this new state-of- the-art facility. This is a proud time to be an Aggie.

I showed up in September 1953,a bright egotistical 17-year-old, fresh out of high school. Being an only child magnified my egotism and sense of self-righteousness. These characteristics were sure to clash with the hard-core military discipline at A&M sooner or later. But surprisingly I really took to it as a freshman and liked knowing the boundaries. Some referred to A&M as a school for "poor boys" while the University of Texas down at Austin was the school for kids from "richer families". But no one would deny the strong academic program at A&M the ethics, embodied in "The Aggie Code of Honor", and all the traditions making A&M such a unique place.

 It was clear there were no women on campus, and to get a date you could go to neighboring Bryan, to Waco or one of the rural communities around Bryan-College Station. But the academic program and life in the Corps of Cadets was so demanding it was clear you would not have time to fool around. In fact the Commandant of the Cadet Corps announced at the beginning of my Freshman (Fish in Aggie parlance) Year, "Look around boys, those on your left and right will probably not be here by the end of the year". He meant a high percentage of us would flunk the academics, or reject military training, meaning you're out either way!

I got off to a fast start in my first year, earning a straight A average, with particularly high marks in chemistry, thought to be a killer course designed to eliminate weaker students. Induction into Phi Eta Sigma Freshman Honor Society and winning the freshman engineering contest which awarded me a brand new Keuffel & Esser slide rule and case were my big first year achievements. In my third and fourth years, I was inducted into Tau Beta Pi engineering honorary and Phi Lambda Upsilon chemistry honorary, and wore all three golden keys with pride on my watch chain. My GPA earned me a Distinguished Military Graduate (DMG) designation with a Regular Air Force commission. This was a career type commission as a Second Lieutenant, one of a handful, meaning I was destined to an Air Force career, unless I chose otherwise after three years of mandatory service.

The largest extracurricular activity at Texas A&M was "Bonfire", from early October to Thanksgiving Day Eve. It touched every single person on campus. All cadets participated, downing huge trees in the Brazos or Navasota river bottoms, loading flatbed trailers, dropping these huge logs at the build site, and stacking them tepee style around a tall center pole.

When not in class or studying, you worked on some phase of Bonfire. It was grueling, exhausting, hot physical labor, around the clock. But everyone was emotionally supercharged, working with their buddies on a crew to perform a common objective that was bigger than any of us. Bonfire was an awesome experience. Everyone worked, few if any were slackers. Professors, however, showed no mercy, giving major exams in all courses during "Bonfire Build".

It was torched on Thanksgiving Eve to the wonder of many thousands of adoring fans and the entire student body. Bonfire represented the "Burning desire in every Aggie's heart to Beat the hell out of TU" the next day!

Bonfire is no longer a core part of campus life in Aggieland after the tragedy that took the lives of a dozen of our brightest and best when the stack collapsed in the pre-dawn hours of November 18, 1999. There was no choice but to lose bonfire after this tragedy. In the old days, our bonfires were inherently safer and more stable, because logs were stacked in the style of a tepee or pyramid. This design put a physical limit on its size.

Somewhere along the way, Bonfire took on the form of a tiered wedding cake, logs in each layer stacked vertically on ends, reaching higher and higher. Each of the five or six tiers was wired together around a tall center pole. Too late, it was realized this design was unstable compared to shorter tepee stacks of old. We always believed our old Bonfires burned bright enough and long enough to serve everyone's purpose! The bonfires of old still burn in this old Aggie's heart, as I happily recall the intense joy, passion and fervor as thousands of Aggie faithful gathered for "Burn" to the stirring marches belted out by the "Fightin' Texas Aggie Band".

There is no way to replace Bonfire as a cornerstone of the "other education", together with life in a Corps Dorm. Texas A&M lives in my heart today with as much fervency as I had six decades ago, and nothing can ever replace it in my life. The education and experiences I got at A&M are forever....

After finishing at A&M, I went on to post graduate school in chemical engineering at the University of Colorado (CU), Boulder. They offered me a very attractive scholarship package. An additional bonus was learning to ski at a nearby area. After four years in the highly structured and disciplined environment at A&M, I didn't care for the laid back laxity at CU. Decent academically it lacked the pride, discipline and vigor that characterized Texas A&M. The best thing I can say about CU is that I earned a post graduate degree there and got introduced to skiing, a cornerstone of my life.

Eventually, called to active duty as a lieutenant in the Air Force, I had the excellent fortune to be assigned to the Research and Development Center at Wright Patterson Air Force Base, near Dayton, Ohio. There I enjoyed three wonderful years, having great facilities, a great mentor and terrific success. Although my commission at A&M gave me the option to spend an entire career in the Air Force, I opted out after three years, my contractual obligation, choosing instead a career in industry.

For the first time, I was exposed to different styles of managing large, complex organizations. I had no formal skills in business that would have prepared me--I had to learn as I went, and had the benefit of excellence mentorship. I gave serious thought to getting an MBA from a reputable place like Harvard, as Wayne Stark my old mentor at A&M urged, instead of going into industry. But I decided against this after being offered my dream job at Humble Oil and Refining Company (Esso) in Houston. I couldn't imagine getting the kind of job they offered me without first earning a reputable MBA. I was soon to find a new mentor at Humble in a job that would set me in a direction for the rest of my life. This was the best job I ever had.

FAMILY VACATIONS

O ther than trips down to the farm in Omen, I remember only one family trip during my childhood.

We joined two other families for a trip to Dallas in 1940 to see the just released epic, "Gone With The Wind" starring Clark Gable and Vivian Leigh. I clearly remember all of us staying overnight in a "tourist court". The adults attended the movie in shifts, someone always staying behind to look after me. I had to stay because foul language was used in the movie. It must have been that famous line spoken by Clark Gable, "Frankly my dear, I don't give a damn".

Until I could drive, my summer vacations were train trips with my mother to wherever my uncle was drilling oil wells. Sometimes it was out west near Lubbock, Leveland, or Snyder. Sometimes in the south central part of the state not far from Corpus Christi or Alice near Banquetti or some other remote location. Some years he drilled in southeast Texas near Livingston, Liberty, Saratoga and Kountze. It was during the War years and trains were pulled by gigantic huffing, puffing steam locomotives. Many passenger cars were not air-conditioned, so it was always hot as blazes in the Texas heat. We rode along with windows open, buffeted by superheated air and an occasional hot cinder thrown from the locomotive's firebox.

Trains were packed with soldiers in uniform, moving from place to place on leave or to a base where they had been reassigned. Some even squeezed into luggage racks above rows of seats, trying to snooze in hot, jerky discomfort. For the most part, passengers were congenial even with discomfort. Long train trips made me realize the vastness and diversity of Texas. It took the better part of a day and night to travel from Longview west to Lubbock. Army bases seemed to crop up everywhere along the route, and soldiers got on and off at every stop. They were just kids, only ten or twelve years older than I going off to war.

Seats on many rows faced each other, making for six pairs of knees, knee to knee. I once struck up a conversation with a soldier directly across from me and must have said something that rubbed my mother the wrong way, because she promptly told me to "quit popping off" and be quiet. I didn't strike up more conversations with soldiers after that, though I wanted to.

71

This was the only kind of summer vacation I knew. My dad stayed behind, never joining us on these trips. His idea of vacation was fall deer and squirrel hunting in the Sabine River bottom. Or, attending a conference of law enforcement officers in Houston, San Antonio or Tulsa. He got acquainted with Texas Governor Allen Shivers at one convention, a real treat for a staunch conservative like my dad. He visited family in Oklahoma once or twice, traveling by train.

He was fascinated by the vast caverns at Carlsbad, New Mexico, traveling alone by train, spending a week, making daily visits to the caverns and other ancient Indian sites in the area. He was deeply moved by the pipe organ rendition of "Rock of Ages", echoing deep in the bowels of the earth. He brought back a small stone from the cavern he cherished for life, keeping it in a special spot near his bed. I never understood its significance, though it held some special or maybe spiritual meaning to him.

My parents once sent me alone on the Santa Fe single car diesel powered " jitney" to Silsbee, deep in southeast Texas to visit my aunt and uncle. I was eight and really felt grown up, taking this hundred and fifty mile trip by myself. I rode with Aunt Fannie Mae from Silsbee to Saratoga where she and Uncle had rented for the summer while he drilled several oil wells. The nearest town of any size was Kountze. Saratoga was a tiny town and, like many small towns, had no central sewage handling facility. Sewage was piped from clusters of houses to several spots, impounded in small putrid "ponds", which were covered with pieces of metal roofing material. These so-called "cesspools" were definitely off limits. My home town was a civilized place, disposing of wastes in a modern system — I'd never heard of the crude way it was handled at Saratoga, and nobody thought to warn me.

I soon made friends with a few neighborhood kids, even borrowing a bicycle from one who had a spare. Not knowing about the hidden peril of cesspools, I drove innocently across what I thought was just a scrap of sheet metal. Smelling the foul odor, maybe I should have associated it what was beneath, but I didn't. Coming from a civilized place like Longview, even with my acquaintance with outhouses at the Omen farm, it never occurred to me that wastes would be handled like this. Before getting completely across the fifteen foot span, the sheet gave way and I sank, bike and all, up to my chin in the foul contents. I screamed and yelled with all my might until my aunt and nearby neighbors came running. Someone shoved a pole out to me which I grabbed for dear life as I was pulled out of the filth to safety. Awful slime covered me from head to toe. Aunt Fannie Mae washed me down with a garden hose, nozzle set full blast. My soggy clothes weren't salvageable and she burned them. My Aunt saw to it that I spent the entire afternoon in a tub of warm, soapy water. She scrubbed me with a stiff brush until I thought I would bleed. I learned an important lesson that day----don't walk or ride over anything that has even the slightest odor!

To assuage my feelings after this terrible experience, Uncle treated me to a pro baseball game that night at Beaumont, plying me with soda pop and hotdogs. Next day he retrieved the bicycle out of the abyss with a long handled rake, washed it off and returned to the neighbor who knew all about my baptism in the cesspool. I imagine everyone in Saratoga knew about it, as I took my share of good natured ribbing from the kids.

Our first family vacation was in 1950 following dad's resignation from the Longview Police Department. He grabbed a golden opportunity which sought him out, becoming Chief of Security for the Texas Eastman Company, a Division of Eastman Kodak. Their new petrochemical manufacturing plant was to be built on several thousand acres outside Longview near the Sabine River. Leaving that demanding and extremely dangerous law enforcement job behind gave our family cause to celebrate. The only trip the three of us had taken together in my first fourteen years was back and forth between Longview and the farm at Omen, or a time or two to call on relatives in Tyler.

I was fourteen by a few months, a newly licensed driver and World War Two had ended. Dad bought our first family car, a big black 1948 Chevy four door sedan with manual transmission. It had no radio or air conditioning, but I thought the big Chevy was magnificent. Dad's job change, the new car, the war's end and my new driver's license meant things were really looking up for the Adams' family.

Dad had taught me to drive on a manual transmission automobile, so I was right at home with the Chevy. The tricky part about driving such a vehicle is letting out the clutch just right so you don't go bucking down the street. The sight of a bucking car and a green horn driver behind the wheel wasn't the kind of image of I wanted to project. Stopping for a traffic light on an incline is really tricky because of the need to avoid rolling backwards as the clutch is let out. This maneuver has to be done carefully and smoothly as the accelerator is depressed. Too much of one or too little of the other results in killing the engine or worse, bucking ahead until you could regain control. Some old timers held the view that "When I can't shift gears myself and have to depend on one of those automatic transmissions, I'll just stop driving". Longview had several down-under-then up underpasses with traffic lights atop the upside, presenting challenges to me and other new drivers. The up side stoplights always seemed to be red, posing a challenge when it turned green.

Dad's driving lessons during two years before my legal driving age were comprehensive, emphasizing safe driving practices. Safety was higher on his list than competence, whether handling an automobile, a firearm or tracking game in the woods. He drilled safety into my head every step of the way, and I have to say those lessons have lasted a lifetime. I might have failed passing these principles on to my children because I wasn't as effective as dad in getting key points across.

Dad was the ultimate "defensive driver", thus his instruction was built on principles of driving defensively. During driving lessons, he put me through the paces at intersections posing threats from an imaginary automobile, maybe bursting through a stop sign or traffic light---how would I handle that? What would I do? He used this technique to sharpen my senses, making me realize that anything, even the most unexpected, can happen on the road. He stressed driving in such manner as to always give the other driver plenty of room, don't crowd—even if you have the right-of-way. Don't hog the passing lane, always give the other driver plenty of room to pass.

Yet he was not a slow poke by any means, usually cruising at 65 or 70, combining caution with reason and good sense in everything he did.

Things changed in a big way in our home after the war ended in 1945. Grandma had moved on, and her choice room was now mine. I couldn't believe the changes that came over my dad after he left the City for his new job at Eastman. Dad was the first person Eastman hired, and his first job was to recruit a crew to string barbed wire around the property. With his horse and saddle, he seemed happy returning to his old cowboy days in Oklahoma, riding Big Red throughout more than 2,000 acres of Eastman property. He was outdoors all the time, loving every minute of it. He and his new employers got along famously together. He was pretty much his own boss, really enjoying his role as construction started on the big new chemical complex. He was a new man, fun to be with, relaxed and easy going. It was the first time in my life I had seen him this way.

Dad was no longer the deadly serious Police Chief whose life was often in danger. Still reserved and serious, he often laughed and joked with us at home. There were no more emergency phone calls in the middle of the night—no longer did he have to deal with the "criminal element", as he called them. He was relieved to finally be able to live each day without the threat of having to use deadly force--- or being a victim of it.

He was in high spirits, even lighthearted as we prepared to drive west to New Mexico. I was the "designated driver" with my new license. We were heading 700 miles across the plains of Texas into New Mexico for a family visit to Carlsbad Caverns, dad's favorite place, our first (and only) family getaway. He thought Carlsbad was such a great place, wanting mother and me to share the experience with him. I couldn't have been happier, having the chance to enjoy our first vacation as a family. Most decisions in our family had been very difficult because of so many stresses and strains. Finally, making a trip like this was a miracle.

We left at the crack of dawn on a June morning in 1950, driving west on Highway 80. I was behind the wheel, dad rode shotgun, mother was behind him on the backseat. We must have been a sight to behold in the big black Chevy. Dad and I wore khaki pants and shirts, dad his white straw hat. Mother did her best to be comfortable in the backseat in her print dress, windows rolled down. Things went well until we got to Mineola 40 miles from home. Mother suddenly realized she had forgotten her corset, left cooling in the refrigerator, her usual summer practice. There was just no choice but to go back and get it, otherwise she couldn't go on.

There was no blowup, and we dutifully drove back home for the undergarment. We set out again but now in the heat of the day, windows open, still in high spirits. After Dallas and Fort Worth, we decided to pack it in for the night at Seminole. Pushing steady all day at 65 to 70, I was glad dad was pleased with my driving.

Driving on the next morning, west of Seminole, we came upon a large trailer truck loaded with cattle. You could see them through the wide gaps between trailer railings. I decided to pass, and carefully pulled out, starting around the trailer. Suddenly a huge yellow stream of cow pee erupted, flying straight through dad's open window. He was drenched, khakis, hat, shirt and all- -mother avoided the drenching. I accelerated on around the rig and found a safe place to pull off the road. Dad was so flabbergasted he couldn't speak. Fortunately mother was well-prepared and blotted him with a bath towel. She even had a large jug of clean water she used to wash him down. Then the three of us just stood beside the car and had a big laugh.

We stopped at a store a few miles further, got sandwich fixings, and dad washed up. Finding a nice shady spot for a picnic, we really enjoyed ourselves.

The rest of the trip was uneventful. It was chilly deep in the caverns and, like dad, I got goosebumps as the pipe organ played Rock Of Ages, echoing through the depths.

This was our one and only "family trip" when I was growing up. Yet life in our family got better than I had ever known. My new room provided a place for all my treasures, including a spot for my 30-30 Winchester hung below the newly mounted deer head. A new driver's license meant I could enjoy a few freedoms to go and come within reason, in the family car. My mother's work life greatly improved now that we owned a car. She could be home at evening meal time, like "normal" families. Sometimes I drove her to and from work, and on occasion she drove herself. My dad was virtually a new person out from under the pressure and frequent danger associated with running the city's Police Department.

And above all else, the long war in Europe and the Pacific was finally over. Life on Harrison Street got good!

WORK

I t was never my goal to "get rich". I've known people who really made it big.

Invariably, they built their own successful businesses. Others made it big as screen, television, stage and political personalities, authors and public speakers. Still other gifted individuals made big bucks as sports stars of one kind or other.

Either way, they built their own thing, riding their own horse. Many sold a successful business to someone else and cashed it out that way after years of grinding. Some took their own companies public and did it that way. Some big personalities made fortunes on product endorsements or residuals.

One way or another all followed the old tried and true principle-- "buy low, sell high". There is no other way to "make it big".

It's almost impossible to save your way to a fortune. If your goal is to "make it big", you'd best grit your teeth and bear the arduous grind of building your own thing, figuring out how to capitalize on what you have built, regardless of the product or service.

Buying low and selling high sounds simple—it is, yet it isn't, because doing so flies in the face of human nature. People want to follow the crowd, jumping into a situation when everyone else is jumping on the bandwagon because it's more comfortable that way; and jumping off when everyone else is exiting, often in a panic. Inevitably this results in just the opposite of what you want---instead of buying low and selling high, you may have bought high and sold low, losing instead of gaining.

It takes a special kind of person to launch out on his own with nothing but a plan and little else. That's the sort of entrepreneur it takes to build a business of his own, eventually selling it to a buyer or selling shares publicly, creating value that perhaps would be your fortune.

I always knew I was creative, entrepreneurial and didn't really fit into anybody's mold. I began learning this about myself working summers in the engineering department at Eastman in Longview. I worked two summers as a draftsman, in the company of engineers and draftsmen who had been with the company for ages. I was a young kid learning the ropes. It was good work and helped out a lot to pay for my education at Texas A&M. But I came to realize I wanted to do more in life than trace lines of pipe, draw process flow diagrams or try out new catalysts in the pilot plant, all of which I was being groomed to do as a chemical engineer.

But more than anything else, I was being trained to think analytically at A&M, then CU....how to formulate, analyze and solve complex problems....and even how to recognize when I didn't know enough to solve a particular problem.

After earning undergraduate and graduate degrees at Texas A&M and the University of Colorado, I spent a few months as an engineer in the pilot plan at Eastman, getting my hands dirty and doing the things a newly minted chemical engineer does. I discovered--- surprise, surprise---I didn't want to spend my life this way. There had to be something else I could do using my strong technical background. I just didn't know what. I needed more life experiences to even know where to begin.

At different times I played with various entrepreneurial ideas-- businesses I could go into or create from scratch. I didn't have any idea where startup money would come from or how my family would survive while I was chasing some pink dragon. I played around with different ideas including such daydreams as building a private branded cosmetics company; I explored the idea of a chain of funeral parlors years before that kind of thing actually occurred; an environmental recycling business; and even a management consulting firm. Once I explored the use of finely divided inert wood powder instead of flour to bake dietic cakes, pastries and breads.

Each time I got through the analysis and planning stage and ready to proceed to the next steps, I discovered I was unwilling to accept perhaps a meager income for an indefinite period of time during startup. Most new ventures require this kind of sacrifice unless, of course, they are very well financed. I wasn't, and didn't believe I would be! I actually explored entrepreneurial daydreams while serving in the Air Force and from time to time later on. Obviously I did these things on my own time, not company time. I simply lacked enough confidence or determination or something to pull off one of these grand schemes, as a way to "make my fortune".

There was no question in my mind about what it would require. You had to buy low and sell high no matter what you did. I just couldn't quite push myself over the edge to make this kind of move. I sometimes thought it was because I had been trained as an engineer, and everyone knows that engineers make "good employees". I hadn't learned that some of the largest and most successful businesses were built by people who didn't even have a college education, yet were tough-minded, totally confident in themselves, incredibly persistent and lucky. I even got acquainted with a wealthy man in Dallas who built a very large and successful business who said, "I couldn't get a job and had no other choice". He started out from scratch, living hand to mouth until his products caught on. He became the world's largest manufacturer of plastic cooling chests . And it was all because he said he couldn't get a job. So he created his own job and fortune, never to be unemployed again.

Yet, I had a strong entrepreneurial bent, wanting to be a builder of businesses but was just unwilling to squeak by while getting it going. I realized I was in never-never land, neither fish nor fowl--I didn't want to go out on my own, yet I couldn't stand the thought of being a "regular good employee" for my working life. I realized that successful employees in large firms could do very well financially and in every other way over the long haul. That just wasn't for me.

Eventually I was able to crystallize my personal career goal---- simply to accumulate enough material worth to be, as they say in East Texas, "well fixed". That meant having enough to do pretty much what I wanted when I wanted, specifically hunting, skiing, occasional travel and attending a few sporting events every year at A&M. I figured a net worth of $3-$5 million would make this possible. That's certainly not a fortune by Texas standards, but building a Texas size fortune was not my goal. For me, money simply buys independence, which was and is my heart's desire.

These insights didn't come to me overnight. They only came with experience doing a variety of things over a few decades. Believing that I was not cut out to build my own dream company, it came to me over time that I could be a helper to those who had made that kind of commitment. I could be sort of a "corporate midwife", building businesses within larger enterprises built by those who had already made the plunge. By catching a few crumbs off a larger table, I should be able to meet my financial goals. I could negotiate performance bonuses and stock options to my liking. But I knew I would have to bring considerable value to accomplish this. I couldn't just come off the street a nobody, expecting to be well compensated because of my good looks or degrees. I had to bring real value to the table. The idea of the "corporate midwife" began forming in my mind one night on a redeye flight from New York to Houston. My seat mate was a man much older than I, the principal lieutenant to one of Houston's wealthiest men, had been for years, and had done very well for himself financially. He shared a great deal about himself on the four hour flight, and his words fit me like a glove. I soaked it all up as he described his work, being an able helper to a wealthy entrepreneur (whose name was a household word in Houston). It dawned on me that a career like his just might be what I wanted.

I look at work as a way to obtain what I want, not as an end in itself. I've always looked at my work this way. I realize this view is at odds with the way many look at their work. One's life's work, referring to that body of work describing accomplishments over the span of a career, is the stuff of Curriculum Vitae and Obituaries. In my life I achieved pretty much what I wanted as a result of my work, namely to live free and enjoy living even though I did not always enjoy my work. I am truly fortunate to have achieved what I set out to achieve, namely to be in a position to enjoy living, doing most of the things I love to do. Accumulating money for its own sake has no meaning for me, while doing pretty much what I want when I want has always held enormous appeal. This, of course, requires an adequate resource base.

Whatever I achieved came directly from the largess of God's bounty and by His grace. It always evaded me when I was a self-seeking wolf in sheep's clothing, before I got to know the Lord Jesus Christ as my Savior.

I never liked working very much, but I've worked all my life. Work for me hasn't been a labor of love. I worked to live and not the other way around. I discovered early that the best way to enjoy work was to do something I loved enough to "buy bottles of it off a shelf if was it for sale". Then and only then you'd know the kind of work you were intended to do, regardless of pay. I fortunately found "bottled up love--work" at least twice in my career! Neither experience was particularly financially rewarding. But those two high experiences required me to perform heavy duty analysis and strategy development that required me to stretch myself really far to attain. I'll discuss these experiences later on, in detail.

Suffice it to say that I've thrived best in situations where I was over my head, after being thrown into the alligator pond, while being counted on and trusted to deliver. This was an extremely important Life Lesson for me, because what I learned about myself was that my highest and best performances came when I was put into an unknown situation requiring me to conquer a process and deliver the goods. I like to think of myself as a "pressure cooker kind of guy".

My work life began before I was ten years old, not in a pressure cooker but in the security of our yard on Harrison Street. Dad had trained me to care of our yard---cutting the grass, edging, giving shrubbery a haircut, raking and watering. He was fastidious about his lawn and shrubs and picky about his equipment. Everything had to look just so, no more and no less. Equipment had to be kept in tip top condition. He was a wonderful teacher, letting me work alongside him; giving me pieces of work he thought I was capable of handling. I worked my way up to finally taking the whole yard, admittedly never quite getting the hang of trimming hedges to dad's satisfaction.

There were no power tools for yard work, everything operated manually. Our lawn mower, typical of all mowers in the 1930's and 40's, was the push type---you used your own power to push forward, whacking the grass. Before weekly mowings, we removed and sharpened the cutter blade, oiled all moving parts, then put the whole contraption back together. The basket to catch grass clippings was attached, and then away we went. Thursday was our usual lawn day, as it was dad's normal day off from the Police Department. We placed grass clippings into a large laundry tub, dumping them into a mulch pile out back. We trimmed the shoulder high hedge between our house and Mr. Loden's next door every other week. Dad clipped and I raked and gathered the trimmings. Then we moved to the front where I trimmed the shorter shrubbery and dad raked.

By summer's end, our healthy mulch pile would have been the envy of today's composters.

The backyard was home to three tall China Berry trees. During the summer they were lush with hard green thumbnail sized berries that made ideal sling shot ammo which were lots better than rocks. But the mushy yellow stinky mess they made on the ground every fall was another story. My list of chores included raking the leaves and getting rid of the mush beneath the trees.

I wasn't paid directly for doing our yard, it was just expected of me along with other chores for my weekly allowance. I realized I knew how to do something that would be useful to other homeowners and thought I'd try selling my services around the neighborhood. Using our equipment, I could pocket the proceeds. After getting dad's permission, I went all around, knocking on doors asking for the business. I was successful and went to work right away. Bigger jobs paid $5.00, others two or three. Disposing of clippings and keeping up the shrubbery was the customer's problem, not mine. I figured I could do maybe two yards a day to earn five or six dollars. That would produce a pretty decent week's savings. I started around our neighborhood with four or five customers.

My labor was worth money, and money could buy things I wanted. I was proud of myself and shopped now and then at Hurwitz Mans Shop downtown to buy a nice outfit, pants and shirts. My parents bought clothing for me like all kids' parents, but buying a few things for myself with money I earned gave me pleasure and made me proud. I certainly didn't enjoy doing people's yards in the torrid heat, believing there had to be a more humane way for me to earn money. Still I thoroughly enjoyed buying what I wanted with my own money. This experience turned out to be a Big Life Lesson.

I did a repeat the following summer and in addition had a chance to work for Mr. Boyd, owner of Boyd's Dairy in our neighborhood. Late most afternoons, before supper time, I rode along on the running board of Mr. Boyd's old black Ford pickup. The bed of the truck was loaded with glass quart sized bottles of fresh raw milk, jingling merrily along as we drove from house to house. My job was to run to the door of each house, delivering one or more bottles of milk and retrieving empties. This was really easy and convenient work and a lot cooler than cutting lawns. I cut back to only one yard per day. The milk looked magnificent in those necked down glass bottles with their cardboard stoppers, a thick layer of cream on top. You poured the cream off in a pitcher for use in coffee, for whipping cream or cooking, and refrigerated the milk for drinking. Mr. Boyd recycled the empties back through his dairy. Of course you couldn't get away with selling unpasteurized milk now. The pay wasn't great but it added to my stash.

Summertime in my high school years afforded the opportunity to work on a local ranch, owned by the parents of my school friend, Frank.

Frank and I both worked as ranch hands, putting in long hours from sunup to sundown. The heat was stifling, but we didn't care because the pay was good. We spent most days driving large John Deere Super G tractors, plowing, cutting hay for the winter, baling and loading hay. Working shirtless most of the time in jeans and cowboy boots, we got stronger and stronger, tossing around those 75 pound bales of hay. Today we'd be scared to death of getting skin cancer!

We usually relaxed with our homemade sandwiches and iced tea at noon, and skinny dipped in a "tank" (a tank in Texas is usually called a pond elsewhere--it's a convenient way to water cattle). Often a few cows and an occasional water moccasin joined us. We had a grand time working on the ranch, in spite of the hard work and intense heat.

It was all worth it when Frank and I visited Dallas (Big D) to shop and buy special clothes for the new school year. I absolutely loved spending money that I had earned and saved from the summer's work.

MENTORS

T he Mentor is a wise and trusted counselor who takes you under his wing and shows you the ropes.

He can be a mentor for a lifetime or for a shorter time. But the key is this person exerts considerable influence on you. Your life is changed because of what you take away from the mentor. It can be life skills, technical skills, social skills, business skills, or even your spiritual being. I'd like to tell you about several of my mentors--people that have played a very important part in my life after taking me under their wings.

I've introduced you already to my dad, Albert. He was my first and greatest mentor, teaching me everything he could about life, woodlore and animal life, shooting, hunting, playing fair and working hard. I was more fortunate to have him as a mentor than I can ever tell you. Kids that don't have a parent/mentor have really missed something big. They will need to find one somehow, later on.

By the way, not all mentors fit the mold of one who cares for and nurtures you, taking you under his wing. Neither are all mentors wise. I've broadened the definition of mentors in my life to include one who, though diabolical, I trusted and with whom I cast my lot before learning his true nature. I'm referring to John (Jack) Andresen. My experiences with Mr. Andresen were life changing. Even with predominant negatives in my brief but intense association with him, I learned many deep, insightful, and lasting lessons about business and investing. Actually I learned a great deal about myself from "life with Jack". For this reason, I've placed Mr. Andresen in the company of truly wonderful mentors in every sense of the word, not because he was a positive influence in my life, but because I learned so much from him.

I'd like to give you now just a very brief summary of the kinds of things I learned from my Mentors, one by one....

From my father, Albert:

To love the great outdoors and enjoy God's many creatures that live in the wilds... to safely enjoy and take care of firearms...and automobiles...and the virtues of honesty and hard work in all my dealings. An example himself, dad showed me the value of study, learning and improving myself, throughout life.

From John Wayne Stark at Texas A&M:

I can do far more things than I think I can...I am better equipped to tackle bigger challenges than I ever believed...believe in myself and the good sense God gave me

From Colonel Lee Roy Standifer, USAF:

Keys to effectively managing large, complex organizations, especially those with a technical mission...He threw me into my first alligator pond and cheered me on as I survived.

From Guy V. Mallonee, Esso/Humble Oil/ExxonMobil Corp:

Guy supported my ideas and my work in the biggest corporate alligator pond in the world...under his watchful eye and through his mentoring, I learned I could not only survive but I could prosper in the dreaded pond of alligators...Guy helped make me a believer in myself and my abilities.

From Jack Andresen, Andresen & Company, New York:

My most unusual mentor whose lessons were as much about what not to do as what to do...I'll never again accord a budding start-up business idea with as much respect as I do the investment money that would give arms and legs and breath to the idea...seed money, venture capital, investment, or whatever one may call it. You've always got to buy low and sell high, even if doing so means going against "the herd".

JOHN WAYNE STARK, TEXAS A&M UNIVERSITY

M r. Stark was my mentor because he was the first person, outside
my family, who recognized qualities in me that I didn't know I
had.

In spite of my strong technical orientation, and little interest in the
extracurricular, he believed that there were latent qualities of
leadership in me that I had never recognized or developed. He saw me
as a sort of "a diamond in the rough". He urged me to go on and
develop skills that would serve me well in business after I completed
my first degree in chemical engineering.

Mr. Stark was the first and only Director of the new Memorial Student
Center (MSC) at Texas A&M. The MSC opened in 1950 as the living
room for the University. Mr. Stark served in that capacity for over 30
years, retiring to leave his proud legacy behind. I got to know Mr. Stark
because he hired my wife as his secretary and personal assistant when I
was a third year student. She had already graduated from the
University of Texas at Austin, and was well qualified for this
responsible position on campus.

Mr. Stark was an Aggie himself, Class of 1939. After the war he went to
the University of Texas to earn a Law Degree. Instead of practicing law
he returned to A&M, becoming head of the new MSC. In other
universities, he would have been the officer in charge of "student
activities". The MSC was the hub of student life on campus,
augmenting the strong military bearing of corps life. It was the center
for extracurricular meetings of all kinds. Mr. Stark introduced the
student body to the arts including opera, Broadway shows, exhibits
and lectures by noted figures. With my wife's assistance, he created
and implemented the Student Conference On National Affairs
(SCONA) which brings political and business leaders from over the
world to campus for this annual weeklong workshop.

These kinds of activities are mere examples of Wayne Stark's efforts to
broaden the Aggie experience. Every year he took a group of Aggies to
New York City and Boston for a week to have the experience a lifetime.
Aggie Alums hosted these visits, providing housing, hosting tours and
special dinners at places like the Waldorf Astoria and the Plaza Hotel's
famous Oak Room. He arranged other trips for students to Asia and

Europe. Aggies who were privileged to fall under Mr. Stark's spell were enriched for a lifetime.

Wayne sponsored many graduating Aggies to enter the Business School at Harvard University in Boston, where he had a special "in" with the Dean. Most had engineering degrees and fared well at Harvard. Wayne even persuaded me after I got out of the Air Force to visit the Dean and check out going for an MBA. One visit was all it took for me to decide that was not what I wanted to do. Just why did I feel I didn't need any more arrows in my quiver? I was young, egotistical and rarin' to go! In fact, I might have been shortsighted and naïve about the kind of help Harvard could give me.

Many years later, after all my "on the job learning experiences", I realized that Wayne Stark's idea of attending Harvard's B School wasn't restricted to what I'd learn there. It had more to do with getting my ticket punched, with getting credentialed, with the people I'd meet and the image I'd be able to convey in the future.

But the key for me was to find exactly the right job and get the training I needed if I wanted to do it on my own. I might have been ahead of the crowd initially had I heeded Mr.Stark, yet over the long term it probably didn't matter.

LEE ROY STANDIFER, COLONEL U S AIR FORCE

C ol. Standifer pulled me out of the research labs at Wright Patterson Air Force Base (WPAFB) to work on special assignments during my third and last year of active duty.

Although I had received a career commission at Texas A&M, and it was my option to stay on for a career in the Air Force, I had pretty well decided to get out when my time was up and go into private industry. I have to say the idea of an Air Force career was very attractive, complete with benefits of all kinds and the opportunity to pursue education to the extent I wanted at government expense. (Careers in military service continue to be attractive today as then). Col. Standifer hoped I would stay on when he pulled me up as a special assistant.

Research at Wright Patterson was done primarily by civilian scientists and engineers with military officers sprinkled in. The head man at the Materials Research and Development Center where I worked was slotted to be a high-ranking Air Force officer Level 06 or above, like Standifer. Both Col. Standifer and Mr. Stark at A&M saw something special in me I hadn't seen in myself, and challenged me up to the hilt.

Wright Patterson Air Force Base has played a key role in the development of aeronautical technology for many years. The Wright Brothers tested some of their early ideas at an area that became known as Wright Field. Their famous bicycle shop was in nearby Dayton, Ohio. Air Force procurements and design specs for many airframes (called "platforms"), guidance and propulsion systems and airborne weapons systems were initiated by or otherwise came through WPAFB.

The development of advanced materials has always been key to aeronautical technology. The Materials Central where I worked employed over 500 engineers and scientists, most with advanced degrees. About 50 of us were Air Force officers, half were careerists.

One of the problems I worked on was lubrication techniques for very high temperature environments, such as critical moving components such as valves and swivels reentering the atmosphere after flights in space. Conventional methods will not work under such high temperatures. Another big element of research dealt with materials that would burn away (ablate) on the surface of a reentering vehicle, maintaining safe conditions for the crew inside. (Abalation for controlling high temperature heat dissipation during re-entry predatd the tile technology, now used.)

Requirements for new systems such as fighters and bombers were generated, speced and procured by Wright Patterson. WPAFB usually participated all the way through proof of concept and flight testing.

After World War II ended, large numbers of German engineers and scientists who had worked on Hitler's advanced technologies were brought to Wright Patterson for interrogation. Dr. Werner von Braun, Hitler's chief rocket scientist, was among this group.

I was among an elite group of young Air Force Officers on active duty at Wright Patterson's Material Central Laboratory. My duty station was a laboratory which included highly specialized devices, instruments and technical support staff for doing research on advanced lubricating materials and techniques. Much of the work involved the deposition of a wide variety of solid materials on metal surfaces, and testing under extreme temperatures and loads. My work was supported by several university contractors, including Rensselaer Polytechnic Institute(RPI) and the University of Utah. I had contracts with several local machine shops and vendors to support our in-house research. During two years in the lab, I co-authored and published several technical papers in professional journals. I was especially proud of the work done under my direction by Prof. Fred Ling at RPI. We devised techniques for measuring and calculating temperatures between sliding metal surfaces--only guesstimated before our work.

I'm sure Col. Standifer had gotten more than one report from my civilian overseers that I was a maverick. Probably he was told I was difficult to supervise, if not impossible. Frankly I didn't suffer fools easily then, and I still don't. I quickly learned that Col. Standifer and I saw many things the same way.

He was right out of the mold of Gen. Curtis LeMay, the heroic Chief of Staff of the US Air Force. LeMay was a consummate cigar smoking, gruff, no nonsense commander who took no BS from anyone. Col. Standifer's manner was identical, though he smoked cigarettes instead of cigars. He was a highly intelligent P-47 fighter pilot career officer from Tennessee, having flown in the awesome Eighth Air Force in the air war over Europe. Standifer earned a PhD in metallurgy after the war. He didn't spare the rod and he took no prisoners. I've never had a boss I liked more or with whom I was more compatible.

Col. Standifer gave me a man sized assignment that probably was beyond my level of experience and maturity. He assigned career Air Force Major, Claude Hollifield, a fighter pilot with a chemistry background as my cohort, to keep me from getting into too much trouble. We were to report directly to Col. Standifer weekly, briefing him on our progress. Specifically, Col. Standifer asked me to visit and analyze several large research and development centers to see how they were organized, how they were managed and to gauge their effectiveness. He wanted us to compare our findings with his organization and to recommend options for improvement that he could take forward for approval.

Col. Standifer had seen something in me he thought was special. He gave me a man-sized assignment and trusted me to do it. I had six months to do the fieldwork and three to analyze data and information, write a report and make recommendations. I undertook the work enthusiastically, competently and I relished every minute of it. I got my first real look at management styles and organizational development. I began to see some of the things Wayne Stark had stressed, urging me to go to the B-school at Harvard. Still I didn't quite buy in, because I wanted to go to work without any further delay and "start making money".

At my going away party, Col. Standifer laid down a moniker for me that to this day I don't know how I earned. He called me his "QEO"--- that stood for Quiet Effective Operator. As swashbuckling as I am, I thought I was anything but quiet. But I accepted this complement from Col. Standifer gladly, hoping I could live up to his expectations in my career. By the way, I don't think Standifer was being facetious....he really meant it.

GUY V. MALLONEE, HUMBLE OIL & REFINING CO/ESSO/ STANDARD OIL OF NEW JERSEY

Please note that I use Esso throughout this section. Esso was the more widely recognized name of the Standard Oil Company of New Jersey empire.

I have taken the liberty of using this name instead of long forgotten Humble Oil and Refining Company of Texas simply because Esso is more recognized. I was never part of the Esso organization, always a Humble employee. The corporate names have continued to evolve over the past five decades, to the highly recognizable Exxon Mobil brand now across the country and around the world. Actually the first Car Care Centers flew the Esso brand east of the Mississippi River and Enco west of the River. Certain legal restrictions prevented Humble, the US parent company, from using the Esso brand coast to coast, thus the Enco brand appeared in the west. It was a brighter day for the company when Exxon became the single domestic brand, coast to coast, then acquiring Mobil Oil to become the world's largest company under the single ExxonMobil flag.

He was the epitome of the Southern Gentleman---tall, slender, silvery white hair, cobalt blue eyes, chiseled features--he looked like he had just stepped off the filming set of Gone With The Wind, as he ambled down the 37th floor of the new Humble Oil Company headquarters office building in downtown Houston. His southern drawl gave away his native roots in Virginia, which was home to numerous executives in the company. You might even say Guy was courtly in manner and speech.

He spent his entire 40+ year career in Esso, starting at the bottom and working his way up through the ranks, to become the Corporate Marketing Director, overseeing the entire US sales and marketing operation. Humble Oil (pronounced with silent H---Umble Oil) was the large, important domestic affiliate of the Standard Oil of New Jersey's worldwide empire of founder John D. Rockefeller. Guy's job was truly a Big Deal in the world's largest oil company. I admired him right from the start from my very junior position as an Analyst in the Corporate Marketing Research Department. I knew I could learn a lot from Guy if I ever got the chance to work close to him.

I landed at Humble in the early 1960s, after my term of service in the Air Force. It was a propitious time in the life of the company, as all of the Jersey affiliates were being reorganized and merged into new US and worldwide corporations. The opportunities for a newcomer like me were tremendous, on the upside.

Coming to the end of active military service, I had boiled my job search down to three and only three opportunities. One was to stay on as a career officer in the Air Force, a tempting possibility with my career commission at A&M. An Air Force career carried terrific benefits including worldwide travel, further academic studies at Air Force expense and management of large, important global enterprises. Another option was to leave the Air Force, becoming a full-time civilian researcher at Wright Patterson in one of the advanced air research programs. Starting pay, perks and benefits were very attractive, and of course I already knew the ropes there. The work was critical to the US aerospace effort.

A second opportunity was with Corning Corporation, the major manufacturer of glass and related products, based in the Finger Lakes Region of Upstate New York. This too was a very attractive opportunity with a great starting salary, getting in on the ground floor of the potentially mushrooming fiber optics business. Living and working in beautiful Upstate New York replete with extensive year-round outdoor activities including hunting, fishing and skiing, was a huge attraction. I would be reporting directly to one of the top officers in Corning. A member of Corning's Board of Directors, Mr. Russ Mariner, my putative boss, oversaw all of the company's new product development activities. The Corning opportunity was absolutely outstanding.

The third opportunity, albeit with the lowest starting pay, was in Houston in my native State of Texas, with the Humble Oil and Refining Company. The opportunity to come in to work at a corporate level, learning about the business from seasoned executives, outweighed the disadvantage of the starting pay. Even without an MBA Degree from Harvard or Wharton, I was invited to join a small group of professionals at Corporate Headquarters, most having backgrounds in engineering and business and quite a few years' experience with the company. Few outsiders were hired into the kind of job I was offered. They must have had confidence that I would be able to learn all I needed to know about investment analysis and market research on the job. Knowing little about present value analysis, discounting and investment analysis was daunting, but I was confident I could learn on the job instead of the classroom. Mr. Stark at A&M continued urging me to get my MBA at Harvard instead of going directly from the Air Force to industry, but I was determined to bull my way through. I was convinced Esso provided this unique opportunity.

We relocated from Dayton, Ohio to Houston, Texas in the fall of 1962, and I quickly settled into my new job. I absolutely loved it! I couldn't get enough of it, applying myself more fully and working harder than I had ever worked in my life. Soon I was given responsibility for two analysis projects — 1) the ongoing work by A.C.Nielsen evaluating and advising on television media and advertising buys---and 2) management of Esso's experimental Marketing Laboratory in Altoona, Pennsylvania.

In the Nielsen job, I found myself serving as a sort of handmaiden between three disparate groups: 1) McCann Erickson, the large and powerful New York advertising agency charged with creating, producing and placing all Esso advertising; 2) A.C.Nielsen, the New York research firm who developed metrics and measured the effectiveness of McCann Erickson's; and 3) Esso, who presided over this triumvirate, who directed and paid all of us. I was responsible for managing the Nielsen work, analyzing the field data, interpreting and presenting findings and results to management, of course with help from my very able boss.

My second job, the Altoona project, was equally interesting and challenging. It too had lots of unknowns for me. It was one of the most ambitious undertakings in market research and analysis ever attempted. It had been conceived and put in place two years earlier in response to repeated questions from Esso's Board of Directors concerning the efficacy of advertising. This was a perennial budgetary issue, some Board members wanting to know "How much is enough"? More caustically, "What happens if we just suspend advertising"? And "Just what are we getting in return for our money"? Tough questions needing solid answers.

The challenge was especially difficult because quantitative answers were needed to satisfy Board members nearly all of whom had strong technical backgrounds. They were by and large engineers, geophysicists and geologists, with many years experience in the field.

All were hard-nosed businessmen, the kinds of individuals you'd expect to pose penetrating questions, going right at the heart of any issue. They were accustomed to the kinds of hard hitting, pithy presentations they got from "upstream" entities dealing with oil and gas drilling, production, transportation and refining, a far cry from the "soft science" of marketing and certainly advertising. Some would even say advertising is some kind of "black art" that defies solid analysis.

After lots of soul searching, Marketing Research came up with the ambitious idea of creating a sort of laboratory where quantitative information about advertising effects could be obtained. My predecessors screened markets all over the country to find a suitable test market. They desired a market with reasonable but not overwhelming Esso market share; and a captive media so "leakage" of advertising into the test market from other markets would be minimized. They concluded that Altoona, Pennsylvania, filled the bill better than any other market. Television from Johnstown, Pennsylvania and Altoona were the only sources entering the market, so there would not be encroaching ads from elsewhere.

It's hard to imagine anyone but a group of engineers, thinking quantitatively, could devise the kind of methodology used in Altoona. Along rigorous socioeconomic and statistical lines, panels of individuals representing cross-sections of Altoona's population were devised. The central premise was that the behavior of a particular statistical sample of consumers in Altoona, Pennsylvania should be a reasonable proxy of the way the same stratigraphic sample would behave elsewhere. Panel members were induced to maintain diaries of their television viewing, radio listening and their fuel purchases at predetermined periods of time, fitting into an overall calendar framework. This was done in such a manner as to build up a "synthetic year" of media exposure and fuel purchasing within each stratigraphic sector. Such formulation would result in a record for a typical Thursday in November, or a Monday in June, for example. These data could be matched against our known schedule of advertising in the Altoona market.

With this information, it would be at least theoretically possible to determine how many "hits" a stratigraphically average individual received, and from additional questions in his diary how his attitudes about Esso were influenced. Was there a threshold number of "hits" needed in a particular amount of time to stimulate the consumer to try a tank of Esso next time? How were Esso's already loyal customers affected, if at all, by the advertising? Done correctly, we hoped to get down into the fine granularity of how advertising works to expand market share and to determine if it helps to reinforce the brand loyalty of existing customers.

We hoped to find linkage between advertising "hits" and consumer behavior. Skeptics doubted there was any linkage at all, that spending $20-100 million or so per year contributed little or nothing to Esso's business. The Altoona approach could be best described as "mechanistic", wherein we would attempt to describe at a fundamental level how, or if, advertising works. From the beginning it was believed to be a high-risk project, a bold and daring approach that might or might not produce meaningful insights even after sinking a few million dollars into it.

Other less mechanistic approaches could well have been devised, the most obvious being to select say five different test markets, subjecting each to different advertising messages and intensities. Effects could be measured in terms of sales, brand switching, consumer attitudes and other indices. This gross approach wasn't taken because it wouldn't provide a level of fine-grained detail needed to answer the persistent critics who questioned the value of advertising at every budget cycle.

Esso's Advertising Director and advertising agency hoped to goodness for a positive result supporting their position, otherwise the naysayers would have a heyday. But trying to explain the complex Altoona project to the non-technical yet brilliantly creative types in Esso's Advertising Department and ad agency to win their support was nightmarish. To no one's surprise, they never really got on board.

Safeguards were needed to ensure against all the negatives or biases that could creep in--- panel tedium, dropouts, failure to keep records, and dishonest responses. It was believed a contract market research firm, J A Ward Inc. in New York who had served Esso well for many years, could do a better job than we in managing and maintaining the Altoona field work. It was their job to ensure against bias, maintaining continuity and integrity in the panels, collecting and collating the all data from Altoona. We retained Computer Usage Corporation of New York to handle and process the massive amounts of field data. Advertising logs and schedules were provided by McCann Erickson.

I had authority to change the frequency and timing of Esso advertising coming into the Altoona market in order to fit a design matrix, letting us measure the effects of increasing and decreasing advertising levels. Some Board members held that we should be able to buy advertising over the course of several years in a sawtooth manner, up and down---- one year high, next year low, etc., resulting in lower net outlays over a period of time. We hoped to be able to measure this kind of effect. Brand switching was another hoped for nugget of information--what would it take to get Amoco buyers, for example, to switch to Esso? Would there be a point at which our messages would be so dilute as to lose Esso customers to other brands?

Guy Mallonee often sat in meetings where I was presenting interim findings. Impressed with his astuteness, I was amazed at how well he handled groups of individuals holding sharply divided views. He had a special touch when he was in the room. I wanted some day to be like him.

The long-run hope was to create a mathematical model of the marketplace that could be exercised through a variety of perplexing marketing problems. To help with modeling formulation, I brought in a group of mathematicians from the Esso Research and Engineering Company, Esso's wholly owned brain trust in Linden, New Jersey.

We were never completely successful attempting to quantify the effects of advertising. While many insights were developed, advertising continued a magical and creative process, remaining slightly under the radar avoiding overly rigorous analytical scrutiny. The Esso Board's penetrating questions were never fully answered, and the Tiger in the Tank went on down the road, defying extensive quantification. We were able to glean enough first order effects to convince many critics that advertising was a good thing within sensible budgetary constraints. At least, they didn't throw it out the window.

For many years, I've believed the approach was sound enough to justify some wonderful PhD opportunities for university researchers. Certainly the need existed. Esso certainly had the right idea, a framework to rigorously measure advertising effectiveness. This kind of thinking should have led to the creation of a mathematical model as step one, which would guide more accurately and efficiently the kinds of data required. They just got the horse before the cart. They structured an intensive process in the field to collect vast amounts of data and information before deciding on an analytical framework and what questions they were really trying to address.

As I moved along, in Esso, additional jobs came my way. It was my good fortune to be assigned to a research project to determine the efficacy of continuing to produce and market a specialized automobile tire made from an Esso Chemical Company product, butyl rubber. Bulk quantities of this special rubber were reformulated by Firestone Tire and Rubber Company, then cast into a private label Atlas brand tire called the Bucron. The Bucron was an upscale aftermarket product promising a soft cushioned ride, reduced road noise and quiet cornering. The Bucron was sold through Esso, Amoco, Sohio, Socal and other stations carrying private branded Atlas automotive products.

But its superior handling qualities were tarnished by customer reports of poor tread wear, many claiming they got only 15 to 20,000 miles on a set of pricey Bucrons. Esso had a vested interest in getting to the bottom of the problem, factually and quickly for the well-being of our dealers and Esso Chemical Company. Preservation and protection of Esso's quality image was and will forever be a supremely important asset to the company. Esso would never market any product believed to be inferior and would never engage in activities of any kind that could reflect poorly on its good name. The allegedly poorer than expected performance of the Bucron had to be analyzed and corrected quickly, one way or another.

The purpose of the study was then clear. What are the real facts about the Bucron, and how serious is the problem? Depending on our findings, what options do we have? Is the problem severe enough we should entirely stop producing and marketing Bucrons, even though they utilize our own butyl rubber? What about a reformulation of the rubber — is that a possible solution? And if so, what new marketing approach should we consider for a reformulated, repackaged tire?

The research was needed to address these and related questions in only a short three month window. We were expected to report our findings first to Corporate Marketing, i.e. Mr. Mallonee et.al. then to the Board of Directors. It was decided I should be the lead analyst. This was my indoctrination and baptism of fire in Esso's vast retail complex.

I learned Mr. Mallonee had been involved in the decision to appoint me lead analyst. Someone must have been trying to determine how much load I could carry, since I still   managed the A.C. Nielsen and Altoona projects. I felt overwhelmed at times, but pressed ahead, trusting my teammates and secure I could hire consultants if needed.

Fortunately a related major parallel study was getting off the ground at the same time, analyzing all aspects of Esso's retail marketing business, with major emphasis on the automotive aftermarket. The usual products sold by gas stations---gasolines, tires, batteries, accessories (TBA)---were to be included in the study. But it needed to go much deeper into the automobile service and repair business across the board, examining major competitors such as Firestone and the tire manufacturers, Sears, JC Penny, PEP Boys, automobile dealers and the full array of our oil industry competitors. We needed to determine whether this was a business Esso should jump into with full force, or not. Were there significant dollars to be made in this business, beyond the pumping of motor fuels?

We were expected to assess the importance of TBA sales and service and the automotive repair business to Esso and select competitive dealers. We planned to rely heavily on Esso's outstanding field organizations to identify examples of successful dealers in their areas, then to line up appointments for team members to meet with those selected.

Views at the top about where the company should be heading varied widely, from exiting the retail service station business entirely, to going for broke with bold new retail level approaches. The "Automotive Aftermarket Study" was enthusiastically awaited up and down the line, including Esso's worldwide parent in New York, the Standard Oil Company of New Jersey. Top management expected the study to be thorough and comprehensive, a serious aid in helping to decide Esso's future posture in the US, and possibly overseas.

I quickly learned that "upstream" in integrated oil companies means everything connected with getting oil out of the ground, all the exploration, analysis and interpretation of exploratory geology and geophysics, drilling and completing wells; and   "downstream" is everything else, transporting, refining, and selling petroleum products. You didn't have to be a genius to figure out what stood where in the vast Esso culture----clout clearly was among "upstreamers". "Downstreamers" were the step children in the family. There was good rationale for the disparity---downstream operations clearly were a drag on the otherwise robust profits and the healthy return on investment earned upstream.

A standing joke, which was actually true, was that it cost more to pump gasoline five feet out of a hose at the gas pump into your car than finding, drilling, producing the oil, transporting it across country to a refinery where gasoline and other products are produced, then transporting it to the gas station. A continuing issue was what if anything could be done to make marketing pay its way and contribute to overall profits.

We developed a design and budget for the more modest Bucron project. Because of the broad nature of the Aftermarket Study, management decided to include the Bucron study as a subset, making better use of resources. Accordingly, I became a member of a working group of analysts, led by one of Esso's rising young stars, a seven year veteran chemical engineer with a Harvard MBA. What a coincidence. He had the very same credentials Wayne Stark at A&M wanted me to have!

While designing the major Aftermarket study, we went ahead with the Bucron study, ably assisted by the Princeton, New Jersey consulting firm, Opinion Research Corporation (ORC).They were retained to help gauge the severity of the Bucron's tread wear problem and any carryover effects on customers. ORC responded quickly and did an outstanding job. Mr. Mallonee was the primary recipient of the Bucron study results before proceeding to the Board. Our presentations up and down the line were well received, in fact earning me accolades from top management. In the end I was branded a "hardass" by Bucron diehards in the company. I didn't mind that moniker one bit! Bucron ultimately bit the dust.

By this time, I'd offloaded both the Nielsen television work and the Altoona marketing lab. I was more than fully consumed by the Aftermarket project and delighted to be relieved.

Fortunately or unfortunately, the project leader for the Aftermarket study, the rising young star, decided to leave Esso for an opportunity in consulting. This came as a total surprise to the Corporate research group. I don't know how or why, but I was named his replacement. Suddenly all eyes were on me. I knew I had to succeed at all costs-- failure was not an option. I was replacing an individual who appeared to be eminently more qualified than I.

This was one of those times in my career I was expected to do a job which challenged every fiber of my being. I had to rise to the occasion--

-there simply was no other way. With relish I took up the challenge. This was my first plunge into the huge Esso mega- alligator pond!

First it would be necessary to establish baselines. We had no really solid data on our share of the national TBA and automotive aftermarkets, only speculation and "company lore" from old timers. We didn't have good data and information about how our major competitors operated, especially Sears and other big retailers. We believed that TBA and service business was extremely important to most Esso dealers, but it hadn't really been quantified and analyzed. We knew, in fact, that a dealer really couldn't make a go of it on motor fuel sales alone because his margin of profit was so small, maybe 2-4 cents a gallon. He had to rely on off-island sales and service to his customer base to make ends meet. Obviously some were far more successful at this than others.

Amoco was market testing a new service business concept in the Chicago area, a huge facility with many service bays, offering a very wide range of automotive products and services. We knew it was operated directly by Amoco and resembled large Sears automotive service centers. It bore absolutely no resemblance to traditional oil company service stations. We knew from the start we didn't want to go in that direction. Mr. Mallonee made it clear in the beginning that we were to steer clear of any plan that might do injury to Esso's proud network of independent station operators across the country. In turn, he directed us to explore approaches that could enhance everybody's business in the Esso family, virtually lifting everyone's boat, direct Esso stores and independent dealers alike. It's important to note that Esso's independent dealer organization was the pride of the industry and our assignment was to figure out a way to enhance it, a very tall order.

During phase one we developed business models of typical and exceptional dealer operations in each Esso region, working closely with regional personnel to gain access to people and data. We looked closely at our competitors in the aftermarket business, including competitive dealers as well as the extravagantly large Amoco and Shell test facilities. We conducted several important large-scale consumer surveys to estimate how well Esso stations actually were selling TBA and off island services compared to our oil company competitors.

Early results were eye opening. It appeared that we somewhat lagged Mobil Oil, for example, in off island sales of TBA in relation to motor fuel sales. This early insight was controversial, hitting a number of proud Esso marketing executives between the eyes. Regardless of naysayers, the notion was undeniable that our loyal gasoline customer base, with Esso holding the largest motor fuel market share in the US, represented the greatest potential for new products and services we could offer. Customers trusted Esso. They were positively disposed to trying out our new products and services. An added bonus would be brand switchers, new customers trying out Esso fuel products, attracted to our new lines of automotive products and services.

Consultants were brought in as needed to help us better understand and model the large retailers like JCPenny's automotive service business. By far, our most successful consultant was a recently retired Merchandising Manager for Macy's Department Stores in New York, Mr. Louis Bernstein. He was enormously helpful, and together we evaluated advertising practices of aftermarket competitors, including prices of TBA and services and special sales promotions. Oil companies historically avoid price advertising of goods and services to absolutely ensure the truly independent status of dealer operations. Dealers are free to set their own prices on all products and services including motor fuels with no undue pressure from their fuel suppliers. Esso would need to brave these turbulent retail advertising waters in order to compete effectively with big retailers and tire companies. We would obviously need extensive involvement by our corporate legal staff to devise practical remedies and ways to ensure fair pricing. I have to say here that Esso corporate legal staff performed superlatively, sparing no effort to ensure in every way we were on solid legal ground in our quest to be fully competitive. The last thing anyone wanted was to be accused of unfair competitive practices. We would take all steps necessary to avoid this at all costs!

Special side studies probed all aspects of parts supply, cost and pricing, guarantees and warranties, sales and service training.

Analyses were conducted to help understand the profitability of different repair services, from brake repairs and tune-ups to large complex jobs such as engine and transmission overhauls. These analyses clearly showed we should not tie ourselves up with large time consuming repairs and overhauls, concentrating instead on the faster, lighter services such as alignment, tune-up, brakes and TBA sales and service, needed routinely by a high percentage of our customers.

We presented results up, down and across the Esso chain of command almost constantly to keep everyone abreast of findings and our team's thinking. Mr. Mallonee wanted to be sure our communications were clear, and there would be no big surprises. We practically lived on airplanes and in hotels the year of the Aftermarket Study. Stakes were high across the company on the outcome of this work. Everyone wanted in on the action which might shape Esso's future in the marketplace.

Guy Mallonee's many years of experience determined the guiding principles for our work, namely that whatever we recommend must not bring injury to or breach the mutual trust and respect of the healthy, prosperous independent Esso dealer organization. Phase One clearly showed that gigantic service centers similar to those of the Amoco test and large retailers like Sears would do nothing to enhance the health and well-being of our independent dealers. We discovered, in fact, that if Esso went full blown with such an egregious concept, many of our dealers might be damaged. This looked to us like a mistake in the making for Amoco and possibly other oil competitors, one that we would steer clear of in whatever path we recommended.

Guy Mallonee oversaw the vast Esso retail complex of more than 30,000 stations, a high percentage of which were independent dealer owned and operated. His business was conducted through four regional Vice Presidents across the country, each strong and independent with clear profit and loss responsibility and wide latitudes of authority. Guy's focus was mainly on policy and overall performance and profitability. He was responsible for results, up to and through the Board. In this way, policy was centralized at headquarters and operations decentralized through large and very powerful regional field organizations. Implementing a new marketing approach would require approval at Headquarters and the Board and be dependent on regional operations for implementation under headquarters guidance. Executives had to buy in at all levels or no new scheme would work.

Centralized policy and decentralized implementation may seem to you like a cumbersome way to do business. Yet this management approach has undergirded Esso's success for many years to become the largest company in the world, with the largest gasoline market share in America. Everyone everywhere knew the Esso slogans, "Happy Motoring" and "Put a Tiger In Your Tank". When a significant move was made or new direction taken, the entire company from top to bottom needed to line up behind it.

Esso's vast operations around the globe still follow this model, centralized policy and control in Headquarters, strong decentralized operations in every country and region. By the way, Presidents of Esso's regional subsidiaries around the world are enormously powerful within their realms. They deal at every political level in host countries, including the country's President, or dictator, as the case may be. Often, top Esso executives are considerably better acquainted with the host country than the US Government and its corps of diplomats. I've seen this with my own eyes around the world. Esso personnel could often make things happen when our own diplomatic corps couldn't.

We needed several more definitive pieces of information before returning to the Board for further approvals. We needed to define the specific approach we would recommend, including types and numbers of facilities. Guided by Mr. Mallonee's imperative, Esso's retail operations in toto, dealers and all, would need to be favorable disposed toward a new approach. For openers, one test market in each of Esso's four regions needed to be selected.

We decided to recommend an approach based on what we found in our own back yard — several large, highly successful Esso dealers. The best examples were in the greater New York City and Baltimore markets. Without exception, these large Esso dealers were completely open with us, cooperating in every way, giving us total access to their business records. It grew clearer by the day that this handful of our own dealers were already pointing the way and that our approach needed to borrow from and expand upon their good practices. Some of our top executives were flabbergasted to learn that more than a few of these big independents earned very high incomes from their businesses, comparable to the earnings of many top executives.

Clearly, loyal Esso motor fuel customers were our best source of expanded off island sales and service. Trusting Esso for motor oil, gasoline and diesel fuels, our challenge would be to convince them we could take care of most of their other automotive service needs, competently and at a fair price, fully guaranteed. As I mentioned, a few of our big independents had achieved this. Could we replicate and add to their successes broadly across Esso's marketplace, while earning attractive profits and returns on investment for the company? That was the $64,000 question!

We needed to harden our recommended approach and prepare a full up starting budget request for the Board, complete with timelines, sales and profit objectives, and projected returns on capital invested. Mr. Mallonee was with us every step of the way, making invaluable suggestions.

Meetings with the Esso engineering and construction group resulted in several renderings which helped describe our two generic types of designs — 1) existing Esso facilities that could be modified, rebuilt, or in some acquiring additional adjacent land — or 2) totally new grass roots facilities on parcels already owned or to be acquired specifically for new Car Care Centers. Whether modified or new, we wanted to have a minimum of five service bays, preferably more including one for diagnostics, others for service including at least two with hydraulic lifts. The Parts Department needed to be large enough to carry substantial inventory, far more than a normal gas station. A nice, clean customer lounge type waiting room was needed, competitive with those at Sears and automobile dealers. This, of course, would be a far cry from the dirty, dingy areas and restrooms found in most stations across America. Gasoline islands had to be configured so that effective new merchandising and service displays could be shown on driveways.

Finally, we needed to recommend specific test markets and numbers of locations in each--this would be essential for preparation of a notional start up budget request. We believed four to six centers in a market the size of say Baltimore would be about optimum for our advertising and sales promotion coverage, product inventory and parts supply, employee recruitment and training and other management considerations. I believed it would be a serious challenge for us to come up with any more qualified sites than this in most major metropolitan markets.

Having worked out most of the critical parameters, it was time to set up an organizational structure in Headquarters and the Regions and begin to involve them deeply in selecting test markets and site locations. Mr. Mallonee designated me the Headquarters Coordinator together with Carl Yantis, a senior long time company executive with heavy experience in all aspects of Esso marketing. Carl had recently spent a stint as number two in Corporate Advertising and was the original "Tiger in Your Tank" man. Carl's contacts, skills and vast experience in the field would be vital for our success. Delighted to be partnering with Carl, we were organizationally reassigned to Mr. Mallonee's corporate operations group, no longer part of Corporate Marketing and Business Research and Corporate Advertising.

Mr. Mallonee called together a meeting in Houston of key managers from the field to discuss the new concept. Attendees were expected to be prepared to commit their Regions, designating management personnel totally dedicated to the Car Care Center program, and recommending test markets. The designated managers were to be released from all other duties, assigned strictly to the Car Care Center program, reporting directly to Yantis and me on all Car Care Center business.

Test markets in each Region were discussed and four selected— Baltimore, Memphis, Dallas and Milwaukee. We had looked previously at Los Angeles, rejecting it because we were new there. Houston would have been an obvious choice, but we decided against it in the initial test because of the terrific corporate scrutiny it would attract---we wanted to get a little experience under our belt before we took on Houston. The four lead individuals named had strong marketing and business backgrounds with outstanding experience in Esso. Others would be made available to them as needed, on whatever basis was required.

Detailed criteria for the kinds of locations needed were developed, based on groundwork studies with specialized consultants directed by Mr. Gerald Rolling, whom we hired from the Ford Motor organization in Dearborn. He developed a math model including critical factors such as traffic count, socioeconomic data for the area, customer base and competition. Land area, building requirements and other criteria were communicated to our Regional managers so lists of candidate sites could be proposed and screened through Rolling's model. We went on site to review and approve those that passed muster.

It would be necessary to operate all facilities as "company-owned and operated" in the beginning as we were gaining experience. This would permit direct control over all aspects of the business, simplifying legal hurdles we faced in placing competitive price advertising for products and services. Our attorneys advised that we could advertise prices and services available strictly at Car Care Centers, with absolutely no implication we were directing independent dealers to charge similar prices. This would preserve the right of independents to choose for themselves, free to offer whatever products and services they chose, setting their own prices, even beating ours if they so choose.

Obviously some of the most desirable locations were owned and operated by independent dealers. We would make every attempt to convert them over to direct company operation. This would require a great deal of persuasion by key people on the ground. The dealer would have to see how he would be better off in the short term and over the long haul, by going our way. We knew this would be an uphill battle in some cases, and we'd have to back off, seeking an alternate site. We stressed the importance of maintaining a totally cooperative and supportive atmosphere throughout the dealer organization. In no way did we want the new Car Care Centers to be perceived as threats. Conversely, the new breed of exemplar operations had to be seen as a help, giving the regular operator something to shoot for.

With this information, we returned to the Board to present our initial budget request. We provided a full briefing that included scale models of Car Care Centers. We were supported by several critical elements of the company in our meeting with the Board, including Legal, Engineering, and Finance and Accounting. I was thankful for all the guidance and support from Guy Mallonee and for the thoroughness of our preparation. We were able to effectively deal with every question raised that morning. The Board gave the go-ahead and asked us to come back periodically with updates and status reports.

> *At this point, I want to stop and make sure you realize that we were plowing totally new ground, not just in the world of Esso, but in the oil industry as a whole. If you've gotten the idea based on what I've said so far that these were just going to be "bigger gas stations", you're dead wrong! We were undertaking a huge departure from past industry practices. The Car Care Center program was set up with its own organization, carved out of the whole of Esso; with its own unique retail accounting system, from Yantis and me, down through each individual Center, capable of rolling up sales and other data on command; having its own Profit/Loss and return on invested capital statements for which we were accountable; neat, clean, orderly five, six or more service bay facilities with customer amenities that could compete with most car dealerships, including customer pick-up and delivery; clean, uniformed and courteous service personnel, inside and on the driveway, all well trained and competent; pricing for parts and service, fully competitive in the marketplace. We regularly advertised prices of tires, batteries, and such services as tune-ups, brake repair, and front end alignment. From time to time we offered special deals on engine diagnostics and other services. We ran full or half page ads on our services and products including tires and batteries together with prices in the metropolitan newspaper, often in two or three colors. Such retail advertising by an oil company had never before been done. We were competing head to head with major retailers. And we had to walk a legal tightrope to do it! The thing that was at stake here was the very future of oil industry retail operations. Could our approach succeed in getting Esso's retail marketplace off the dole from "upstream" operations? Could we make it pay for the company? And for our dealers?*

With the Board's blessings, we proceeded to definitize plans in each test market. We spent many days on the road, reviewing in detail every proposed site in each market. We were pleased each region moved out rapidly and enthusiastically. In the meantime, we asked Corporate Accounting to set up a separate profit and loss center for our new operation and to develop all necessary training for Center employees on bookkeeping and clerical requirements. We anticipated accounting for parts and supplies inventory would present a challenge.

We tasked McCann-Erickson to prepared retail advertising formats for our approval. We prepared training for all Center employees with the help of equipment suppliers, such as Hunter Manufacturing for wheel alignment; Allen Diagnostics and others for engines, diagnostics and tune-ups. We utilized brake equipment people for everything concerning brakes. By the time we put it all together, our training program was comprehensive and our training manuals came together. Training would be provided for Center personnel at field locations by our equipment vendors.

With the help of Louis Bernstein our special consultant, we devised sales training materials and programs for all employees expected to be in contact with customers. Emphasis was placed on driveway selling techniques while customers' windows were wiped and oil checked—long lost gas station services. Tread wear and wear patterns revealing alignment problems and other commonly overlooked problems would be quickly noted by a competent technician. Louis did a fine job encouraging just the right amount of aggressive salesmanship, neither too much or too little. He actively trained most of our driveway personnel himself.

Great care was used in recruiting employees for Car Care Centers. Obviously each Center Manager was responsible for recruiting his employees. A Center required one or more Service Managers, a Parts Manager and a Sales Manager, all under a Car Care Center Manager.

We often recruited personnel from automobile dealers and major retailers. Job descriptions were developed for each position, together with pay brackets, benefits and incentive packages. Automobile dealers turned out to be a very good source of Service Managers and service employees. Driveway and sales personnel came from a variety of sources including tire dealerships. All were intensively trained in our new systems, with great emphasis on giving excellent service to our customers. Employees were expected to be clean and neat, wearing special Car Care Center uniforms we provided. We were striving to render a whole new level of service on driveways, in service bays and in clean, comfortable customer lounges containing tasteful sales displays and useful literature. We had to be sure all our employees were on the same page. Some Centers employed as many as 40 to 50 people, depending on volume of business and hours of operation. Most were in the 20 to 25 range.

In some cases it was quite a reach to persuade a successful independent dealer to convert over to employee status, even with assurances of becoming independent again in the future--we had to make it worth his while. Some top managers in the company were shocked to learn that we had to reach for the sky in some cases to make it worthwhile due to their high incomes. But it was occasionally necessary if we were to procure the best locations.

We developed an ingenious plan for procuring and maintaining parts inventories at Centers. Searching through many options, we knew we needed a single source. The only single source that could take care of our unique needs was the Mopar Division of Chrysler Motor Company. We learned that Mopar could supply parts locally for all makes and models of automobiles, the only vendor having this unique capability. We looked at NAPA and others, concluding they couldn't meet our needs.

After visits back and forth between Detroit and Houston, we cut a deal with the President of Mopar to deliver and fully supply our needs in the four test markets. They gave us a unique capability---basically a complete inventory warehouse backing up our Centers; prompt delivery of parts, usually in a 2-3 hour window; excellent quality products; and training for Center personnel. No other oil company had struck this kind of deal with Mopar. What's more, Mopar was a large and robust company and could go with us into new markets in the future.

The terms we negotiated were attractive, making good business sense for us both. We worked out normal as well as extraordinary delivery schedules. Mopar assisted us setting up initial inventory levels and inventory accounting systems at Center level and taught a section in our training program. The entire Mopar relationship worked like a charm and was a good deal for everyone.

Designs and architectural drawings were required for each individual site, while maintaining an overall Esso family appearance. Yantis and I required our approval on every project before proceeding to construction. Some required additional land acquisition. It was almost always necessary for us to appear before local zoning boards for approvals or variances. This was particularly challenging in the large Baltimore market. But we succeeded in almost every case. Esso's excellent reputation and outstanding local businessmen were always a huge help, greatly easing zoning approval hurdles.

Monthly business projections and budgets were required for each Center, before proceeding to construction. Our accounting system picked this up and provided variance analysis every month so we would know where we were long and short. If sales fell below expectation in some product areas such as tires, we could apply special emphasis and training to get back on track. Variance analysis was very helpful to us in controlling expenses, as we had committed to profit estimates and returns on investment to the Board. Our corporate reporting was rolled up on the basis of each test market, then an overall picture of performance was proformaed.

Special logo, signage and identification were needed to differentiate Car Care Centers from everyone else in the Esso family. We retained the well-known creative firm of Jack Tinker & Partners in New York to give us a hand. (Tinker had recently achieved rave reviews for work with Braniff Airways, "putting an end to the plain plane" concocting an extravaganza of colored Boeing 727's in its fleet). They came up with a colorful logo featuring the Esso oval resting atop horizontally framed CAR CARE CENTER. We met with Esso's sign vendor in Dallas, worked out the details and placed an initial production order for twenty molded internally lit plastic signs.

Memphis turned out to be our earliest and best test market. The Esso management team there was simply outstanding. They had designated five wonderful Memphis locations and were well ahead of the other markets. Our very first grand opening was slated for the Car Care Center on Summer Avenue in Memphis, November 1965. This was a huge event, with Mr. Mallonee hosting a delegation of top company brass. Our newspaper advertising was outstanding, with teaser ads beginning well ahead of time to whet appetites in the Memphis market. The facility itself was nothing short of beautiful--it was a rebuild of an existing facility, accompanied by the acquisition of more land. It had eight service bays and other features that made it the flagship of Car Care Centers from that day forward. Powerful searchlights on the driveway beamed into the night sky, drawing crowds to the grand opening. Louis, our retail consultant, spent a week on the driveway ahead of time with employees, training and ensuring everything would go right. Esso was graciously complemented by Memphis city fathers and newspaper editorials welcoming the new wave of Esso service facilities into the market. Automotive News magazine, Wall Street Journal and other media covered the event. People actually observed a major departure from anything they had seen before at gasoline service stations. Our service bays were chock-a-block with business, and sales of gasoline and motor oil soared.

We went on to develop twenty-one Car Care Centers in four test markets. None was as beautiful or successful as that first grand opening on Summer Avenue in Memphis, with lots of storefront glass, searchlights and traffic . I had a large portrait photograph made and framed which was my prized possession hanging in my office at Esso. Implementing the new Car Care Centers in giant Humble Oil /Esso was like changing the course of the Queen Mary in mid ocean. It was a companywide effort from the Board down through the entire organization.

These were halcyon days for me. I was at the top of my game. Someone once said everyone should get five minutes of fame. This was mine. Wall Street Journal, Automotive News and local news media sought interviews with me. The new Center in Memphis was a colossal success, widely acclaimed throughout Esso and the automotive service world. It even enjoyed support and positive comments from Esso service station dealers in Memphis. Many saw how to benefit from the new breed of center, especially wanting in on some of the training. Memphis dealer response was without question one of our highest and best achievements.

My work was all consuming. I sometimes went for three weeks without a day off or even to spend a night at home in Houston with my family. We could never have done all this without the able and persuasive help of my mentor, Guy Mallonee. He put his stature with the company on the line time and again to secure cooperation from every element including Regional and field operations, Corporate Accounting, Advertising and Sales Promotion, Legal and Esso's Credit Department as well as Design and Construction. Guy Mallonee was my role model as a courageous, intelligent, incisive businessman who knew what he wanted and pursued it with tact and force. He was my "Angel" who I'm sad to this day to admit, I let down by leaving.

I was arrogant before. But now, having enjoyed multiple successes at the largest company in the world, I was over the top! More and more I thought about leaving the Mother Ship and somehow going out on my own so I could make serious money. I wasn't exactly sure how, but I thought about everything from building a chain of funeral parlors to making oil deals. But nothing seemed quite right. I managed to hide my secret desires from Guy Mallonee and others at Esso who believed I was good to go for the duration, as I was on the "fast track". One of the first lessons I learned at Esso---just like any real life family — you're in it for life. No one could imagine any sane person wanting to leave a management position such as mine in the Esso corporate world....but just maybe I wasn't sane.

We don't always know when we are well off in life. It's more often than not hard to tell. Looking back, Esso was the best company I ever worked for, my jobs at Esso were without a doubt the best jobs I ever had, I was happier in my work than I've ever been, and Guy V. Mallonee was the best boss I ever had! Now today with my 40 years of hindsight, leaving Esso was the single biggest mistake of my career!

Then my world turned, and along came Jack Andresen, life in the Big Apple, my bouts of hard drinking, and my life would never again be the same. I had no idea how poorly grounded I was and how wonderfully I'd been mentored, sheltered and protected by Guy and my Esso family. I had little idea about the dog eat dog world of big money New York and Wall Street, and I had yet to learn how much I needed Jesus Christ as my Lord and Savior.

Postscript

Esso's Car Care Centers failed to make it, in the long run.

Neither did Amoco, Shell or any of the ultra large oil company approaches. No one has 20-20 vision about "what might have been" or what will be in the future. The world is replete with "woulda, coulda, shoulda's". But here goes mine.

Not only did leaving Esso pave the way for serious problems in my future, it possibly changed Esso's future as well. I now believe my departure from Esso in 1969 resulted in two things: I headed down a career path full of alligators the likes of which I'd never seen; and Esso changed course.

I was a very hard and persistent flag carrier for what we were trying to accomplish, basically bringing into being a whole new level of customer service across Esso, the largest, wealthiest company in the world. We were trying to make "downstream pay its way". My untimely departure (for what I thought were greener pastures) left nobody behind with my unique drive and zeal. I am bold enough to believe there simply was no one who could lead the effort through obstacle courses as well as I. Knowing as I did who was left behind and their capabilities, all were excellent long-term employees with great experience. But none would dare go up against the system as I did, time and again, to keep plowing forward. Mr. Mallonee's sponsorship, backing me again and again when I got into tight spots with our field organizations, meant everything. Without his consistent support the business would not have gotten off the ground. But without my aggressive drive, who was he going to support?

Esso and the other majors were faced with the likelihood of losing important off driveway product and service sales to big retailers, cutting in more and more to capture business that historically belonged to service station dealers. How long until they started making big inroads into motor fuel and motor oil sales as well? These were daunting prospects for the industry in the late 50's and 60's.Questions were frequently asked at oil industry Board levels about the industry's future in retail. Dr. Peter Drucker and other academics filled the professional literature with excellent papers, warning about industry's abdication of its automotive service business. Drucker's "Marketing Myopia" was perhaps his most salient and foreboding work on this subject.

The fact was that most independent dealers depended heavily on off island sales and service for their principal income. Gasoline sales arguably didn't put food on the table for the dealer---that had to come from services, repairs, maintenance and sales of TBA. Fuel sales basically paid for light and heat---you had to sell tires and batteries at a minimum if you wanted to get beyond the basics. Smart operators cultivated their fuel customers, who were sort of a bird's nest on the ground, for these additional sales.

In my opinion, the industry failed to measure up to competitive threats, and now four decades later the genie is out of the bottle and can't be put back in. All one has to do is drive down any busy roadway in America to observe that "gasoline sellers" are predominantly self-serve islands, where customers pump their own gas and squeegee wipe their own windshields. Inside, they buy milk, soda pop, candy, pizza, and magazines. They have absolutely nothing to do anymore with the care and upkeep of customers' cars. The industry abdicated all responsibility for car care to specialty repair shops, automobile dealers, Sears and other big retailers, Firestone and other tire company stores. The retail level of the oil industry now bears absolutely no resemblance to the industry it once was and at one time tried to become. We, in turn, failed in our quest to make retail pay its own way through more robust off-island product and service sales to customers.

Is this a good thing? Maybe so, in the larger scheme of things, as cars are now built to be more reliable, needing less frequent attention. Tire blowouts and plugged radiators are almost a thing of the past. Still automobiles and other vehicles are far more complex than they used to be with computer controls for engines and other critical components. I don't know the answer to this riddle, and like many conundrums the answer isn't simple. It is a fact, however, that Exxon's profits certainly haven't suffered. The decade of the '60's saw Esso experiment with a number of non- petroleum adventures, including its own venture capital operation, Jersey Enterprises, Inc., as well as a move into manufacturing solar cells. Car Care Centers came along during Esso's venturesome period. Some, like Conoco, were experimenting with automatic car washes. Others were testing out mini-quick stop milk, bread and short order convenience stops. (At Esso most of us thought the idea of selling foodstuffs together with gasoline was disgusting, but look where we are today). Ultimately, wise heads at Esso decided to pull away from all superfluous ventures and strictly focus on its core oil and gas resource business around the world. Who's to say that was the wrong decision? Not I.

The entire industry, and especially ExxonMobil, continues to grow and prosper mightily with new discoveries of oil and gas around the globe, including the revolution in natural gas produced from shale formations here in America. This certainly validates Esso's decision to focus on its core resource business....producing crude oil and natural gas. The business of ExxonMobil now is clearly to produce oil and natural gas, wherever in the world it is found. ExxonMobil is virtually a "Company State", dealing with principals and Heads of State all over the world, whether they are friends of America and the Western World or not. ExxonMobil is basically its own nation! It is not strictly an "American Company"....Less than half its earnings come from North America....ExxonMobil is truly a citizen of the world, a virtual "Company State".

Other than selling motor fuel at the pump to self-serving customers, Esso and Big Oil are out of the retail business.

Hats off to the few surviving gas station independent dealers who take care of customers' cars while gassing them up, cleaning windshields, checking oil and examining tires. Some competently perform many automotive and product service needs of customers and earn a good income doing it .

Once upon a time, budding entrepreneurs could go into this service business for themselves, even without college degrees, and make a real go of it!

Life Lessons from ESSO

- *Under Guy Mallonee's mentoring, I came to realize my capacity for carrying a very heavy, demanding workload. I learned to trust myself in business and management decision making.*

- *I developed strong skills in formulating and presenting detailed and complex information and data to executives at the highest level and the Board of Directors.*

- *I became proficient in structuring and conducting all aspects of business and financial analysis. This included present value, discounted cash flow analysis and return on investment.*

- *I learned to create a new business, get it up and running, and operate it profitably.*

JOHN (JACK) ANDRESEN, ANDRESEN & COMPANY, NEW YORK

Bear with me, dear reader, for it's a long and twisted ride through my saga of Jack Andresen.

At times I may sound repetitive, and at other times my verbage might sound "too loud" for the situation. Please humor me and keep reading until you reach the end. My experience with Mr. Andresen covered only a two year period, 1969 - 1971,but that was more than enough to last me a lifetime. I consider Andresen a mentor not in the usual sense of one who has stimulated you to do positive things in life, but one whose impact has been large, including many lessons in what not to do as well as what to do.

I got on board the big new Eastern Airlines jetliner in Houston for a Monday morning flight to New York and was struck immediately by the appearance of my first class seatmate. He was tall, physically fit, middle-aged, impeccably dressed in a handsome gray suit, fancy French cuff shirt with his initials, and a tasteful blue tie. With horn rimmed glasses he looked like a university professor. His facial features were sharp and chiseled. He sat staring at a lined yellow legal pad with pen in hand and brow wrinkled, obviously deep in thought. Air travel in the 60's and 70's was luxurious, pursers and stewardesses looked neat and sharp, and onboard meals competed with upscale restaurants in appearance and quality. It's hard now to imagine the way things were then. Blue jeans and other casual dress were rarely seen on airplanes and air travel was considered luxurious.

No warning light went off in my head, and I heard no announcement alerting me that the man sitting next to me would change my life... forever. That's how quantum changes sometime come, without warning. In an instant your life and the lives of your loved ones can be changed permanently.

Before the 707 started taxiing, he looked over and said, "Do you know what a creative man is"? Normally you'd introduce yourself to the person next to you, maybe with a little chit chat. Raising such a deep question before even saying hello was sort of off the scale. I had work planned for the three-hour ride, not conversation with a total stranger.

Turning his question over in my mind, I responded as thoughtfully as I could and obviously struck a resonant chord. Surprisingly, we were off to the races in nonstop conversation about life and business, all the way to New York.

I learned he was John Andresen, everyone called him Jack, Chairman of a stock brokerage and venture capital firm bearing his name, Andresen & Company. He described his considerable investment success in the 1950's and 60's,growing to become a large investment banking firm. He had been in Houston for a weekend conference and was returning home.

He told me about his life's journey, coming from small town Iowa to Wall Street. After starting out in a modest job with an investment banking firm, he parlayed meager holdings into a fortune, hitting the jackpot in a particular stock, White Shield Corp. Attracting several well-heeled investors into the stock, the value of all their shares soared. After this and other early successes he climbed the ranks of venture capitalists, and had been recognized recently by Newsweek Magazine as an up and coming source of venture capital.

I was intrigued by Jack's amazing success story and wanted to know more about him and his company. He asked what I thought about many things, including the future of the oil industry ---what I believed characterized outstanding managers—my thoughts about sizing up investment prospects. He asked about my goals in life, and how I planned to achieve them. I was flattered that someone of Jack's stature with his many achievements cared about my views on so many things. I should have wondered why he gave a hoot about what I thought. What "coin of the realm" did he see in me? Maybe I should have been less forthcoming, but I was captivated. I'd never met anyone quite like him.

Landing at Idlewilde Airport, now called JFK, he offered me a ride into the city. Normally I would have taken the helicopter for a quick trip to the Pan Am Building at Grand Central Station, but thought it would be interesting to spend another hour with my intriguing new acquaintance. An inner voice was telling me to cut it off, but I didn't listen. I was in for another surprise--his vehicle was a big black Cadillac limousine and he had his own driver. The ride in was luxurious, aided by Glenlivit on the rocks and more lively conversation.

Dropping me off at the Berkshire in Midtown, Jack wanted to stay in touch, inviting me to stop by for a visit. His office was at 120 Broadway in the financial district. It didn't work out that trip, but I hoped it would at another time. I couldn't get this compelling man out of my mind in the days and weeks that followed, and wanted to know more about him.

More than 40 years later, I realize this was not just a "chance meeting"--God doesn't play Russian Roulette. Being a follower of Jesus Christ now, I realize things don't "just happen" by chance to me. And I didn't even know Jesus Christ as my Lord and Savior during my Jack Andresen period. God, in His infinite wisdom and mercy, is present every moment of my life and has always been. He loved me even when I was mired in sin. My guiding light is Romans 8:28, Paul the Apostle telling us to be thankful in all things because they work together for the good of those who love the Lord and are called according to His purposes. I didn't know whether I loved the Lord or not back then. In fact I hadn't thought much about spiritual things since my childhood church experiences. But I know now He loves me and was working out his purposes in my life, though I was in sin. Otherwise I might not have met those crises in life that ultimately plummeted me into despair, when I cried out for Jesus to save me. I would have had to come to Jesus in some other way, lovingly orchestrated by God. God in His wisdom allowed my overwhelming ego and vanity to be shattered, getting my undivided attention.

Jack was the instrument that started my ball rolling down the road to destruction, desperation, conversion and rebirth, ultimately to sanctification and to a wholly new life in Christ. I believe God's plan for me would have come to pass, one way or the other. My plans and God's plan for me were at odds until I finally got on board. His plans don't change no matter how hard we try to change them.

Jack Andresen was raised in the Catholic church, but I doubt he ever had a personal relationship with Christ Jesus. God can and does use carnal men to work out his purposes, and nothing and no one is beyond the love of Jesus Christ. I came to learn over time that Jack was brilliant but deeply flawed and amoral. Eventually, I came to detest Jack even though I learned many things from him that helped me down the road in business, including what not to do.

Jack and I kept in touch over the ensuing months, and I visited his offices during a trip to New York. Andresen & Company was high up in the impressive shiny black-glassed Marine Midland Grace skyscraper on lower Broadway, in the heart of the financial district. The offices were attractive, well organized and geared for efficiency and production. There were two main parts of his company--- an extensive stock brokerage and trading operation under Jack's partner, Frank Rubenstein; and venture capital and investment banking under Jack. Beneath one organizational roof, startup and seed capital could be raised and invested, looking ahead to downstream public stock offerings in successful ventures. Rubenstein's operation included several Wall Street heavy hitters with worldwide client bases. Rubenstein had made a fortune in the dry cleaning business on Long Island before partnering with Jack.

This kind of cradle to grave operation appealed to the entrepreneur wanting to concentrate on building a company while getting financial support from a single lead entity. This way he could avoid having to beat the bushes up and down Wall Street, frantically searching for money.

Jack's venture capital brain trust occupied swanky offices and suites, separate from the rest of the firm. Several former 3M Company executives worked in this area. Jack enjoyed close relationships with a senior officer and research director at 3M, opening many doors for him into the world of advanced technology and materials sciences. The ex-3Mers were bright young engineers, holding respectable MBA's. They were formidable technology analysts. Their job was to seek out businesses with strong technology bases, sift through and evaluate them, and present the best for possible investment banking or venture capital relationships. Jack and his group had put together several successful high-tech deals, including computer peripheral equipment and advanced material manufacturers.

I wasn't surprised when Jack asked me to leave Esso to come aboard to round out his venture capital operation. This was more or less the natural outcome I expected from his mating dance with me since we met. He wanted me to participate directly in managing one or more companies in which he was heavily invested, helping them grow. He saw development of new ideas, products and markets as the pathway to prosperity and believed I was the catalyst he needed. He offered a whopping increase in my salary and benefits and said he would provide options and warrants to purchase stock in ventures I would be working on. He didn't want me to spend much time, however, prospecting for new investments as the 3Mers and others in his brain trust had that base covered. He assured me my fortune would be made by building up one or more companies already in his stable of investments.

He showed me the office I would have in his suite, a large beautifully furnished space overlooking the mammoth construction site of the World Trade Center towers 1 and 2. This was heady stuff, playing into my grandiose fantasies, ego, vanity and hopes for fame and fortune. Jack's deal sounded almost too good to be true---and it was.

I was conflicted about what to do, being fully committed to my work with the outstanding high quality people at Esso. The thought of breaking away, moving my young family to the Big Apple where we had no friends or family, was daunting. Jack encouraged me to take my time, that his offer would be there as long as necessary. It was a tough decision because so much was involved, considering that my family was happy and settled in Houston, I was being catapulted by my successes at Esso, and the scary but tempting uncertainty we would be getting into.

I didn't realize the gaping holes in my knowledge of Jack's firm and what was really expected of me, and I didn't have a clue about the internal power struggle over control of Andresen & Company. Because my research was inadequate and my thirst for financial bonanza immense, I didn't investigate thoroughly enough to uncover the fact that Jack's brain trust was not really loved by the other side of the house. Also I should have insisted on knowing more about the company or companies Jack had in mind for me to help grow.

These failures on my part proved costlier than I could imagine — and were my undoing. I let the prospect of riches cloud my vision.

A few months passed after Jack's invitation. Throwing myself fully back into the Car Care Center work, the allure of New York and Wall Street and its pot of gold never left my mind. Staying in Houston versus going to New York was a daily topic at home, as there was much to be said for both choices. I had a long visit with my boss at Esso about the situation. He gave me every assurance that I was on Esso's fast track, that my future was golden if I continued the pace I had set. He'd do everything he could to help me get the right opportunities and exposure, including experience overseas, so essential for top executives in a worldwide integrated oil company. He even had a couple of Esso's senior officers stop by to encourage me to stay. I really didn't believe I deserved this kind of attention, though admittedly it boosted my swollen ego.

Difficult decision that it was, my wife and I eventually came to believe that living and working in Manhattan, children in private school, weekends enjoying the grandeur of the big city could be a tremendous growth experience for us. And we thought the pot of gold was real enough to take the plunge. Having the opportunity to make all this happen, I was scared to death but at the same time excited about the prospect, a perfect storm for poor decision making. We wanted to live in the city itself, suburban commuter life was out of the question in our first year or two.

I phoned Jack before Christmas, taking him up on his offer, saying I'd report during the first week in January, 1969. He had hoped I'd be able to come up for the firm's Holiday party, but that wasn't to be, as my hands were full in Houston.

Resigning from Humble Oil and Refining Company (Esso), we made arrangements to pass on my Car Care Center duties. Guy Mallonee threw a nice going away party--I hated to say goodbye in the worst way to my fellow workers and bosses. People just don't leave Esso period; you expect to sign on for life. I felt a deep pit in my stomach, knowing what I was leaving behind. We sold our home in Houston almost immediately to friends of our neighbors, wanting to live in our wonderful neighborhood near Rice University. It was a done deal, almost overnight including our Buick. We didn't want the burden of owning and garaging a car in Manhattan.

I left for New York the day after New Years to find an apartment for us in the city, to search out the school situation and to report in to Jack. Family and household effects would follow in a week or two. I was fortunate to find exactly the right kind of apartment on the Upper East Side, near the East River, close to shopping, wonderful parks and the Mayor's home, Gracie Mansion. A high quality private school was near, children picked up by private carrier every morning and returned after school. I believed commuting to Wall Street via the IRT two blocks away would be no harsher than my daily drive to downtown Houston in traffic.

Jack assigned me to shepherd a high tech company located in Farmingdale, Long Island, that was built around an inventor, Louis

Bucalo.(I'll be referring to it as Company K). Bucalo's proprietary technology seemed ingenious. It was an entirely new way to manufacture complex metal shapes and appeared to have many promising applications. Bucalo had demonstrated the concept at laboratory scale, but so far had gotten no orders that would permit him to establish anything near commercial scale production. (This was the classical case of a technology looking for a product, a situation most seasoned investors try to avoid getting into).

The process itself involved electrolytically depositing a metal surface on a dissolvable shaped substrate; then dissolving the substrate to leave behind a metal piece shaped exactly like the substrate it had covered. Then, for example, this newly created metal piece could be covered with yet another dissolvable substrate, and a second metal surface could be deposited; then by dissolving the second substrate, a second metal surface would remain, precisely conforming to the shape of the first metal piece and fitting snugly against it.

This technique could be used to produce a variety of complex shapes and products that might be difficult and costly to machine and fabricate by conventional methods. The Bucalo patents were as strong as process patents could be, like Jack required in all his technology investments.

Jack introduced me to Mr. Bucalo, encouraging us to be innovative to accomplish great things at Company K. Happily, Lou and I hit it off from the start, immediately spending two intensive weeks, going through every aspect of the company, visiting with employees, getting familiar with Lou's technology, and exchanging ideas about technology, potential new products, marketing, management, our families and life in general. We talked about our individual goals and how they might be achieved.

But after going over the company's books and reviewing recent financial transactions, I was troubled by some of the things I found. Experienced managers, including the well compensated President of Company K, a former key executive of a major chemical company, had been hired by Jack and his investor group to build and run the business so the talented Mr. Bucalo could concentrate on product development. Yet, after more than a year, they showed no progress. Two acquisitions of compatible specialty machine shop businesses had been made the previous year. It was expected these two profitable businesses would undergird Company K. Still, none of the hoped for synergism had been achieved. Worse still, I believed Bucalo wasn't comfortable batting new product ideas around with the hired guns, because nothing came of these discussions. I was happy that he seemed perfectly comfortable kicking ideas around with me.

I could see no end to the subsidies required from Jack and his investor group, amounting to several hundred thousand dollars at a bite just to keep the company afloat....nothing lay ahead but continued losses and more red ink. Company K was headed for a collision with the ground with the particular team Jack had put in place.

The job Jack expected me to do now became starkly clear, and it was scary. There was no clear way forward except to somehow come up with a product or application that would quickly hit the jackpot. I felt uncomfortable about my ability, or for that matter, anybody's ability to achieve this in any reasonable amount of time. Coming up with one or more new products that could attract a production size order was quite a hill to climb.

I started thinking I had made a serious mistake coming into the Andresen cabal. Some of the heavy hitters at Andresen were invested in Company K, and I learned they were less than happy about the lack of tangible progress. Maybe I was paranoid, but it occurred to me that I could become some kind of "sacrificial lamb". In several chance hallway interactions with Frank Rubenstein, he pumped me pretty hard about progress at Company K. Frank was very soft-spoken and a master of tact, yet always seemed to drop dimes on Jack about Company K and his approach to venture capital generally. These few chance conversations made me very uncomfortable. I wondered how much more he knew about the whole situation at Company K than I. Jack had made it clear he didn't want discussion outside our wing about Company K.

Once or twice I mentioned Rubenstein's comments to Jack, thinking that was the right thing to do. He brushed aside any concerns about internecine struggles at the firm. After several attempts to discuss it with Jack, I decided to keep these suspicions strictly to myself, not knowing whether anyone involved with Company K or Andresen could be trusted. I was suspicious that Company K was one part of someone's grand scheme to "get Jack", and I didn't want to be part of whatever game was being played. I just wanted to make money, but the once alluring promise of earning a pot of gold was growing dimmer. I didn't think it wise to discuss my concerns even with Bucalo, not knowing for sure where he stood with Jack and Rubenstein.

Bucalo and I agreed we needed to bring Jack up to date on where we stood and to devise a plan for Company K. Our meeting soon came to pass, after hours, in Jack's office, with Jack, Louis, me and a bottle of Scotch. This would be my first close quarters decision making meeting with Jack, typically after hours with plenty of Scotch and no time limit. Bucalo said this was the way Jack liked to operate. Bucalo and I had hashed and rehashed the things we wanted to go over with Jack and we were in complete agreement. Our job was to include Jack in everything we knew and come to a boil on what was needed.

We recommended that Jack take three steps: 1) fire the highly paid managers he had brought in; 2) make Bucalo the President; and 3) designate me a special consultant to the President. As we expected, Jack's first reaction was to shout that Louis, gifted engineer that he was, knew absolutely nothing about running a business and would be a disaster as President, even with my help. He believed it would be a complete waste of Lou's time to be bothered with business administrivia. We stuck to our guns, and the meeting ended late after much discussion, lots of Scotch, but no decision.

We let things percolate a few days before scheduling another meeting after hours. This time Jack came around, agreeing with our recommendations and deciding to begin making management changes immediately, that very evening. Louis and I sat quietly by in Jack's office late that night as he wielded the axe by phone, canning all of the old management team.

At a special meeting of the Company K Board the next week, Jack went over proposed changes, and Mr. Bucalo was elected President. It was a short meeting, since Jack voted the lion's share of stock, even though there was a small public market the result of an earlier IPO.

Other problems of a financial nature surfaced as we cleaned out the company, including obscure accounts that didn't make sense, raising questions in my mind about subterfuge. My concerns grew about me and my family if Louis and I didn't make the grade. I never had any doubt in my mind about Louis Bucalo's honesty and integrity. It looked to me like Lou, Company K and the investors had been poorly served by the "hired managers". And I couldn't stop thinking I had taken the job without getting enough information about what was expected. I had been blinded by money and what I had been led to believe was great upside potential. I hadn't realized that I would be slotted into a single company that was riddled with technical and financial problems, one in which the investors obviously held very high expectations. And if my suspicions were right, I just might be thrown to the wolves.

Others in Jack's group were out prospecting, investing, having a great time and apparently making money while I was stuck. My salary was good, but I didn't see how I was going to make any real money unless I too could prospect and bring something in. I didn't see how my warrants and stock options in Company K would pay off in the foreseeable future. Even worse, I wondered how my handsome pay could be justified (perhaps to Frank Rubenstein) unless we could show tangible results, soon!

Louis and I continued to hammer away, coming up with ideas for several new products. He made various prototypes in the lab, and we tried them out on prospective customers. The most promising product appeared to be a type of valve, known as a ball valve. This snap action type of valve could be made electrolytically in many sizes and shapes---as small as a pin head, or as large as 10 inches in diameter. We just needed to find the right applications. We believed the ball type valve could find a place then held by so-called gate valves or other valve types that were cheap to make. If we could offer a competitively priced ball valve with its inherently superior flow control characteristics, we hoped to get orders for commercial quantities. Company K's electrolytic process could potentially produce a ball valve that would be fully competitive with other valves, but would be superior in many applications.

But making progress was like pulling teeth, because this type of valve challenged the state of the art in controlling fluids, whether medicinal sera or back yard water hydrants. Along the way, we explored various business arrangements such as licensing, subbing out manufacturing, or setting up a production line in house at Company K. Either way, we needed a production size order whether we produced the order ourselves or farmed it out. But getting such an order in the first place was a high marketing hill to climb. Pioneering any new product is challenging, even products that offer significant potential benefits over those that are tried and true. Inertia, continuing to do things the same old way, is hard to overcome for any new product seeking a place in an established market. We were aggressively seeking a niche for the new ball valve in the building trades among such manufacturers as Kohler, Crane and Moyno.

In spite of suspicions and doubts about Andresen and my job security, I was learning a lot about investing, investors, how they think and act. I was getting exposure to a different world from any I had ever known. I wanted to learn all I could in the time I had, whether a day or five years. One that has served me throughout my career concerns the relative value of "an idea" and "investment capital". A cornerstone of investing at Andresen and many other venture capitalists was " Money Is More Important Than Ideas". I regularly saw entrepreneurs with ideas in search of investment capital. While not exactly a dime a dozen, inventors and people with ideas, some admittedly brilliant, shopped all over Wall Street seeking funds. It was a world long on ideas and opportunities but stingy with capital. Investors have their pick of places to invest, but most idea peddlers can't be so choosy. I observed investors who wouldn't have a serious discussion with a prospect unless it was understood from the start that the investor would have control of the business, i.e. over 50% ownership, not the entrepreneur until certain milestones were met. Then and only then could the entrepreneur regain control, under pre-agreed upon terms. While discouraging to some, such stringent measures were acceptable to others, giving them ready access to capital so they could concentrate on building the bushes instead of having to beat the bushes every few months for money.

Venture investors expect returns of ten, twenty or more times their initial investment. Though this may sound like usury, it reflects the extremely risky nature of most new ventures. The high risk associated with drilling a "wildcat" oil well in a virgin area with no previous production, is analogous. The mortality rate for new ventures and startups is very high, and venture investors rightly need to be compensated for taking extraordinary risks.

I knew Jack saw me as an "operating guy", not the "investor type" — a guy who knows how to get a business off the ground, making it hum. Jack admitted most investors don't understand operations, nor do they have the necessary temperament. And he was sure I'd never be a good stock picker. That was a hard pill for me to swallow, although it was perhaps meant as a compliment to my operating expertise. My ego and pride never accepted being told I was limited about much of anything, once I made up my mind to do a thing. "Pickers" at Andresen told me they were happy to have an operating guy like me on board, babysitting one of their stepchildren. And why shouldn't they be? Was I playing a fool's game with me the fool and I just didn't know it yet?

Jack eventually relented, letting me look around, trying my hand at prospecting for up front or near up front funding prospects. But the few I brought in didn't measure up to Andresen's investment criteria. First and foremost, the quality of the principal — Jack's actual proposition being "Is He Able". And his close second, "What Is The Razorblade and What Is The Razor". Holding a solid patent position that could stand up under careful legal scrutiny was yet a third hurdle, once you got past the first two. For one reason or another, my attempts turned out to be futile. Jack's contention that I am an operator, not much of a stock picker, was truly verified in his mind.

I actually introduced three prospects to the firm, only to have them leave town after what amounted to a kangaroo court, unhappy they came to New York on their own time and expense, learning little and accomplishing nothing. I learned by the experience and actually understood why these particular prospects did not make the grade at Andresen. Two of them, by the way, went on to build healthy, profitable companies without the benefit of Andresen venture capital. One became a household name in cooling chests and recreational equipment, Igloo; the other a successful synthetic marble manufacturer, supplying the building trade. I pretty much stopped looking for prospects after these, digesting where I had gone wrong and concentrating on Company K.

I continued working with Bucalo at Farmingdale, but my questions about the motivation behind my hiring didn't go away. I believed it would take a miracle for us to achieve Jack's goals, and while we were making progress, it was slow. I felt I had little or no job security without major success at Company K, and I had placed myself and my family in a vulnerable position by moving out of the hallowed and relatively secure halls of Esso into the wiles of Wall Street. I didn't think it wise to discuss my feelings with Bucalo, in spite of our excellent relationship, because I didn't really understand his relationship with Jack. Now I had no mentors like Guy Mallonee and other fabulous executives at Esso, and nobody had my back. I felt terribly out of place and unsure about my future with Andresen.

Jack and I disagreed frequently about the business on Long Island and business in general. I thought he resented my attempts to bring in prospects, and I believed I would never make any real money doing Jack's bidding at Company K. I believed Jack had misled me, and I had no one to blame but myself for falling for his yarn. Our relationship deteriorated, and he once fired me in a fit of pique. Next day, he hired me back, wanting to get things off to a new start. We went out, drank our lunch and calmly talked business. I laid out my concerns about Company K investor disenchantment and pressures, and I pushed him to tell me point blank if I had been hired to simply assuage the investors. He just swept my concerns aside. He insisted he was under no threat from the other side of the house, and assured me that I was not being set up to take the fall for Company K.

I had blundered seriously, falling for Jack's beguiling lure, believing there was a future for me at Andresen & Company. Whether Jack knew the seriousness of the problems at Company K before I laid them out I'll never know. Someone must have suspected problems, given the pressures on Jack and the informal comments Frank Rubenstein made to me. I had grown to disrespect, even to detest Jack, thoroughly repulsed by his mendacity. I got the distinct impression from Rubenstein that Jack's venture capital operation was thought to be shoveling the firm's money out the window on speculative deals like Company K. In my crystal ball, it was just a matter of time before Jack would lose control of the entire firm to the other side. If that happened, I didn't need an Ouija board to see what would happen to me and others in Jack's brain trust.

I knew I had to get out of there before it was too late. Unfortunately, I didn't have a clue about how to get out or where to go.

The full truth about my suspicions, who knew what about K Company, and my forebodings about internal warfare to gain control at Andresen probably went to the grave with the principals. Mr. Andresen died in the mid-1990s, reportedly in severe stress over one of his ventures gone awry. Mr. Bucalo died a few years later. According to public records, Mr. Andresen did in fact lose the internal war for control. He restarted in Greenwich, Connecticut a few years later. He seems to have continued the search for proprietary technology investments, emphasizing medications and medically related miracles. I don't know whether any of his pursuits led to a bonanza, though I doubt it — he might have simply suffered more heartache.

According to public records, Mr. Bucalo ultimately developed a miniature ball valve that could be implanted in males to effect a reversible vasectomy. It seems the technology was carried forward by a major pharmaceutical manufacturer on some basis outside the U.S. I don't know whether Bucalo hit the jackpot. It would surprise me if he did. We might have been on the trail of what ultimately became a product used now everywhere in homes across America — some version of the old ball valve. Still, it's clear to me the big manufacturers weren't about to give us a production order, letting us break into their lucrative markets. They obviously developed new generations of valves themselves.

Finally, I know nothing about the ultimate fates of Andersen & Company or Company K.

What I know now is that my life and the life of my entire family changed forever once I pulled up roots in Houston and relocated to New York City. A chance meeting with a charismatic seatmate on a morning plane ride permanently changed everything. Our lives shifted to an entirely different trajectory from then on.

Robert Frost's brilliant, insightful poem about coming to a fork in the road is so true. It fits my journey in life, perfectly.

THE ROAD NOT TAKEN
by Robert Frost

Two roads diverged in a yellow wood,
And sorry I could not travel both and be one traveler,
Long I stood and looked down one as far as I could
To where it bent in the undergrowth;

Then took the other, as just as fair,
And having perhaps the better claim,
Because it was grassy and wanted wear;
Though as for that the passing there
Had worn them really about the same,

And both that morning equally lay
In leaves no step had trodden black.
Oh, I kept the first for another day!
Yet knowing how way leads on to way,
I doubted if I should ever come back.

I shall be telling this with a sigh
Somewhere ages and ages hence:
Two roads diverged in a wood, and I---
I took the one less traveled by,
And that has made all the difference.

Yogi Bera had a different take on life saying "When you come to a fork in the road, take it"

.

POSTLOGUE ON JOHN ANDRESEN

M y two years in New York with Jack Andresen amounted to a watershed period in my life, finding myself up that old proverbial creek without a paddle — a period that was amazing, eye-opening, educational, scary and frustrating, all at the same time.

It was amazing and eye opening because I found myself in the mainstream of life in a dog-eat-dog world where making big money on the last deal was all that mattered. Feelings about losses and empathy for the less fortunate didn't amount to a blip on a screen. It was scary and frustrating because I knew I couldn't produce all the magic needed to fix Company K, and this meant I had absolutely no job security. I knew what I needed to do. I needed to pull up my big boy pants and step out of the trauma that encased me. But I seemed to be in a state of shock — unable to look for work, believing that all my skill and talent had evaporated. I should have been able to easily locate a better fit for my skills and background, but jumped to the conclusion that my family and I didn't belong in New York. Once again, I jumped the gun.

Jack tried to persuade me to become a specialist in the oil, gas and energy industries, and get set up in one of the large investment banks with clients around the world. I researched the idea, identifying only one such critter of any prominence, a Frenchman named Marc Millard with the firm of Lazard Frères. This was one of Jack's better ideas, but by the time it came along, I just wanted out, period. I didn't trust the words that came out of Jack's mouth or the ideas from his head.

I was contacted about a new job in Esso's global propane business, starting out at Corporate Headquarters in Rockefeller Center. The opportunity was outstanding and was under a friend from the Esso Research and Engineering Company, Dr. Myles Connor. After a year or two in New York, Myles expected us to be relocated to European headquarters in London. I interviewed and was offered the job. After first saying it was a go, I decided I didn't really want the big worldwide life in Esso any more than life as an energy analyst in New York. Actually, returning to Esso would have made abundant sense as I look back on my life. Rarely does a departed one get the opportunity to return to the Esso flagship under any conditions. In fact one of my regrets in life is that I left in the first place, at the top of my game.

Lessons Learned from Jack Andresen:

Lessons I learned on Jack's watch were timeless, influencing my life in business from then on. I'll attempt to summarize them because they have been important to me. Please try to look beyond the personage of Jack Andresen I've described, and beyond my foibles as well, digesting these important points for what they are.

1) *Why stocks go up*
   Three factors make stocks go up, or down---psychological, technical and business factors. Jack was a self-described genius on psychological factors, believing few others were so gifted as he. Technicians can be hired to assess the technical aspects of a deal. Jack believed I had the bases covered on business factors, that my skills in this regard were unique to Wall Street.

2) *Buy low, sell high.*
   Not as easy as it sounds, because it goes against the "herd instinct" which we all have to one extent or another. It's human nature to "want company" when making important decisions, such as where and when to invest. Successful investors have learned this lesson, and often go against the herd. Doing this is a lot easier said than done. This basic principle applies across the board in life, whether stocks and bonds, real estate or show business. Develop skills that enable you to buy low and sell high, not the other way around, buying high and selling low, resulting in loss.

3) *Investing is the highest form of business activity, everything else is lower.*
   Jack evangelically believed in owning pieces of many companies, i.e. stocks, in which owner-managers were "beating their brains out trying to build a business". This is a debatable principle, at least in my book, yet Jack lived by it. We argued about this, among many other things. How could Jack place such a high premium on my business operational skills while feeling my genus was somewhere lower on the business totem? This was just another of many paradoxes about Mr. Andresen.

4) *Evaluate potential managers of ventures very carefully, your aim being to determine if the prospect is "able".*
To Jack, being "able" meant virtually being superman. His requirement went beyond being "capable". It superseded being versatile. And went beyond possessing technical strengths. He was fixated on finding the "total man", a virtual godlike multifaceted person, capable of doing nearly anything. In the beginning, Jack believed I was one of the superman genus. He was disappointed to learn that I too had many shortcomings, including my growing dislike of him and his firm. As impractical as his ideal was, Jack instilled in me a deep sense of what constitutes a good manager. I learned to more skillfully recognize good managers in the tribe of would-be managers, to recruit and set them up to be successful, and to motivate and reward them. This skill has been one of my long suits, and I credit Jack for helping me.

5) *Secure a proprietary position in your business if at all possible.*
Investment prospects with a strong patent position, also satisfying the "razor blade and razor" criteria, usually offer maximum proprietary potential in the marketplace. Strong product type patents are usually better than process type patents which can be gotten around more easily. The "razor blade and razor" strategy can provide large continuing sales to customers that already own the "razor". The Verizon cell phone ,by example, is a "razor" and continuing cellphone services the supply of "blades". Colgate Palmolive can practically give away toothbrushes if they are able to hook you on their toothpaste. Several years ago, the folks at Schick sent me an unsolicited free razor. I tried it, liked it, and have used their shaving products ever since.

6) *Money is more important than the idea.*
    *I previously discussed this important principle saying that
    people with good ideas were all over the financial district,
    seeking investment funding. In fact, ideas were a dime a
    dozen. Funding, however, is a scarce commodity, and venture
    investors can and should be very picky. Most often,
    entrepreneurs over estimate the value their ideas, making a
    deal with venture investors hard to come by. The nature of
    venture funding is high risk, and investors are entitled to a
    premium return, ranging from ten to thirty or more times
    their investment in a reasonable timeframe. Some investors
    may require absolute control of the stock from the outset,
    allowing management to reacquire control over time as certain
    negotiated milestones are met. Giving up control to secure
    funding can pose a serious stumbling block for the
    entrepreneur. Some aren't willing to give it up, believing their
    idea is worth more than the money. My experience is that
    entrepreneurs showing reasonable flexibility when seeking
    venture investment are far ahead of others.*

7) *Marketing research on a new product or system is best
    done by trying to make a sale.*
    *Even if you have only a prototype, or maybe just a good set of
    drawings and schematics. Asking someone what they will buy
    doesn't get to the nub of the problem, which is whether I can
    actually sell one of what I am trying to sell. I've actually made
    several large sales based strictly on renderings and product
    descriptions. Admittedly the sales were conditional, depending
    on my ability to actually deliver.*

I took Jack's assessment of my skills to heart when I set out to find
what was to be next. Deciding against returning to Esso and knowing
Jack didn't think much of my stock picking attributes but said good
things about my operating skills, I decided to become a "corporate
midwife", helping grow new businesses within existing companies .I
needed to be judicious in selecting whom to work for. I expected to be
remunerated by stock options, bonuses and warrants plus salary and
benefits, meaning I'd sign on as an employee with operational
authority to make things happen. I thought about packaging myself as
a consultant, but decided against this route, as consultants have no real

authority to get things done---they only suggest and recommend. If I could hire on as a midwife in the right kind of company, I would use those skills Jack believed I possessed in abundance.

I wasn't motivated to start up my own company from scratch, like the Lou Bucalos of the world and Company K. The risks I would have to assume would be unacceptably high for my family and me. I just didn't have the stomach for it, and didn't want to make such a large personal sacrifice. I'd seen many struggling entrepreneurs come through the financial district seeking capital, some going without pay for long periods as they tried to get a new company off the ground. My personal financial base was too limited to weather a startup storm, and inadequate to buy a significant existing business. From what I'd seen, I didn't want to be involved with Andresen money in any way, so that was not an option.

Frankly, I wanted to have my cake and eat it too. I wanted to be involved with a company that was already off the ground, flying well, in the black, with aggressive owners who wanted a new spark, one that I could provide by taking the company in new directions. Owners would need to have the stomach to be supportive and patient while the new business is built, and accord me the incentive to make it worth my while. I wasn't bothered by the fact that neither the New York Times or the Wall Street Journal carried job vacancies entitled: "Wanted – Corporate Midwife". Even so, I knew I'd have to find a way to demonstrate my abilities to prospective employers.

I knew there was a handful of successful "turnaround specialists" who were connected with banks and large investment bankers. I realized they were masters at coming into a troubled situation, quickly scoping out the problem, and turning the company around to earn their pot of gold in resuscitated stock. I was a long way from anyone trusting me to take on this kind of situation. The best I could aspire to near-term was to start out small, build my reputation and credibility, while getting to know selected banks and bankers.

At some point in your life, big breaks start to winnow down, maybe disappearing entirely. In my mid-30's, I had gotten spoiled by having so many big breaks, expecting them to continue showing up just like always. But they stopped dropping out of the sky, and I needed to refocus my thinking. I discovered what successful people have always known – you have to get off your butt and make your own breaks.

You can't do it being passive. You MUST actively, maybe even aggressively, seek out and create your own breaks. Maybe the opportunities were as abundant as always---but my vision had changed. Also, now there was more noise in my system and I questioned the clarity of what I saw.

NOTES ON MY LIFE AFTER ANDRESEN

After leaving Andresen and turning down a great opportunity to return to Esso, armed with new thinking about the general direction I wanted to pursue, I took my family for a long ski vacation in northern Maine to clear my head and get my feet on the ground.

I've skied to clear cobwebs out of my head ever since I was a graduate student at the University of Colorado. Long ago, I discovered I simply cannot worry about life's problems, finances or anything else when I ski. I totally focus on the skis beneath me, my syncopated body movements, and the trail ahead, while enjoying God's beautiful scenery and the rush of icy air across my cheeks. Some claim golfing, diving or flying brings this kind of mind clearing experience. My passion has always been skiing on beautifully groomed slopes in somewhat steep terrain, as I regain my mental and emotional bearings.

I found all this and even more during our sabbatical in Maine's mountains, deep in the winter of 1971-72. Our children were nine and eleven, able to be on their own for most of the day in the huge expanse of Carrabasset Valley's mountains. Just give them a couple of bucks apiece for snacks and lunch during the day and they were gone! Both already had become pretty good skiers.

I occasionally scouted around for work, telephoning contacts during my skication and turned up a few opportunities in Texas and New England, roughly fitting my new "midwivery" criteria. Unfortunately, I had started drinking more than I was willing to admit during our time in Maine. Down deep I began feeling like I was starting to fall apart. Daytime brought me back to great joy and exhilaration, cruising down the groomed steeps, always with a flask in my pocket to warm my spirits on those long chair lift rides back to the top.

But in the après ski hours back at the lodge, I was gradually becoming a wreck, trying to hide my feelings from my family. Most nights I went to bed after drinking too much, waking in the morning hung over, with a lulu of a headache. I believed I had decent plans for my career moves, but wasn't sure I could find the right opportunity. I fooled myself into believing alcohol was a confidence builder and imagined I could do about anything after I had drunk to excess. Of course I could turn that or any other company around and make a fortune for the owners and myself doing it. Just stand back and watch!

Drinking, I became Mr. Corporation Superman, a hero in my own mind!

I blew through three jobs over the course of three years, after the sabbatical in Maine. It wasn't the drinking that brought me down as much as my personality. Entrusted each time by founders who had poured their souls and pocketbooks into getting businesses going, placed in highly responsible positions, my progression wasn't fast enough to suit my out of control ego. I ran each opportunity into the ground, insisting on doing things my way, with scant regard for others, including those that brought me in.

Yet, even with my out of control ego, I still pulled off some Martin Magic for my employers. For one employer, I took over the reins of a pharmaceutical company with operations across the Canadian Maritimes and in a year turned it around. Then I successfully negotiated its sale on excellent terms to a large Montreal based retailer. So while accomplishing some good things for employers, in three short years I found myself without work, no decent prospects for work, few friends and I was drinking heavily.

I found my way back to Texas with one set of contacts, and after relocating my family to the Dallas area, ran that one into the ground. I was out of work again, struggling to figure out what to do.

My wife was finally fed up, taking our children and moving over a thousand miles away to begin a new life for herself, back in graduate school at the University of Colorado. Without much acrimony, I turned over all our assets, meager at that point, to my wife for their use during her two year doctoral program. There wasn't yet a divorce---just separation, over a long distance.

For the first time ever, I was alone, totally alone and pretty well destitute. I thought how foolish others had been for failing to grasp all the magical things I could make happen in a business. The thought hadn't occurred to me that I had serious problems that needed to be addressed. I believed others predominantly were to blame for my predicament, including Jack Andresen. In one particularly bright moment, I actually believed the world was going to be deprived of my genius, just because I might decide to never work again, professionally. Admittedly, I felt this way after drinking heavily.

This once proud Texas Aggie, rising star in the Air Force and in Esso, had crashed and was burning, losing family, business and income. I saw a true to life axiom unfolding in front of me—the more I drank to build my confidence the more I lost confidence in myself, and the more I lost confidence in myself, the less others wanted anything to do with me. I was convinced others, including my wife, were to blame for my failures. I hadn't yet taken ownership of my situation.

My life was in a vicious spiral downward. My dear mom and dad, only a hundred miles away, were worried sick about me and couldn't do anything but be there for me, which was understandably more than anyone else and maybe even more than I deserved.

I dressed and groomed, making calls on several bankers, explaining my outstanding experience, my unique abilities, and the kinds of companies I wanted to serve. Not surprisingly, nothing came my way. I called on several individual investors with the same result. It never occurred to me that I was my own worst enemy. While trying to put on a show outwardly, I was falling apart on the inside, thinking I was the only one who saw it.

I had no idea whatever that I was on a road leading to the salvation of my soul through Jesus Christ, and that there would be changes ahead in my life I couldn't imagine.

SAVED BY GRACE

I know what it is to be lost. And I know what it is to be saved.

I've been in both places. I know how it feels to be almost totally lost to any moral principles and scruples--in fact so lost that you don't even realize you are hopelessly and obliviously lost, and you keep making the same miserable mistakes over and over, never learning from them. Then I know clearly how almost deliriously joyful it is to be saved from perdition, earthly as well as eternal, by the grace of God through Jesus Christ, my Lord and personal Savior. Having been there, I know how low sin and rebellion against God can bring a man. And, I am blessed to be able to see the hand of God at work in my saved life, giving me a peace that truly passes all of my ability to understand, just as the Lord Jesus promises.

This peace grows fuller and richer with every year of my life. Sure, turmoil comes from time to time--but I can honestly say that I look at events in my life more and more through scriptural and spiritual lenses. I don't react now in the same way I used to when faced with challenges. The old Martin reacted to every circumstance, looking out for himself, often with indifference to others, sometimes in rebellion. I didn't worry much about detriment or hurt to others, maybe even those I loved. Quick on the trigger--shoot before you are shot--turn every situation to your advantage---always have the last word on any subject. I can honestly say now that ideas like this and such memories are painful to me ---it's hard for me to believe that I was the way I was.

I grew up in the Baptist Church in Texas, hearing great sermons every Sunday by Brother Wharton, Kerney Keegan or Bible scholar Dr. W. Morris Ford. The pulpit was occasionally occupied by luminaries such as grocery store magnate Howard E. Butt, Campus Crusade's Bill Bright, industrialist R.G. LeTourneau and others. My mother and dad made sure I was in church every time the doors were open. More than once I responded to the altar call, re-dedicating my life to the Lord, somehow feeling moved by the Spirit — after all, nobody else was responding so maybe the altar call was meant for me. I remember the clarion call from the pulpit, "Now I know somebody out there needs to come forward", after about the fourth stanza of the invitation hymn.

Attending Sunday School every Sunday--Vacation Bible School every summer--church twice on Sunday and sometimes midweek service

Wednesday, I knew every hymn by heart and could quote lots of Scripture. As far as I knew, I was saved from damnation. Yet it never occurred to me that my physical body and my mind were "temples of the Lord".

Through college, Air Force and into professional life, as I began to encounter life's little tests and temptations, my faith was shallow but this didn't trouble me much. Eventually I put on the mantra of the intellectual, even coming to question Christ's virgin birth and His miracles. Somewhere along the line I even began questioning the authenticity of the Bible. How could it possibly be the true Word of God? After all, the Bible was all about miracles and hard to believe events. I never stopped to think that God's Word was filled with mind bending miracles that challenge our faith — that just maybe God intended it this way — you have to have faith to believe! Now I know it's impossible to believe except by faith!

I was dumbfounded, realizing that it is possible to be immersed in Bible teaching, dogma and catechism, yet be "lost as a goose". In my heart of hearts, I knew I didn't really believe. I knew I hadn't truly trusted Christ Jesus to save me. The storms of life came and I had absolutely nothing to fall back on. Like everyone else, I would pray at the last minute when there was nothing left to do---" Lord please save me from this or that calamity--Lord please give me a good outcome", etc.--- a poor excuse for prayer and prayers like this must be insulting to the Lord.

I came to realize I didn't really have as much as a casual relationship with Christ Jesus, whether the chips were down or life was great. Instead of trusting that God was in charge and things would somehow turn out the right way, as Paul promises in Romans 8:28, I fought every step of the way. I was absolutely sure I knew my needs a lot better than God or anybody. I couldn't think in terms of "thy will be done". It was more like "I want it this way and no other way and I want it now and I want you to give it to me". It scares me to realize this is how so many think and pray---if this can be called prayer.

I knew in my mind I could never "be good enough" or "do enough good things" to earn salvation. That didn't keep me from trying. While I was in the Air Force, I taught Sunday School and attended church regularly. I tried taking my Sunday School classes of teenagers on interesting visits to museums and other places. I earned accolades from for my efforts. Yet everything left me empty. Nothing was satisfying or fulfilling. I hadn't really taken Christ Jesus at His word when He said that He was the only way to salvation--sometimes we keep looking for any other way to get there except the clear, simple way Jesus Christ told us. I had certainly fallen short of understanding that God's salvation was strictly an act of grace, made possible because of the sacrifice and resurrection of His only begotten son, Jesus Christ. He even reprimanded the Pharisees for exactly this kind of piety---having the form of belief but not the substance.

I knew all about the church, its history and principal players; I certainly knew all about Jesus Christ, His disciples, and Paul the Apostle. But, I didn't know Jesus Christ the person, I never had an ongoing personal relationship with Him and with God the Father. My considerable "head knowledge" didn't do me much good when the chips were down. And in just three short years, I had gone from being a bright star on the rise at Esso to a dim mortal in danger of drowning in a bottle.

I first met Pat Booth on a beautiful morning in Dallas in 1974. Pat was known as an investment broker who made his way finding deals and hooking them up with well-heeled investors in Texas. Someone along the way, I don't remember whom, suggested that I should call on him during my search for work, that he might know of something that would fit me. I found out that Pat, a descendent of Salvation Army founders William and Catherine Booth, was a member of a family of inventors and entrepreneurs in Dallas. Pat's "Uncle Jack" Booth was the inventor of the multi-selection drink dispensing hand held device used in bars and soda fountains everywhere. His grandfather invented a food freezer technology and founded the Zero Plate Corporation of Dallas. So I learned ahead of time that Pat had "entrepreneurism in his blood".

Pat Booth was the first person to confront me about my spiritual condition. Unannounced, I stopped by his office in suburban Dallas to make a cold call on him. Arrogantly, I just thought he'd be in his office and, from what I'd heard, would be glad to meet with me. Before I could even open the glass door to his office and go in, he saw me in the hallway and darted right out. I was taken aback that he insisted on talking to me in the hallway, and he made it clear he preferred me not to come into his private office area. I thought he was rude, but shrugged it off. After all, I called on him without an appointment – he hadn't called on me!

Our hallway meeting was brief, and I barely got a chance to give him my spiel. He ended it abruptly, wanting to know how to reach me if he had anything further to discuss. Weeks later, I asked why he'd been so rude to me, not wanting me to enter his office. Pat looked me straight in the eyes and said he saw Satan working in me and wanted to keep me at a distance. I was shocked! I've known and loved Pat as my brother now for four decades, and I've learned that he is one of the most unusual, unpredictable people I've ever known. Pat was just being Pat on that auspicious morning in 1974.

He called that same night, inviting me to come to his office for an early morning breakfast the next morning, that he'd been thinking about me and wanted to have another visit, this time in his conference room. After our iffy initial contact, I didn't know what to think. But I accepted the invitation — I needed to find work!

I was surprised to see that Pat was joined by two other men for our breakfast meeting. I just assumed they were associated with a deal they planned discussing with me. But it quickly became clear I was grossly mistaken. Business wasn't on the agenda at all. One of the three, a man named Wes, stood and took us through a kind of flow diagram, like chemical engineers use all the time to describe processes. He drew it on a white board at the head of Pat's conference table. However, I soon saw that Wes's diagram depicted steps through the life of a person, beginning at his birth, ending at his death. Eternal hell and damnation and Heaven lay at the end of his diagram. Wes looked at me and said, "You, Martin, are hell-bound ".

These three obviously hadn't been briefed on my temper. I had more than a few choice words for these well-meaning gentlemen. After talking a little longer, they shared several pertinent passages of Scripture with me. I exclaimed it was obvious to me that there was no business deal to discuss, that this had been another complete waste of my time. Without further ado, I left the meeting, expecting never to hear from Mr. Booth again. I was sure I'd been misled and deceived once more!

My condition continued to worsen as frustrations grew, trying unsuccessfully to find work that met my criteria. I didn't realize the more I drank the less appealing I became. More frustration heaped on top of frustration, and I was caught in a vicious downward spiral.

Pat stayed in touch with me in spite of my negative reaction at his office. Almost daily he called, asking me to join him for lunch. At first I declined, thinking time with Pat would lead me nowhere. But he persisted and I finally accepted his invitation. Then, utterly embarrassed, I wanted to hide as Pat thanked the Lord for our food and time together. To me, this was an outrageous thing to do in a public place. What if people saw us, heads bowed in prayer at a restaurant? What would they think?

Before much longer I came to the end of my rope, pretty well deciding I'd never work professionally again. I'd convinced myself that the old "Martin Magic" was a thing of the past, serving me well until I got off the straight and narrow. Already I had turned over all worldly assets in my name to my estranged wife. I no longer had a proverbial "pot to pee in", I was drinking heavily and had no desire to work---or to live anymore. I was clearly on a path to doom---and hell, just like Wes said.

Pat called late one night and said he and his wife, Amy, would be coming for me in fifteen minutes. They wanted me to come with them. I hadn't yet met Amy, and was afraid she might be a female version of Pat. Having reached the end of my wits, I agreed to go with them. Later that night, in the wee hours of April 14,1974, at Pat and Amy's home in Highland Park, I prayed to receive Jesus Christ as my Lord and Savior.

This was another Big Watershed event of my life! Again, my life would change directions…forever…this time for all eternity!

NEW WORK

"I can do everything through Him who gives me strength." (Phil 4:13).

"Trust in the Lord with all your heart and lean not on your own understanding; in all your ways acknowledge Him, and He will make your paths straight." (Prov. 3:5-6).

April 14,1974 started me down a new road in life. But I was riddled with doubts, actually believing I'd screwed up things so badly nobody would ever give me a chance to work professionally again! After all, just how many good opportunities come your way in life? How many times can you afford to blow these?

My highest immediate priority was to put down the bottle. Pat and I both realized I had to really sober up quickly and stay sober to have any hope. Fortunately, I hadn't yet become so repressively hooked and addicted to alcohol that my system craved it. I used it mainly to blot out my sadness and bitterness, getting a dose of courage to face the next day. I found that stopping drinking was pretty easy to do on my own this time, though twenty years later it would be a lot harder.

After spending a few days together, driving around, talking endlessly about life and salvation, Pat nudged me to apply for a menial job as a night watchman at a large grocery warehouse. Pat was acquainted with the owners, and it turned out had used this connection once before in behalf of another forlorn executive who'd gone astray. I was hired on the spot with no questions asked, given a uniform to wear and assigned to the night shift, starting that very night.

My little hourly job paid just enough for me to get by, buying food, paying rent and little else. Throughout the night, I made the rounds every hour, checking off time clocks along my route to prove I'd been by at scheduled times. I'll assure you this was a humbling experience for yours truly, the Corporate Superman!

My work schedule was a blessing because my days were free for Bible study with Pat, and I had time in the afternoons to do research at the Dallas Public Library as I sorted through possible options for my future. This research helped me conclude I wanted to return to the energy world — I just didn't know the specifics. I was amazed to learn how much had changed since I left Esso!

After I'd been on the job for three months, Pat asked me to quit being a night watchman and move into his office to help him out. This was a bold step, for he knew I'd left lots of broken glass behind. He trusted the Lord to bless this change, knowing I was sober and had been attentive to my warehouse job. By trusting the Lord, he didn't necessarily have to trust me!

Six months into my new life with Christ and three months after I'd moved in with Pat, we got a" miracle telephone call from the sky" one morning. The Head of Personnel for the new Federal Energy Administration (FEA) called to see if I would be available to come for a meeting in Washington. They wanted to talk with me about a consulting stint on the so called Project Independence Blueprint (PIB) study, aimed at getting the country off foreign oil imports. I agreed to meet the following week in Washington to discuss the PIB and what they wanted me to do.

The government was gearing up for major efforts in the wake of the devastating Arab oil embargo of 1973, that had churned up major problems across the US and the entire World. Cars were lined up for many blocks to fill their gas tanks at stations, often to find no fuel was available when it came their turn at the pump. It all stemmed from the embargo of the Suez Canal by the Arabs in the Persian Gulf. The effects on life in America were devastating! The Nixon/Ford Administration had asked Esso and other majors for help, including personnel who could be assigned temporarily to the FEA in Washington. They were referred to me by my Esso and oil industry contacts who probably didn't know anything about my current predicament. I can't begin to describe how this inquiry boosted my spirits, after the treacherous path I'd been on for three years!

Pat was just as happy as I, and gifted me a surprise airline ticket for the quick trip to Washington. My interview at the FEA went well. They asked me to come immediately and I agreed. The consulting pay was outstanding, and I liked the work they wanted me to do in energy finance. I drove up from Dallas the following week with blessings from Pat and Amy and the love of my mother and dad. They were greatly relieved that once again my life appeared to be headed in a positive direction. As it turned out, my overnight stop by Longview to say goodbye was the last time I'd see my beloved dad, this side of Heaven.

In August, 1974, I settled into temporary living quarters Pat arranged for me in Tacoma Park, MD, a Washington suburb. Pat was acquainted with the folks who owned and ran the place, called Cornerstone, a "half way house". He believed they'd understand my needs as a four month old Christian, just finding his way. I planned to commute back and forth to work at the FEA in DC, while looking for an apartment in the city near work. This arrangement didn't last very long. Everyone at Cornerstone took evening meals and fellowshipped together, but work didn't usually give me this option. I moved out after only a week, taking an apartment just two blocks from my office in the city.

I didn't know a single soul in Washington, so living and working there was an entirely new experience for me. My only previous contact there might have been fortuitous. Seven years earlier, I'd had the good fortune of meeting several times with Esso's Vice President of Governmental Affairs, Randal Myers, in Washington about Car Care Centers. Then in 1972, he became President of Esso. I never knew whether Mr. Myers had any part in my call to Washington. I do know one thing for sure---don't ever sell anyone short! You never know for sure whom or what you're dealing with.

One of my favorite Bible stories, recorded in Genesis 18, describes Abraham's interaction with two Angels he mistakenly thought were simple travelers on the dusty road to the city of Sodom, which God intended to destroy because of its wickedness. Don't think for a minute I'm ascribing angelic status to the Esso President, because I'm not. This is just one more among many experiences in my life demonstrating God's love and his often unfathomable way of doing things!

Washington turned out to be a whole new chapter in my life. I performed well enough to catch the attention of several higher ups who asked me to stay on after my consultancy. They wanted me to lead a planning and analysis division in the new Energy Research and Development Administration (ERDA). My rank would be "Supergrade" Federal employee.

Six years passed like a flash! My work had been challenging, personally rewarding, and hopefully good for the nation. Once again like at Esso, I moved into operations after managing planning and analysis for two years. Operationally I managed the new Department of Energy's work in oil, gas and oil shale technology development, and renewable energy. I settled into life in Washington, setting up home in a Northern Virginia suburb, commuting to and from work. My wife and children returned from Colorado, and we tried to make a go of it. But too much water had flowed under the bridge in the past twenty years, and it didn't work out. Without too much acrimony, we parted, and decided the children would live with me to be near their school.

The earlier Chapter entitled, "Leta, My Mother" discusses her move to live with me and the children after the death of my dad. She literally stepped into the breach for us, making home the best it could be under the circumstances. Our home was in her capable hands, as we proceeded to redirect our family life. I was able to continue the important work before me, because I had total confidence in mother's abilities and I knew how deeply she and the children cared for one another.

Soon I purchased a small ski place in Stowe, Vermont, an eleven hour drive north, where we could all get away on long weekends and holidays to pursue our favorite pastime. Mother enjoyed the little condo as much as we did, and busied herself preparing stews and other delicious things for us to enjoy after the kids and I came in from a cold day on the mountain. This place was a wonderful rallying point for us, as we made our new life. Without question, my successes in Washington were made possible in large part by mother's helping hands to make a comfortable home for the children and me. She held down the fort while I met the heavy demands of my job.

The long and short of it is, I couldn't have done it without her!

————————

The world's energy markets were turbulent during three decades following the end of World War 2. Oilfields in Europe, especially in Romania which supplied the Axis Powers with crude oil, had been heavily bombed by the Allies. Europe and Japan struggled to rebuild after the war's devastation. Saudi Arabia, the US, Venezuela and Canada were the world's primary oil producers. Major US oil producers, Esso, Royal Dutch Shell and others drilled and operated oil fields in Venezuela and the Persian Gulf region under special royalty payment arrangements with host countries.

By the early 1960's,Venezuela and other host countries joined forces to form an oil cartel, the Organization of Petroleum Exporting Countries, known as OPEC. Its founding member was Venezuela where Esso had operated successfully for many years. Using its newfound cartel powers, OPEC demanded higher royalty payments from the visitors. Not satisfied with these richer arrangements, they eventually nationalized oil production and established entirely new protocols with Esso and the other producers. In less than a decade, OPEC became a force to be reckoned with, able to dictate crude oil pricing across the entire world.

America experienced its first OPEC oil shock in 1973 with the blockade of the Suez Canal, the main thoroughfare for oil transport from the Persian Gulf to refineries in the US and the rest of the world. Long lines at gas stations from coast to coast illuminated two facts: 1) America had grown too dependent on foreign oil; and 2) the suppliers of that foreign crude oil, e.g., OPEC, operated in their own best interests that were frequently at odds with American interests.

The disruptions in 1973, almost bringing America to its knees, created political earthquakes in the halls of Congress. America, strongly sovereign, was not in the habit of turning its future over to foreign powers. America's dependence on OPEC member nations was growing, and in just a few short years we would be dependent on them for over half our oil needs. There was great distress across the land and outcries for America to "do something". It was thought America simply had to become less dependent on foreign sources, as quickly as possible. All kinds of proposals made the rounds in Washington.

Step One was to undertake a massive effort in the Federal Energy Administration (FEA) called Project Independence to determine how America could obtain "energy independence" by 1985 or '90.The very idea that this could be achieved in such a short timeframe was preposterous, demonstrating how poorly leaders in Washington understood (and still don't understand) energy.

Even so, this activity brought me to Washington when I was a new baby Christian in August, 1974, for new work and to start a new life.

It's serendipitous that this arch conservative was thrown a lifeline by Washington, and the Federal Government was my "employer of last resort"!

The new Energy Research and Development Administration (ERDA) brought practically all energy related research from across the entire US Government under one single organization. The new agency was headed by two very able executives — Dr. Robert Seamans of MIT, and Mr. Robert Fri of McKinsey & Company consultants, appointed by President Nixon. The new agency encompassed Research Development and Demonstration on nuclear power, coal, oil and gas and all renewable forms of energy such as solar and geothermal. R&D on energy conservation was included as well as R&D on all modes of transportation. Fundamental and basic research in energy technology would be supported by ERDA through the National Laboratories and universities. Once these entities became the new ERDA, and organizations and personnel were housed in one major facility, top management immediately had to decide R&D budget levels across the board. It was clear no rational analytical technique existed to support this process, and one was needed.

The government finally came to the painful realization that there was no quick and easy panacea to America's growing dependence on OPEC oil. The Nixon Administration set out on a more sensible course, supporting research, development and demonstration of new, better energy technologies, all under the umbrella of ERDA. The more realizable goal of ERDA was to promote and support the development of technologies which could reduce America's dependence on foreign sources of oil, over the longer term. Of course, the RD&D that private industry would and could do without assistance from the government needed to be considered. This way, an appropriate role for the government to play could be carved out and defined, focusing funding where it was most needed.

Importantly, ERDA was completely separate from the plethora of arms of government responsible for enforcing and regulating energy supplies, particularly oil and gas, coal mining and electric power generation and distribution. These regulators would reside in agencies like the EPA, FERC, NRC, OSHA, IRS and on and on. The idea behind ERDA was to involve private sector companies in government sponsored RD & D, bringing the best minds and experience in the country to bear on developing energy technologies for America's future. Doing so, achieving the best of industry involvement in developing new technologies, would certainly be more difficult if the researchers and regulators were under a single department of government. (This, however, is exactly what President Carter did by creating a new cabinet level Department of Energy, home to most energy regulators as well as technology developers).

Such analysis would be a large effort in order to examine the unique and wide ranging number of energy technologies being supported by Federal funds. Unfortunately, priorities were often determined by political fiat rather than rational needs-based analysis. Much of the time, Congress funded the wheel with the loudest squeak---or those technologies with the weightiest political clout.

Understand that industrial firms stood to make big money if their technologies made it into the marketplace. Government funding was and will always be sought after by promoters of their favored technology, whether it's an electric car, advanced batteries, solar cells or biomass conversion to oil substitutes. The renewable energy/solar lobby, for example, was and still is a strong political presence, with backers including major manufacturers able to exert enough influence in Congress to ensure disproportionately large funding for photovoltaic, wind, solar thermal and other renewables, with little or no analytic market-oriented rationale behind funding decisions. Renewable energy technologies such as wind and solar were clear examples of those with powerful lobbies---so powerful, in fact, they had the ability to distort rational funding priorities and decisions.

I'm not suggesting that promoters of renewables like solar are the only culprits—virtually all technologies have their backers usually supported by lobbyists, some stronger than others. ERDA, however, wanted to make funding decisions based on a real world market-oriented needs based analytic rationale which could be used to provide some defense against extraordinary political muscle.

150

And so it was that I was chosen by ERDA's top management to lead an effort to come up with an approach, a study plan, costs, personnel requirements and time tables for this important undertaking. Officially my title was Chairman of the Analysis Committee for MOPPS, which is government parlance for the "Market Oriented Program Planning Study". In this capacity, I was responsible for all day-to-day operations of MOPPS, agency-wide. A very capable Deputy, Dr. Bruce Robinson, a brilliant ERDA physicist and Mr. David Beecy, a former Westinghouse mechanical engineer, were assigned to work shoulder to shoulder with me to design and run the effort.

I, in turn, reported to a small committee of ERDA top management, who provided all needed help and support across ERDA and other Departments of government. My principal contact on the management committee was Mr. Harry R. Johnson, a savvy petroleum engineer from Pennsylvania who had worked his way up through the Interior Department ranks. Harry also was my direct boss in my "real life" ERDA job. We got along fabulously, and his knowledge and support helped MOPPS immensely.

Time was of the essence because of the serpentine manner in which the Federal Government's budget is put together. Management wanted to have preliminary results in time to impact the next budget cycle, only a few short months away. By the way, you'd never put budgets together in business the way government does. You'd go broke before you even start!

Throughout my career, I've dealt with large scale systems oriented problems of a complex nature. Almost always, it's been my job to assemble and lead a skilled group of analysts, coming up with solutions. In that sense, I usually served as project manager, given the temporary nature of most projects. Often, I've changed hats after project completion to manage all or part of the ensuing work. MOPPS was clearly going to be larger and more complex than anything I had been involved with, including Esso's major Automotive Aftermarket Study and the Marketing Laboratory project in Altoona.

My approach is to first think through "how to think about the problem" before going any further. Determine at the outset what the problem really is and what it is not. Don't start collecting data and information until you are satisfied you see the problem correctly.

Leading this group of highly talented analysts was one of the most rewarding accomplishments of my career. The approach we came up with was ingenious. It was largely the brainchild of my deputy, Dr. Bruce Robinson. Several other analysts made substantial contributions, but Bruce Robinson's was stellar. David Beecy ingeniously structured the scenarios we planned to examine and their complex macroeconomics. I seriously doubt government could ever implement an approach like MOPPS again.

At the risk of making your eyes glaze over, I'd like to explain what we did.

The bottom line for MOPPS was simple. We had to devise a method to quantitatively prioritize the full array of energy technologies. What better way to prioritize than to rationally estimate the contribution each technology would make at future time horizons — 10, 20, 25 years into the future. This would provide solid rationale for supporting those technologies expected to make significant contributions within reasonable timeframes. Why pour considerable funds into technologies not expected to make any significant contribution until many decades down the road? Obviously such prioritization schemes would certainly mean "somebody's ox is gonna get gored" along the way. Some "sacred cows" would be sacrificed, and ERDA decision makers could anticipate strong political backlash. We recognized it wasn't our job as analysts to worry about the political problems likely to arise. Our job was to render a fair, objective and sound analytic framework for estimating priorities, leaving the politics to others.

The key to our approach lies in Basic Economics 101, the analysis of supply and demand for a product or service. As functions of price, Supply and Demand work against each other to come to a point of equilibrium.

In the supply area, higher prices, or increased values, stimulate production of that product or service. Conversely, as prices fall, people drop out of the market to produce those goods or services.

For a particular product or service, one can graphically express this relationship in what is known as a Supply-Price curve. So called Supply Elasticity is a result of this relationship. A steep curve thus graphed is said to indicate that the supply of that product or service is highly price sensitive, or "elastic". Energy supplies, oil, gas, coal, and electric power follow this rule. Price trajectories into the future for oil, gas, coal and electric power, all from conventional sources, define the competitive base against which any new technology or process must compete to win a place in the market. We would need to have cost and price characteristics of every technology for this approach to work.

The same phenomena holds on the Demand side of the equation. Except it is reversed. Higher and higher prices for a product or service reduces or discourages the demand for that product or service. Lower prices, in turn, stimulate demand. This relationship can be quantified and graphed in what amounts to Demand-Price curves or relationships. A steeply descending curve means that the demand for that product or service is highly price sensitive. Said another way, Demand is highly elastic

Energy is consumed by three broad sectors---Residential/Commercial, Industrial, and Transportation. Each of these three large sectors is composed of many different demand classes, each with its own price sensitivity. ERDA program offices would need to assemble Supply-Demand relationships for all energy technologies, including energy conservation.

For a particular product or service, there is a point at which Demand and Supply balance, i.e. Supply exactly satisfies Demand. This condition is said to be "at equilibrium", and the price at which this occurs is known as the Market Clearing Price. When represented on a single graph, this is the point at which the rising Supply-Price curve and the falling Demand-Price curves intersect.

In simple terms, the price a buyer of a product agrees to pay the seller, and the seller agrees to accept, is the so called "selling price", representing "equilibrium" between buyer and seller.

A large scale mathematical model would mimic this process, if one existed. It would perform iterations like these until arriving at an equilibrium state between supply and demand. But in the mid-1970's, no existent model contained the detail necessary for MOPPS. Stanford Research Institute's (SRI) energy model at Palo Alto was the best available, but fell far short in terms of its ability to estimate market penetrations by new technologies. We decided to use the SRI model to help us find approximate market clearing prices for conventional commodities — oil, gas, coal, etc. All new technologies would have to compete with these in order to win a share of the market. National energy demand and other macroeconomic indices such as population, GDP, inflation and other factors would feed the SRI model to help us find realistic starting points for MOPPS iterations. In other words, we could tweak these variables, conforming to macroeconomic conditions we wanted to evaluate in our construct of Scenarios or Cases to estimate market clearing prices for oil, gas, coal, electric power etc., which we'd then feed into the MOPPS framework to estimate the ability of any new technology to penetrate the market.

Having no such comprehensive mathematical model, it was clear that we had to devise a "human model", functioning in much the same manner a large math model would operate. This would obviously become an extremely intense effort across ERDA, involving all program offices. Comprehensive workups (technology characterizations) on all supply and demand technologies across the board would be required. The Analysis Committee then would initiate an iteration, we called a "pass", specifying the aggregate energy demand, a proxy Market Clearing Price derived from the SRI model, and all pertinent macroeconomic indices.

We asked the General Services Administration (GSA) to obtain dedicated office space and desks to house as many as 300 workers in downtown D.C. to conduct MOPPS' iterations. Each pass or iteration would require about two weeks of working group time, and a week of work by the Analysis Committee to integrate results and readjust price tracks if necessary for another iteration through the same scenario. Each iteration would bring us closer to a steady state equilibrium between supply and demand.

Drawing from all ERDA program offices, we organized a core working group for each of three major demand sectors: Residential & Commercial, Transportation, and Industrial. Under its respective Chairman, a very senior level program manager, each sector replicated the buying behavior and energy consumption patterns within that sector. They used the proxy Market Clearing Price we provided, total energy demand and other indices given by the Analysis Committee and individual technology characterizations to estimate penetrations of all new demand-related and conservation/energy saving technologies. All forms and amounts of energy supplies would be "produced and sent out" to the Demand sectors from a Black Box we called the "Intermediate Supply Group"(ISG). The ISG, under the direction of a senior Planning and Analysis executive, would "produce" all liquid, gaseous and solid fuel supplies and electric power. These commodities would be made available "across the fence" to the Demand sectors in response to the same macroeconomic signals of total demand, GDP, and estimated equilibrium energy price trajectories for conventional supplies.

New Supply technologies entered the mix only as they could successfully compete against conventional supplies for a share of the market. Electric power generation was treated as a special case within the ISG since it requires ongoing sources of coal, oil, gas and nuclear fuel. Central station solar and wind power as well as distributed solar and wind had to compete in this arena. Refined petroleum products, motor gasolines, kerosenes, lube oils, diesel fuels and aviation fuels and heating oil products, were likewise produced by the ISG and made available over the fence to the Demand groups.

I want to repeat for emphasis here — any new technology was in competition with conventional ways market demands were satisfied, in the short, intermediate (1985) and long term (2000+). This is exactly how any new technology has to go up against thresholds established by conventional supplies out in the "real world".

Oil Imports, a critical set of estimates in MOPPS, would be determined by the shortfall in oil demand and supplies, mimicking the "real world".

During "passes" through the MOPPS "human model", several hundred ERDA and support contractor personnel were involved intensively for two or more weeks at a time. If the trial or "pass" failed to close at equilibrium, an additional "pass" was conducted against tweaked (adjusted) estimated energy prices and other factors. Iterations were continued until the Analysis Committee decided the clearing price and the associated total supply-demand closed at a reasonable equilibrium. This would constitute completion of a "Case", such as a "Base Case"; a "High Demand Case"; a "Low Demand Case"; or a rigorous, environmentally driven " Stress Case". We were limited in the number of Cases we could examine by the intense time pressures we were under and the extensive personnel requirements.

We settled on two time horizons for MOPPS — 1985 and 2000.These were reasonable, as our starting point was the mid-1970"s. Ten and twenty five year horizons gave time for new technologies to come into the market and be tested. The new technologies would either find a niche and we could measure their share of each Demand sector; or they would fail and disappear from Supply and Demand sectors. Technology advocates would thus be prevented from accusing MOPPS of unfair treatment because we didn't allow enough time for their pet technologies to find a place in the market. The Analysis Committee wanted to give all ERDA technologies a fair and unbiased opportunity to contribute, and we expected blowback from some advocacies.

After meeting ERDA management's needs for early preliminary results, we continued constructing Cases and conducting passes over the following eight months, briefing top management on results each time a Case was completed. Cases covered a wide range of scenarios, including stressful environmental cases which imposed severe limits on effluents released into the air and water. Other cases envisioned a strong energy demand growth future resulting from robust US economic growth; another a low growth future. We bracketed almost every realistic energy future. With the benefit of more than three decades of hindsight, I believe this is what we achieved.

MOPPS held many surprises for its principal sponsor Mr. Robert Fri, ERDA's Director pro tem, as well as many other executives in the Administration and Congress. Few had realized at the outset that we would be developing comprehensive estimates of future supplies of conventional energy sources, e.g. oil, gas, coal and electric power. As I've explained, these estimates were necessary because they formed the thresholds against which all new technologies had to compete for a niche or share in the market.

Some of MOPPS' more interesting and controversial findings are summarized here:

Huge quantities of natural gas could be unleashed by using conventional and some advanced technologies (horizontal drilling and stimulative fracturing) if wellhead prices increased to more realistic levels. Natural gas sufficient to meet the Nation's needs for well over a Century would be forthcoming if prices were allowed to float free.

Domestic oil production will continue to decline. America will become more dependent on imports, growing to more than 50% of our oil consumption over the next decade. Enhanced oil production technologies(special liquid or gaseous injection, fracturing, offset and multi-plane horizontal drilling technologies onshore and offshore, and deeper drilling) will help mitigate the level of imports required, and should be considered critical technologies.

Increasingly America's oil imports will come from insecure sources, with associated national security implications. The underlying problem for the nation can be thought of as a "fuel form crisis". Liquid fuel forms, largely driven by the transportation sector, is the major consideration.

Synthetic alternatives from coal and biomass will not make any significant market penetration in the foreseeable future, because abundant cheaper supplies of oil and gas will be available. Among synthetic liquid alternatives to crude oil, Western oil shale and tar sands are the earliest and most viable alternatives. Focused emphasis on liquid energy products from crude oil reservoirs, oil shales and tar sands is critical. Massive switching to gaseous fuel forms in the transportation sector is not a feasible alternative in the foreseeable future, except by conversion of gas to synthetic liquid fuels and intermediates.

Vast amounts of naturally occurring gas supplies calls into question large R&D expenditures on synthetic gas substitutes from coal, biomass or other carbonaceous sources. Funding these technologies at disproportionately high levels to create calorific alternatives to the natural product should be questioned.

Coal is arguably America's largest carbonaceous resource, sufficient to last for generations if wisely stewarded. Technologies for cleanly using coal in power plants and steam generation have an important future and should accorded priority.

*There is little or no role for synthetic crude oil production from coal. Other coal based hydrocarbons (alcohols, other petrochemicals) could find a future competitive role.

*Renewable energy (solar, wind etc.) makes no more than modest contributions over the 10-25 year MOPPS horizon, while finding unique niches inwhich other technologies are impractible. Remote locations, or locations far fromthe grid are most amenable.

*A small but important role is found for hydropower, especially low head hydro In rural and off-grid applications. Efforts to continue advancing energy storage technologies should be continued.

*The penetration of almost all conservation/energy saving technologies is enormous in all demand sectors. Energy savings in industrial applications should be a high priority(technologies such as advanced recuperators and others). Energy saving technologies in all modes of transportation (continuously variable transmissions for all road vehicles, high efficiency power plants for aircraft, etc.). Advancements in energy saving technologies for residential and commercial applications achieving large market penetrations include improved glasses, window panes, casement windows, insulating materials and techniques and construction methodologies.

*Nuclear power plays a large role in America's energy future. RD & D on smaller packages should continue as well as efforts to dispose of radwastes and completing the nuclear fuel cycle. ERDA should continue efforts to mitigate technological impediments that prevent nuclear power from reaching its potential contributions to domestic energy supplies.

*We were able to completely prioritize all ERDA technologies based on their expected future contributions in the competitive US marketplace. With MOPPS results and a sense of proper government role, ERDA could proceed to develop defensible, analytically based budget requests. Few agencies of government can lay claim to such a rigorous process as MOPPS to undergird budget requests.   .

158

*Decision makers would need to draw on expertise beyond MOPPS to complete a rigorous budgetary process. We could indeed tell them which technologies would earn a competitive place in markets circa 1985 and 2000, maybe or even a few years beyond the horizon. But advising them on whether funding them would be a "proper Federal role" was another matter. For example, some argued against funding advanced oil and gas recovery RD&D because "the oil and gas industries would do it themselves, without taxpayer monies." They would insist that solar and renewable technologies needed all available funding because no robust solar industry yet existed. The sensible approach we took when asked was, "Look, don't take chances with the nation's energy future---advanced recovery processes were vital to meet requirements in MOPPS projected future, so we'd better be safe than sorry." Solar, in turn, hardly made an appearance at the 1985 and 2000 horizons.

Primer on Synthetic Liquid Fuels and Their Use----

Oil bearing shales in Colorado and other Western states contain vast quantities of kerogen, a precursor to oil. In fact, more oil is contained in these shales than in the entire Persian Gulf. Extracting the oil is a challenging, expensive thermal retorting process, requiring operation of fixed or moving beds of pulverized shale rock at high temperatures to drive out the kerogenic liquids. Huge quantities of these solids must be mined, dug, crushed, moved and processed, creating enormous amounts of dust which must be suppressed. Water spraying is the most used method. Unfortunately water supplies are very tight in most areas containing oil shales. Shale oil usually carries contaminants which poison catalysts used in oil refining. These, including arsenic and compounds of sulfur must be removed ahead of refining and processing.

Shale oil is primarily an aliphatic (straight chain) hydrocarbon, readily yielding kerosenes, diesel oils, heating oil and aviation fuels. Fuels of this type burn smoothly, unlike gasolines, which explode or detonate. Whereas oil from shale has an aliphatic (linear) molecular structure, gasoline is of an aromatic nature, meaning (ring type) molecules, resembling chicken wire. Octane number, displayed at gas station pumps, is a measure of gasoline's detonative or explosive quality. Too low octane number causes the engine to knock, an undesirable condition. The Cetane number is a measure of diesel type fuels' smooth burning quality. In other words, Octane is to gasoline as Cetane is to diesel. If you've ever thrown a little gasoline on a burning fire, or maybe used gasoline to ignite a pile of brush, you know what I mean---it goes WHOOM as it detonates. Compare this with the much slower burning (and safer to use) kerosene. See the difference?

Coal derived synthetic oils tend to be aromatic (ring-type) liquids.

160

Obviously, diesel burning and gasoline burning engines operate on entirely different thermodynamic principles. Gasoline engines, known as internal combustion engines, detonate a measured mist of fuel in a chamber atop the piston, utilizing a timed spark. Most automobiles are powered by this type of engine, also called a spark ignition engine. The piston is thus driven down when fuel detonates, rotating a so-called cam shaft to which the piston is connected by a rod. Thus up and down piston motion translates into rotating motion via the cam shaft which in turn is linked to the drive shaft, moving the vehicle forward or backward. Diesel engines operate with many of the same mechanical principles, excepting the manner in which fuel is ignited. Diesels are called compression ignition engines because the fuel mist is ignited by high compression pressure. Thus, diesel engine blocks are thick and very heavy. Each type of engine provides unique running characteristics and benefits.

Shale oils can be chemically reformed to higher aromaticity, favoring gasolines. Aromatics from coal can be fractured (catalytically cracked) into linear chains, favoring diesel type fuels. Producing synthetic oils from shale and from coal are both extremely capital intensive processes, clearly not competitive with naturally produced crude oils in the foreseeable future.

Naturally occurring crude oil contains the full spectrum of hydrocarbons, from polycyclic aromatics through straight chain aliphatics. Refining is the process by which crude oil is separated into its many constituents—gasolines, kerosenes and diesel fuels, a full suite of oils and lubricants, and heavy bunker fuels, tars and asphalts.

God's gift of naturally occurring crude oil and gas is one of his most amazing provisions for mankind, like air and water!

Georgia Governor Jimmy Carter won a surprising victory in the1976 Presidential race. He had campaigned on a pledge to begin fixing the nation's energy problems that included long gasoline lines and other serious inconveniences during the Crisis of 1973. He persuaded Americans to cast their vote for him, calling our energy situation "The Moral Equivalent of War", blaming previous Republican Administrations for our plight. American bought his campaign promises, electing him our 39th President.

Before we could complete a MOPPS Final Report, the new Carter Administration and a supportive Democrat Congress abolished ERDA, creating in its stead a whole new Cabinet level Department of Energy. All of ERDA's RD&D activities, all NSF energy research, the Atomic Energy Commission (AEC) and its laboratories and nuclear production plants, and the energy regulatory functions from the old FEA were rolled into the new Department of Energy. Dr. James Schlesinger, a long time Washington stalwart, was appointed Secretary of Energy. His Deputy Secretary was long time Interior Department executive, Mr. Jack O'Leary.

The Carter people wasted no time finding out about MOPPS. They were told MOPPS findings flew directly in the face of everything the Carter team stood for. Their "Moral Equivalent of War" rhetoric insisted America was rapidly running out of oil and gas, that price decontrol would only enrich "Big Oil" with no possible increase in domestic production. MOPPS, projecting vast new oil and gas supplies, patently flew in the face of this contention. The Carter team was completely committed to coal and West Virginia's long serving Senate delegation. They saw coal use in all forms, clean coal burning technologies, coal gasification and liquefaction, plus solar and renewable energy as solutions to the nation's energy problems.

There's an old adage that "Washington leaks like a sieve". Committees of Congress learned about MOPPS as a result of a leak to the Wall Street Journal from a mole on our study team. The leak averred that vast amounts of natural gas would be unleashed if prices were decontrolled. The leak couldn't have been more timely, as Congress was heavily engaged in debating oil and gas price decontrol issues. Gas prices had been regulated for years at very low (25 cents per thousand cubic feet, equivalent to oil on a BTU basis of about $1.50 per barrel) wellhead prices. The view that our gas supplies were extremely limited was a self-fulfilling prophecy, because prices were kept so low there was absolutely no exploration and production incentive.

162

Immediately, Congress asked to be briefed on MOPPS. These requests, made through the White House, got the attention of Messers. Schlesinger and O'Leary, who were caught completely off guard. I was summoned to the White House to take them through MOPPS. Harry Johnson accompanied me. The meeting went down hard, O'Leary demanding that we basically lie to the Congress about gas. He tried to intimidate us yelling, "Any fool knows we are running out of gas." He insisted that decontrolling oil and gas prices would only create "windfall profits" for oil companies. Basically, Mr. O'Leary was insisting we perjure ourselves before Congress, a serious offense. We left the meeting very troubled about the directive we'd been given.

Next morning, we were to testify before the House Science and Technology Committee covering all aspects of MOPPS and responding to Member's questions. You can be sure we were white-knuckling our appearance after the fire and brimstone meeting with Schlesinger and O'Leary the previous day. The Hearing Room in the Rayburn Office Building was packed with news media and onlookers, and the full Committee was present. Onlookers obviously expected fireworks.

The Gallery got what they wanted when a Member asked, "How much gas would we get if we let the wellhead price float up to $3.00 per thousand cubic feet"? (The controlled price had been held at $0.25 for a long time, a catastrophically low price). I responded "You would flood the world with gas"!

The Chairman banged his gavel, calling an end to the Hearing. The Congress subsequently decontrolled the price of gas at the wellhead, and relaxed crude oil price controls. Even then, Carter's people continued pressing for a "Windfall Profits Tax" on oil so producers couldn't inordinately benefit from decontrol.

I got banished from oil, gas and coal programs, serendipitously to take the number two position over the new DOE Renewable Energy Program Office. MOPPS, in retrospect, was amazingly accurate about the future with few exceptions.

The Carter Administration's failure to build upon the MOPPS insights remains to this day a national tragedy. Instead, their initiatives were the absolute antithesis of MOPPS guidance. They wasted much time and money pursuing alternatives that didn't have a prayer of helping the nation. After terminating the ongoing effort to develop the Clinch

River Breeder Reactor (CRBR) for nuclear fuels to mitigate the spent nuclear fuel problem, they created the useless Synthetic Fuel Corporation (SFC) which turned out to be a waste and a pipedream. Creation of the Cabinet level US Department of Energy (DOE) was wasteful. Bringing regulatory activities under the same roof with RD&D was a mistake, stimulating further animus between the creators of energy supplies, oil and gas producers, and Government. Little good has come to the nation from the excursion into DOE after nearly four decades. ERDA, as such, was never given a chance, though it had really gotten its act together and had a handle on the best use of RD&D funding in the Nation's interest.

America suffers today, nearly forty years later, because of the blunders of the Carter Administration and its ill-advised energy policies!

MOPPS spoke for itself, notwithstanding Mr. Carter's attempts to denigrate it. Its forecasts of what was to come have been eerily on target. For example, oil imports grew as projected over more than two decades. And by the turn of the century, America was awash in natural gas. Even America's crude oil production future is bright because of new discoveries and improved technology. Many technologies favored and funded by Carter and later Administrations have never seen the light of day. Energy saving technologies (energy conservation) have continued to make enormous contributions in all three demand sectors. MOPPS projections and implications held remarkably true throughout 1985 and 2000 time horizons.

Their final "coup de grace" was Carter's demand that no MOPPS Final Report be published and issued by the usual Government Printing Office (GPO) process. We were permitted to prepare a "Draft Final Report" with a limited "internal only" distribution. We prepared about twenty five bound sets, including the Integrated Summary Volume. Mysteriously, copies fell into hands of the press and several Members of Congress.

Mr. Carter and his band of merry men lasted only one four year term, but the effects of their terrible energy related decisions have haunted America for decades.

I'm proud to say my personal library contains one of the few surviving complete unabridged sets of the MOPPS Draft Final Report. Friends Harry Johnson and David Beecy have others.

In spite of the Carter Administration's attempts to kill MOPPS, it is important to note that a cadre of technical people remaining in DOE put the results to good use. Unsung heroes like Joe Pasini and Bill Overbey with support and encouragement from Harry Johnson and a few others continued to develop technologies to unlock the vast oil and gas resources of America's shales, identified by MOPPS as our highest RD&D priority.

I recently came across an article in the April 24,2013 New York Times by Mr. Clifford Krauss of the Time's Houston office entitled, "By 2023 a Changed World in Energy". I'd like to share just a few of his insights here.

Krausse insists that by 2023, America will be well on its way to Energy Independence. Vast new supplies of oil and gas are coming from new fields in Texas, North Dakota and other places. This abundance is the result of newer, improved technologies and, of course more attractive prices. We will be exporting gasoline and diesel and developing big overseas markets for natural gas.

Electric cars will be more affordable by then, and natural gas will be so abundant that many trains and other vehicles will operate on gas.

Solar electric energy will finally become competitive in many applications, allowing homes across the country to generate more of their energy needs from the sun, competitively. Greatly improved energy storage technology will enable solar and other renewables to find respectable markets.

New previously untapped sources of methane gas will emerge, such as harnessing frozen methane hydrates at the bottom of the sea. Island countries previously devoid of indigenous fossil fuels will be able to harvest gas from seabed hydrates.

Modular natural gas to liquid fuel conversion plants will emerge near major gas fields, including offshore platforms, using improved hundred year old catalytic technology of German origin. These modular plants will convert natural gas into a variety of more easily transportable liquid fuels and chemical intermediates.

It is imaginable that the United States will overtake Saudi Arabia and Russia as the world's largest oil and gas producer by the 2020-2030 time period, making us once again a net exporter of energy supplies. Major foreign policy and national defense issues will arise if we no longer have to continually worry about the Persian Gulf and the Straits of Hormuz. We might even need to reevaluate our role as "the world's policeman".

Two more years managing several high profile programs saw me thinking about returning to the private sector. I wanted to pick up again on my old personal goal of eventually becoming financially independent---not rich, just "well fixed" enough to do a few things I wanted to do, when I wanted, like skiing and hunting. This time, I wanted to capitalize on my knowledge of Washington, how it works, and my contacts, using my old business-building skills and technical know-how.

During my last two years in government service (1978-1980), I'm proud to have had a hand in developing long-run well directional drilling and stimulation technology. At test sites in West Virginia, we drilled the first well into pay dirt with a half mile horizontal run. After stimulating the gas well in a layer known as the Devonian Shale, a simulation model was developed to help guide future prospects. Horizontal drilling and stimulation are now routinely practiced in onshore and offshore projects. Multiple horizontal wells are routinely drilled from the same platform, radiating outwards into the pay zone. This approach has greatly improved the efficiency of oil and gas projects, minimizing the production footprint and associated environmental disturbance.

For the next sixteen years, 1980-1996, I was a "Rainmaker", employed sequentially by two different Washington based contractors that provided technical and management support services to DOE, DOD and other Departments and Agencies of government . A "Rainmaker" in the Washington sense of the word is literally a "hired gun" whose job is to "make it rain government contracts" to the benefit of one's employer. This may sound like an off-color or even questionable vocation. It's Not! It's the way our government works and it's a perfectly legitimate business when conducted legally and ethically.

Besides, successful "Rainmaking" finally satisfied my search for a role as a "Corporate Midwife". It was in that capacity that I was able to profit from growing my own unique business inside existing ones. I achieved this at both BDM and Coleman Research Corporations. An important object lesson here is "Don't give up on your dreams"! When you are sure of you highest and best calling, as I was, don't give it up easily. Hang on to your dreams. After deciding on a goal in the early 1970's, and try and trying yet getting nowhere, I didn't begin hitting pay dirt until the 1980's and didn't really hit a home run until the early 1990's. By then, I was a 55 year old "Rainmaker"!

Contractor support is provided to virtually all Agencies of government by armies of contractor personnel with skill sets that match the particular needs of the Agencies they serve. Contractor personnel supporting DOE and DOD considerably outnumber direct government employees. Many functions require skills that are beyond government's ability or practicability to direct hire. By hiring contractors, Agencies gain the flexibility and specialization they need to carry out their missions.

The "Rainmaker" is an unusual breed of cat, well connected to the wheels of government in one or more Agencies. He is handsomely compensated by his employer because, through his efforts, the contractor grows by hiring more personnel and earning greater profits for owners and stockholders. The name of the game in support contracting is "direct labor", personnel charging their time fully to contract performance as opposed to overhead or "general and administrative" so-called indirect charges. The support contractor's principal asset is People. We used to say, "Our assets walk out the door every day at quitting time."

The Washington Rainmaker doesn't just make it rain. He is usually expected to grow his own business center within the company, recruiting and hiring staff to conduct the actual work of contracts he wins. It's the same as building your own business, except you build it inside an ongoing enterprise. You are responsible for profit and loss and asset management, just as you would be in your own separate company.

Why do it? To me it required less risk-taking than if I'd started up a new company on its own feet. I was willing to sacrifice possible long term gains of outright ownership for nearer term rewards in terms of bonuses and stock options, as the " Midwife".

I mastered the art of putting together winning proposals responding to the competitive solicitations issued by government agencies. Winning large contracts for my employers earned a respectable reputation for me in Washington. Over the decade and a half I was in the business, my efforts were directly responsible for bringing in more than $3 Billion in contract value. I say with some pride that few Rainmakers can boast a record equal to mine. Some of my most visible wins were:

The proposal I led for the State of Texas' award of the gargantuan high energy physics Superconducting Supercollider (SSC) project in the Dallas-Ft. Worth area, a DOE Award;

The winning proposal for Operating and maintaining the US Strategic Petroleum Reserve (SPR), a DOE award ;

A contract to Operate and Maintain INEL, the US DOE's Idaho National Energy Laboratories.

I was instrumental in winning many more DOE contracts, principally of a technical nature. These included technical support for DOE's Radioactive Waste Management Program Office.

I developed and taught courses in Marketing and Proposal Development for my two different employers. These multi-day courses were designed to sharpen the entrepreneurial skills of promising employees. About twenty employees would go through at a time. We offered the course two or three times a year. Teaching the course was tremendous fun for me. Seeing budding entrepreneurs wake up to the prospects for building and growing virtually their own businesses within the larger company was enormously gratifying. It was in fact a lesson in "How to chart your own course to become relatively independent within a large enterprise."

Once contracts were won, management of them on a day-to-day basis, i.e. delivering the goods, was frankly a grind for me. For the most part I was able to delegate management to one of my deputies. My juices flowed best "in the chase". Leading a team to analyze and understand large scale competitive solicitations, then crafting the winning response was my forte'. It was stimulating and highly satisfying to my inner being.

The Lord God had other plans for me for which I am eternally grateful!

BOOK TWO:
MY DRINKING LIFE

MY DRINKING LIFE

T his Book is about my life as a drinker.

Now, with twenty years of abstention and sobriety under my belt, I was inspired to write my story by my incredible wife Margery and my wonderful daughter Sallie Lesue, after I spoke at the Sandpiper Alcoholics Anonymous (AA) group meeting at Merrit Island, Florida. This was a momentous occasion for me, because the Sandpipers had invited me to be their featured speaker on the occasion of my daughter's AA anniversary date. She chaired this particular meeting, making it all the more memorable for us. I really enjoyed myself with the Sandpipers, Sallie's home group. I was very comfortable with this mixture of "recovering alcoholics" of all ages, persuasions and backgrounds, sharing a common goal—sobriety.

I've been the featured speaker at AA meetings a number of times during the past twenty years, and I've discovered what to me is a remarkable thing---I get more honest and down to earth with every telling of my story. My daughter observed that she didn't know I was capable of relating such a plain, unvarnished version of my drinking life, after hearing me speak at Sandpipers. To me, her endorsement was a Seal of Approval, a solid reason for now putting my story in writing. Occasional lapses into vanity and egocentristic yarn spinning with which I might have punctuated my drinking story in the past have been purged, and I shall try to tell my story as it truly was and is.

Actually, I've been a "drunk" pretty much all my life! I don't mean a blubbering, stumbling, falling-down drunk. I simply mean I've had a "drunken disposition" most of my life.

Booze didn't really get its hooks into me until years later, beginning in my late 40's and early 50's. That's when I started believing I had to have it every day---I couldn't do without it! Until then, I always believed I could do with it or without it, even though I always enjoyed drinking socially. After finally crossing over into the dark world of alcohol addiction, I didn't care whether I was in the company of another drinker or not---in fact, I reached the point where I preferred to drink alone.

I've been around alcohol in one form or another all my life. I recall dad's preparation of a morning "toddy" he served my Cherokee grandmother in her bedroom "to get her day started." Her toddy was a strong mixture of hot black coffee and bourbon whiskey. Sitting in her rocking chair, she sipped this potent mixture, occasionally pouring a sip or two at a time into the saucer, blowing it gently, then sipping from the saucer.

My mother was unalterably opposed to this ritual. In fact she was opposed to alcohol use of any kind, period! At best, she tolerated grandma's hot toddies, occasionally rising up to direct my dad to "get that stuff out of the house." Life was really challenging most of the time in our home during my first ten or so years because of situations discussed in Book One. Alcohol, toddies for grandma, a stash of whiskey and beer dad hid in our garage certainly kept the pot boiling at our house.

I can say with all honesty that my dear mother is truly the only person I've ever known who, after living a long full life, went to heaven never having tasted alcohol---of any kind---wine, beer or hard liquor. I suspect the home she grew up in near Troup, Texas was dry as a bone, instilling in her the tee totaling principles that lasted a lifetime.

I had no drinking experience until I went away to college at Texas A&M. Even then my drinking was innocent, a few beers now and then, courtesy of a Senior Texas Aggie buddy from my hometown who had a car and full privileges to come and go. I never had more than three or four at any one time, usually celebrating the end of final exams. During summers back at home, we'd often drink a few beers with dates at one of the local dives---but there was no serious drinking.

My first experience with hard liquor came when I was in post graduate school at the University of Colorado. I went on a one night drinking binge. Unfortunately the binge took place at the home of my major professor in the midst of a student-faculty party. After getting heavily into gin, I somehow went on a destructive rampage---- about what, I don't know. I created an awful ruckus after deciding for no reason that several undergrads had it in for me. In my insanity, I took three of them out, causing some property damage in the process. Somehow I didn't get booted out of grad school, but probably should have been.

I refrained from drinking after the near disaster in Boulder. I actually loved how the booze made me feel. It made me feel powerful, invincible! At the same time, losing control as I did startled and scared me. I would just have to avoid the use of hard liquor if it was going to affect me this way.

I drank sparingly during the three years I served in the Air Force at Wright Patterson AFB, Ohio. The Officers Club at Wright Patterson was known to be one of the finest and largest in all the armed services, offering an excellent dinner, dancing and social events of all kinds. I stuck close to my knitting and don't recall a single episode when I drank to excess.

My years in Houston in the oil industry were another matter. I got exposed early on to the two-fisted drinking habits of some oil men. Most of my excessive drinking bouts were away from Houston, in New York and Chicago. I had a couple of drinking business buddies in both ports who enjoyed partying and drinking hard with me. Often we'd top off an evening with late night visits to the Playboy Club in New York or the Gaslight Club in Chicago. My drinking got out of control only once, an experience I remember vividly because my buddy and I awoke in the same bed in a swanky mid-town Manhattan hotel room late one morning after a long night of partying. It was Saturday, and I was supposed to have returned to Houston late Friday. My friend hadn't bothered to phone his wife in New Jersey, and she was in a panic. Mine was just plain angry! I don't know when or how we got to that hotel room, only that he and I were equally distressed to have awakened, fully dressed in business suits, lying on our backs on a bed that hadn't even been turned down. We considered taking that old remedy, the "hair of the dog ", but decided against it. It took a while for me to live down my escapade.

For the next few years (1972-1980), my drinking was episodic. I continued binge drinking, rarely stopping after one or two or three drinks. I didn't drink all the time, just when I felt like it or when it was warranted in my mind by sadness on one hand; or cause for celebration on the other. I didn't try to analyze my drinking because I thought it wasn't a problem. I was sure I could stop anytime I wanted. It was nothing more than pure denial on my part for me to be so cock sure my drinking wasn't a problem. Objectively speaking, there was hard evidence all around me that I was indeed a problem drinker----my inability to hold a job very long in the 1971-74 period; broken family life, with wife and children gone far away; alienation from friends and family, etc.

Still I insisted I was not a problem drinker. Once even destroying my apartment in a drunken rage didn't wake me up! Neither did it occur to me I was a problem drinker when in another drunken rage I damaged a hotel room, getting visited by the local gendarme! My precious dad came to my rescue, getting me out of that problem. Even his quiet consultation that I was a problem drinker in need of help fell on my deaf ears.

We alcoholics give new meaning to the word "denial." I couldn't admit I had a problem of any kind with alcohol. It was always other people and things causing me to react as I did. It was clear to me that my drinking only came in binges, and when I drank I drank to get drunk. Then I might go for days, weeks, even months without a drink, only to pick it up again if, on some particular morning I thought the sun came up wrong, or something else equally absurd crossed my mind. This is just the way for us alcoholics. Externalities aren't the real reason we drink----we simply use them for an excuse. We drink because we are glad and celebrating something! We drink because we are sad, lonely, or maybe our life is falling apart! It really makes no difference! We drink strictly because we are active alcoholics, and that is what we do....until and unless active drinking gives way to recovery....or possibly death.

The special art and craft of the alcoholic is to arrange and rearrange the deck chairs on the Titanic, while we live in a world bounded only by our minds---not bounded by facts or reality.

I still wasn't about to knuckle under to the likes of AA's Step One that insisted I had to admit being powerless over alcohol. By being a binge type drinker, I might go for hours, days, weeks, sometimes even months without drinking. I was certain that I was in full control. I didn't stop to think about what happened when I drank---that I drank to get drunk---that I liked the sensation of being drunk, regardless of any consequences the next day---that once I picked up that first drink there was no stopping me. It didn't occur to me that my drinking behavior was aberrant.

I was indeed powerless over alcohol once I took that first drink! But I couldn't admit it. Otherwise, I reasoned that I maintained control if I didn't take a drink, therefore I must not be powerless over alcohol. I thought I was an intelligent man---but I came to see in sobriety that alcoholic reasoning defies intelligence !

Step One was a big hurdle for me for another reason. I didn't want to admit I was powerless over anything! I'd yet to learn a well-worn AA adage about having "no control over people, places or things". My engineer's mind said I could control almost anything...it was just a matter of getting the right leverage.

Binge type drinking, going on drinking sprees more or less rarely longer than a day or two at a time, was my pattern until I was in my early 50's. Then I gradually morphed to become a daily drinker. At first I held off til late afternoon, usually about 4:00 or later, depending on my schedule for the day. Ridiculously, I believed waiting until late in the day to drink meant I was in control---sort of like controlled social drinking. I'd reaped considerable business success in spite of my drinking, and believed I was entitled to enjoy the fruits of my labor, including a few afternoon drinks. This would become a daily ritual, in celebration of "my success".

Weekends, at home in northern Vermont, drinking hours usually extended to well past midnight into the wee hours, joined by my wife who drank alongside me. Sadly, drinking together was about all we had left together. We sat in our favorite high back chairs sipping cognac or brandy, in front of a crackling fire in the darkness, with hardly a word spoken, cd's softly playing our classical favorites in the background.

She tragically drank herself to death in a few months. Even this didn't slow me down---I kept right on drinking.

I drank steadily on a daily basis for about five years, getting progressively more dependent. I started by having my first drink in my office around mid-morning, then three, four, sometimes five "Silver Bullets" over a two hour lunch at one of my favorite hideouts with several business associates. Then out for three or four more with a client late in the afternoon, followed by wine with dinner and an aperitif, "for the road".

By the way, the "Silver Bullet" was my version of a very dry Martini....three or four fingers of chilled Bombay gin in an "Old Fashioned" tumbler with four or five plump stuffed green olives on a spear, sunk into the Bombay...no Vermouth....just the straight stuff. It was always chilled, and usually poured over a few ice cubes. This way dilution would be the minimum, and I could enjoy the full, unadulterated blast of Bombay. My closest business associates dubbed me, Dr. Bombay, and for a Christmas gift one year they gave me a framed stylized pastel of me, Dr. Bombay, decked out in ski clothing and ski boots, with my four closest business pals, two on each side.

I developed drinking into an art form, downing colorless liquor, i.e. Bombay gin, all summer, until cold weather came; then switching mainly over to winter colors-- bourbon or scotch whiskey; then back again to Bombay at the first hint of longer days and warmer weather. I never developed a taste for straight whiskey, always preferring a highball of whiskey and coke, or scotch and soda. Scotch and water was usually ok in a pinch, but Bombay gin in the spring and summer was my poison of choice!

My fetish developed to the point I found myself organizing my days around drinking. "Let's see, what meetings do I have today and whom can I drink with? Is anyone on the schedule with whom I have to feign sobriety? How soon can I get out of here and meet my business pals at Clyde's"? Do you get the idea? My whole life was revolving around alcohol. The bottle became my best, most trusted friend.

Unlike so many of my AA brothers and sisters, I escaped the unpleasantness of DUIs. I got a warning once, but it was late at night as I turned into the driveway at home. The patrolman had observed me crossing the center stripe a couple of times only a few minutes before, and let me off the hook because I was home and no longer a threat on the road. I don't boast about this, because driving under the influence as I sometimes did was wrong, wrong, wrong! I got away with drinking as I did because I was usually driven to and from work and meetings with the drinking crowd. Not having to navigate myself spared me from the law, but maybe it helped me be a drunk!

Being successful in business further confirmed my conviction that I didn't have a problem with alcohol. "After all", I told myself, "how could anybody do what I'm able to do if they have an alcohol problem"? I often rationalized my successes by reminding myself, "I'm what's known as a Functional Alcoholic," a drinker who still functions at a high level. Bamboozling coworkers, I was able to get most of them to buy into this functional alcoholic cock and bull story.

All but my Office Manager. I came in one morning to discover that my copious stash of liquor was gone from its cabinet. I simply wanted my usual 10:00 shot to kick off the day. I summoned everyone to my office I thought had anything to do with this prank. Charlotte, the Office

Manager quickly fessed up. After I dismissed everybody else, Charlotte calmly explained her reasoning. She was firm and incisive as she spoke, and wasn't going to let herself be bullied. She explained that she was very concerned because of a recent very large government contract we'd been awarded. Her concern rightly transcended the fact that we'd been awarded this contract in competitive bidding primarily because of me and my special efforts. Her concern was based on good common sense and her knowledge of the applicable regulations. In fact, she was doing her job, protecting the company, and she was doing it well.

I recovered my stash and took it to my apartment. Thus began a new, more sinister drinking chapter for me. No longer able to belt it down at my office because I didn't want to do anything that could possibly hurt our business, I'd simply do my drinking at home...alone. I was beginning to learn that my "best friend" The Bottle was demanding, totally selfish and jealous, wanting me alone with him (or her), without others around to join in our fun. I was even pulling back from my corporate Presidential responsibilities, meeting with employees and clients so I could have time alone with The Bottle.

Soon, my annual physical checkup revealed some troubling information for the first time. My liver was showing signs of degradation, functioning below normal levels and my kidneys weren't up to par. More tests were called for. Still I didn't heed the warning signals and continued drinking with no let up.

September, 1993, came with the blessed event of my son Mason's wedding at our home in Vermont. Margery, the love of my life whom I'd marry in 1994, had participated in our family planning for this special event. The wedding and celebration afterwards was held in our back yard. There was music, dancing, catered food...the works. I started drinking the night before to celebrate this milestone in my son's life and consciously to tone down my feelings. I continued drinking on wedding day morning, standing with Mason while he dressed. I was his Best Man, and this honor meant everything to me. I made my way in and out of the house to my private stash of Bombay, apart from the party. By mid-afternoon I was blitzed, and Margery wisely and tactfully guided me out of the wedding party to our bedroom. I vaguely remember removing my clothes and crawling under the covers. I was asleep in never-never land in no time.

Margery tells me that a couple of hours later, as the party was winding down, I suddenly made an appearance to those who remained without a stitch of clothing on my naked body. Shocked, Margery hustled me back to the bedroom before I could do more damage. Frankly, I have no recollection of this and I don't remember a thing until Margery served me coffee the next morning. As she calmly told me what I had done, I was speechless…for one of the first times in my life.

Realizing the embarrassment I'd caused Margery, myself, and particularly my son Mason, I couldn't handle it. How could I have possibly done that? As we sat together over coffee that morning, it took a while for it to sink in, and when it did, I just couldn't live with it anymore. I realized that Margery couldn't live that way either, and her own successful business was such that she didn't have to. I needed to change my ways, else I stood to lose my precious Margery and everything else.

My mind kept returning to my naked appearance before the remaining guests and what a fool they must have thought my son's dad must be! I just couldn't stand to think about it. My personal nadir had come. It was my low point----in AA it's often called "hitting one's bottom". Liver and kidney deterioration, wild drinking sprees with heavy hangovers, the joy and fulfillment of the birth of my first grandson--- none of these things brought me to the brink like this. Everybody has a point of greatest vulnerability. My Achilles heel must be Ego, Shame and Vanity.

It took bringing discredit to myself and embarrassing my precious wife to be and my dear son to get my undivided attention. Then and there, I told Margery I had to give it up. I didn't know how, but with God's help and her support, I'd do it. We prayed about it, then proceeded to search for AA meetings across northern Vermont.

That night I attended the Happy, Sober and Free Group meeting only a mile from home. I was totally surprised by several men who greeted me with open arms….our personal banker Dan, and a local innkeeper Lou I'd known for years. Other guys at the meeting made me feel right at home, including Marshall who became my deer hunting partner; and computer guru big John. I felt like I had somehow come home to a place I was supposed to be. I thoroughly enjoyed the meeting, the speaker and fellowship with members. Dan agreed to be my temporary sponsor until I decided for sure what I wanted. I was blown away by the intelligence, wisdom, professionalism and friendliness I found there. I'd expected to see a bunch of loser deadbeats, society's dregs. What I found was the polar opposite!

I learned that to get over the initial hurdle of getting sober, I needed to do "90 meetings in 90 days". This is the basic prescript in AA. My sponsor Dan emphasized the importance of seeing this intensive exposure through to the end. We could then begin work on AA's Twelve Step Program.

Committing to do "90 in 90" meant I had to either stay put in Vermont, conducting business from home; or commute back and forth between home and Washington, or wherever else I needed to travel. I decided to be a commuter, still making "90 in 90", wherever I might be. Margery committed to help me meet this schedule, traveling with me when she could. My computer people came up from Washington to set up a computer outpost for us at home.

I actually did "90 in 90", attending meetings all over the country....in northern Virginia, Idaho, California, New York, Houston and Vermont. Marge was with me for over half the meetings. Before any trip, we'd go on the internet and research local AA meeting schedules, times and locations, and we'd plan accordingly. I couldn't have done the "90 in 90" without Margery's help and support. She always helped me remember: Sobriety Is Job # 1 !

Universally, I discovered that alcoholics are by and large an interesting lot. I have to confess my earlier apprehensions and ideas about alcoholics were entirely wrong. And I suspect society by and large has the wrong idea about the alcoholic. I met and got to know people in AA from all social and income strata, representing every kind of job and profession...doctors, lawyers, politicians, plumbers, carpenters, welders, mechanics, top business executives and bankers.

The big lesson for me was "I was not alone"....and "I am never alone". My addiction is not unique. Many, many other intelligent, attractive, interesting people have the same kind of "Green Hair" I have.

Two months after completing "90 in 90", I came down with a serious case of flu at home in Vermont. My lungs became contaminated by material aspirated during violent spells of vomiting. My doctor's diagnosis was double pneumonia, and I was immediately hospitalized. While treating me for pneumonia, tests indicated my gall bladder was the culprit behind the violent spells of vomiting. After discussion with Marge and me, the doctors removed my gall bladder. My recovery speeded up after the surgery, and I soon felt much better.

But lying in the hospital bed, thinking about my quest for sobriety, I remembered I still kept a large stash of liquors in a special cabinet at home. Knowing I'd be discharged soon from the hospital, I didn't want to return home to the copious supply of tempting booze, and I asked Margery to help me. There was no way I could get rid of it myself---for me to do so, I reasoned, was tantamount to executing a close friend! I just couldn't bring myself to do it.

A year later, Marge revealed that she had asked my sponsor Dan to help. Dan went to our house and poured all of it down the drain before I came home. He then got rid of the empty bottles at the town dump. In turn, Margery filled the empty shelves with bottles of juice drinks of every imaginable kind and color. I was pleased and surprisingly satisfied by the sight of these new bottles. I came to enjoy drinking them immensely!

Marge and I proceeded with our late spring wedding at home in Vermont. Friends came from Washington and all over to celebrate with us. I was honored for my son Mason to stand with me as my Best Man, while Marge's daughter Heather was her Bride's Maid. Snowfall punctuated the eve of our wedding and closed one of our mountain passes. But our wedding day was clear and chilly as everyone gathered outdoors. It was a wonderful affair, with dear family, great friends, food and........precious Sobriety.

It's taken time to develop "my program" for sobriety, but I have a program that works for me....it's my program and it might not work for anyone else! I'll keep specifics about it to myself, but I'll tell you it consists of three equally balanced elements. They embrace the Spiritual, Physical and Mental aspects of my life. This program is with me every day, no matter where I am. It's an integral part of my life.

I may never fully understand why I was, am and will always be an alcoholic. I've probed deep in my psyche in search of answers. The fact is, some of us—about 10% of us ----just are that way.

Did I drink because the effects of the alcohol in my system masked insecurities? Why was I insecure in the first place? I always believed insecurity was the result of misplaced trust....that someone you trusted with all your heart let you down, broke that trust. Did my home environment when I was young make me insecure? Certainly the War years 1940-45 or 46 were formative in my life when I was 4-10 years old. I was always worried about my mother, when she worked late into the night.

Growing up, I felt like the odd man out---I had Frank, Jon, Jere and a few other close friends; I was reasonably popular, and I made excellent grades. Still, I was solitudinous, lonely much of the time and didn't really feel like I belonged anywhere...I felt sort of like a misfit.

I certainly felt like an oddball when I was driven around in a police car during those War years. Nobody else was transported that way, unless you were in trouble with the police.

I often made the mistake of comparing myself with others, especially my closest friends. They seemed to have everything! Weekend lake houses, nice cars, mothers whose job was to stay home taking care of their family. I could offer a hunting and rough camping spot in the woods, but little else. On top of all that, our home was run in an odd manner and kept odd hours until 1945 or '46.

By contrast, most of my friends came from well to do families, some with considerable means. They did absolutely nothing to make me feel inferior...just the opposite...they accepted me, Martin, for myself, not what I could materially offer them. They actually liked me because of me! They included me in everything---I was left out of nothing!

So at least in part, my feelings of inadequacy were not well founded. And later on when I drank, I felt like Superman, able to leap tall buildings in a single bound, etc. Alcohol dissolved all my feelings of inadequacy and timidity. I thought I was a normal person!

If I could do one thing for my grandchildren or anyone else, it would be to endow them with a sense of security, that they belong, that they fit right in, that nothing and no one is more important. In my case, the effects of feeling insecure in childhood were long lasting. In fact, so pervasive my life in many ways was shaped by early, lasting feelings of insecurity.

I discovered that alcohol kept me from having a full relationship with Christ Jesus. My love affair with The Bottle restrained God from developing a full relationship with me. God wanted this full relationship and held off until I could truly "have no other gods before Him". Alcohol is one powerful force Satan uses to keep us from

God…keeping us from being all God desires for us. I put it right up there with sex and food in my list of Satanic "tools"….think of alcohol as one of the biggies in Satan's "toolbox".

Then, twenty years ago when I put The Bottle aside to begin a life of sobriety, God through Jesus Christ came into a new richer, deeper relationship with me than ever before. At that point, I could finally be open to Him. I call this new relationship the beginning of my Sanctification. I want the things of God. I want what God wants me to have. I take no pleasure anymore in what God regards as sin. Those sinful activities in my past in which I found at least temporal pleasure don't appeal to me anymore. That includes drinking with the boys, gaining everything I could, maybe even at the expense of others, and adulterous behavior which can take many forms.

God gave me a sense of peace and stability I never knew before. I am generally at peace with myself, and at peace with God. Money could never buy this gift, no matter how hard I tried!

The kind of peace Jesus promises in John 14:27 is a true gift. It's not the kind of peace the world gives, but "peace that passes all understanding". After almost six decades of restlessness, the peace that the Lord gives me is awesome! It gives me the ability to sit still. It gives me a serenity to be comfortable in my own skin. It gives me the time and space to hear my Lord's voice. And it affords me a communion with Jesus Christ which is like nothing I've ever known.

BOOK THREE:
ESSAYS

INTRODUCTION

I 've been a philosophical essayist since the start of my recovery from active alcoholism, twenty years ago.

The Dictionary App on my Tablet gives multiple definitions for the word, "philosophy"....

"A system of principles for guidance in practical affairs". Another defines "philosophy" as "Rational investigation of the truths and principles of being, knowledge or conduct".

In my drinking days, I could make a world of chaos seem rational to my mind. In my ongoing days of sobriety, I began to explore my "new" world, and these Essays reflect my wide ranging philosophies on life, salvation, God's creation, eternity, animals and mankind----all subjects that have challenged and interested my sober mind.

Please don't ask me to prove out most of what I've written, because I can't ! Remember the very nature of a philosophy is a system of beliefs. While a philosophy may well draw upon scientific, historic or documentable fact, it is none of these, because it is strictly an organized set of beliefs.

For example, one of my favorite essays entitled, "We Are Alone in the Universe", defies proof, this side of heaven. This essay is strictly my own set of beliefs based on information drawn from many sources, including the Bible. I believe in spite of man's thirst for finding "intelligent life elsewhere", only with God in eternity will we know the actual truth. I invite you to read this essay and see what you think!

The substance of my essays is a condensation of my own thoughts, observations and ideas. You may or may not agree with many of these---that is your privilege, dear reader. It isn't my purpose to brow beat, argue or cajole you into believing as I do. Instead, my purpose is simply to share my deepest beliefs. If some or all of this resonates with you, great! If it doesn't, I hope you will enjoy the journey and will be stimulated to think about things you might not have thought seriously about before.

Much of my writing is influenced by the Holy Bible, which I personally believe is God's word, written by man and inspired by God....it is His missive to all mankind.

Still other aspects of my essays are shaped by my understanding of physics, mathematics and chemistry and the absolute truth of these sciences throughout all creation. Certain aspects of my thinking have been influenced by the works of Dr. Einstein and others, seeking to understand the relationships between time, space and matter in the universe. God has used the powerful minds of men and women over the centuries to explicate his universal truths though some of the greatest, such as physicist Stephen Hawking, are agnostic or atheistic.

I leave you with a special request.....please read these essays slowly and carefully....one essay at a time. Don't rush through them...take your time, and think about what you've read.

Here's wishing you Good Reading and an eye-opening Journey !

INDEX OF ESSAYS

THE CHALLENGE OF BELIEF

H ebrews 11:1-3, "Now faith is the assurance of things hoped for, the conviction of things not seen. Indeed, by faith our ancestors received approval. By faith we understand that the worlds were prepared by the word of God, so that what is seen was made from things that are not visible". (Harpers NRSV).

Faith is so compelling that God "Accorded it to Abraham as righteousness". This means that Abraham believed and trusted God so completely that he staked his own life and the lives of those he loved most on believing God and obeying His commandments. Abraham believed God and trusted God even when circumstances were contrary to his own "common sense" beliefs...."Go and sacrifice your son Isaac", after you've waited a lifetime for him to be born of your aging wife Sarah...."Leave your home, your friends, relatives and your livelihood and move to a faraway land I will show you" ...a land that you know absolutely nothing about...."There, you will become the father of a great nation, Israel". God chalked up these acts of trust and obedience as though Abraham had done acts of righteousness. He rewarded Abraham for obeying Him, just as He promised He would.

Hebrews 11 goes on to give us a litany of instances when Abraham trusted God, over and above his own reasoning, and it "was accorded to him as righteousness". Then it gives us powerful examples of faith demonstrated by Moses, Joseph and others. If God accorded righteousness to Abraham, recognizing and rewarding his acts of faith, I believe that God accorded righteousness to Moses, Joseph and others in the same way.

God doesn't change, so I believe He credits my acts and your acts of faith and obedience as righteousness, in the same way He did the ancients.

Countless attempts are made every year to "prove" the Bible. There's nothing wrong with this except for so many, "proof" is a necessary prerequisite to belief. Can you prove Jesus was immaculately conceived as God's only begotten Son? Can anyone prove He was born of a virgin? What a stumbling block this presents for those who insist on having proof.

In fact, all of Christ's miracles try our sense of credulity----turning water, a substance which is devoid of carbon atoms into wine, a substance laden with carbonaceous material at the wedding in Cana; bringing dead Lazarus and little Tabatha back to life; His transfiguration in the presence of Peter, James and John high on a mountain, conversing with the embodiments of Moses and Elijah as God Himself announced that He was pleased with His Son Jesus; feeding 5,000 people from just a few loaves of bread a few fishes, with abundant leftovers; healing the blind, the lame, and lepers; and on and on.

In fact, the entire Word of God is replete with stories that, without faith, are hard if not downright impossible to believe----parting the sea so Moses and his vast company could cross safely ahead of Pharaoh's doomed army ; young future King David's slaying of the giant Goliath with a stone from his slingshot ; the walls collapsing around the fortified city of Jericho while Joshua and his small band walked about ; the jackass that talked; Daniel's unique ability to interpret dreams and visions; the profoundly mysterious Ark of the Covenant, with its exotic powers; Noah and his phenomenal ark, full of pairs of living things, surviving the Great Flood; Jonah surviving captivity in a "large fish"...and on and on.

From cover to cover, the written Word of God challenges us, even breaking the bounds of credulity!

Has it ever occurred to you that God intended it to be such a stretch, because----I must accept the Bible by faith, or not at all?

No matter how good my science, I won't be able to prove for sure that "old sol" stood still in the sky (i.e., earth stopped rotating) while a battle raged on down here... or that Christ Jesus came back to life after three days in the tomb!

I will not this side of Heaven be able to absolutely prove to you that these things are true.

So, why am I sure they are true? Because I believe them in my heart---I accept them by faith. And I pray believing that God will attribute these acts of belief and faith as "righteousness" to you and to me, as he did to His servant Abraham and the ancients.

FAITH

Standing chest deep in water, I asked both of my very young children to jump off the side of the swimming pool into my waiting arms. I promised I'd catch them. The first time took lots of coaxing, then the brave jump. I did just what I said I'd do----I was there, to catch each one! How they squealed and giggled with joy and excitement! Next time took less coaxing, and finally none at all. They learned to trust me. They learned that I wouldn't play a mean trick on them. They learned that my word was good.

We've all had similar experiences, learning a simple but basic principle:

"Faith untested is nothing more than hope."

Abraham was a man of faith. His remarkable faith was credited to him by God as righteousness, according to Genesis 15;6 and Romans 4:3.

But my oh my! How God tested Abraham's faith! Abraham actually proceeded to obey God's seemingly outrageous command to put his son Isaac to death as a sacrifice (Genesis 22)....the son for whom he'd waited so long. Abraham took Isaac and a servant up to a spot on Mount Moriah and went through the motions preparing to put his young son to the knife, then burn his carcass on a bier. (Isaac himself probably helped gather wood for his own bier).

Can you imagine the heaviness of that father's heart as he trudged along to Mount Moriah to carry out God's command, sharpening the knife and building up that pile of wood? I don't know about you, but I'm pretty sure this would have been my undoing!

Still, somehow, Abraham found it within himself to follow through, obeying God, believing it would turn out alright. Then God intervened just in time, before the deed was done. Hallelujah! Isaac the beloved son of Abraham was saved!

If Abraham's experience is any guide, and I believe it is, I may have to pass through a foreboding Valley of the Shadow of Death, coming out the other side with the help of God's mighty hand, if I expect to grow in faith. I have to find a way to screw up my courage, believing that God will see me through. This is really hard to do when the Valley is dark, scary and we are all alone. That time of testing isn't fun. More likely it will be painful, possibly even wrenching. It could be costly, like the kinds of losses Job experienced before finally being restored by the Hand of God (Job 42).

There are many kinds of dark Valleys, vastly different from Abraham's, yet dark all the same. There's the Valley of alcohol and drug addiction; the Valley of death of one you love, maybe thinking you can't possibly live without; the Valley of loss of job and income; of severe, chronic illness; of divorce and the heartaches of a family breakup.

Like Abraham, I stare in the face of dark Valleys of a different kind. Each kind of Valley has enough power to leave me bitter and angry, devastated, crippled. But each can grow me to be one who loves God more and more, trusting Him with the outcome He wants for me, which may or may not be the outcome I initially wanted for myself.

This is called getting to know God and learning to trust and obey Him in all the affairs of the world I live in.

ALONE IN GOD'S VAST UNIVERSE

E very time I observe the endless night sky with twinkling, blinking lights from one end to the other, I say to myself, "How can it be that we earthlings are the only ones"? There must be a gazillion other places like earth, capable of supporting intelligent, moving, creative capable beings.

If they are out there somewhere, do they know and worship the same Jehovah God I know and worship? Was the Savior sent their way to be their Redeemer? Was it the same Jesus Christ I know and love? Or in your imagination, do you have to somehow stipulate the existence of yet another God and Savior?

If you believe as I do that there is one and only one God and one and only one Jesus Christ who is God's "only begotten Son"; and if there exist intelligent beings elsewhere who, like we "are created in God's own image"; and if those beings like we are free to choose thus free to sin against God; then you have to admit they need saving from their sins just as we must be saved from ours. Unless of, course, God made them automatons, not in His image.....then you don't have intelligent life at all, as we understand it.....and you talk yourself into a corner with no way out.

Why would the God we know and love create such farciful beings? I don't believe He would! And if those beings, like we, were created in His image, He and His Son must be known to them as They are known to us. I believe He would have told us, if there are others out there, created in His image.

The only way around this conundrum is for you to say there is no God. Then you are free to dream about any and as many kinds of intelligent beings as you wish. To do this, by the way, you have to disavow all that is Holy. I believe God gave you and me the freedom to do this by creating us "in His own image"....we are free to choose! By going this route, you can join forces with those who believe life evolved as a result of exactly the right ambient conditions existing at the right place at the right time. If this is what you believe, there must be huge numbers of places in the vast universe that are conducive to intelligent life. In fact, the Drake Equation (1961) attempts to quantify the number of "advanced civilizations" existent in just our own Milky Way galaxy. Earlier, the great physicist, Enrico Fermi, asked, "Where is everybody"?

Fermi's Paradox says all our logic assures us they are out there, we just haven't detected them yet through radio waves or other forms of communication. Some even postulate that we don't see or detect them because they annihilated themselves through nuclear wars.

I believe in God. I believe God's Holy Word which tells us God Himself created everything that is, from the most miniscule subatomic particle to the cosmos. I claim John 3:16,one of the most powerful in all Scripture, which says: "For God so loved the world that He gave His only Son, so that everyone who believes in Him may not perish but may have eternal life."

I believe with all my heart that God loves you and me to the unimaginable extent that He sent His one and only Son to walk and live here on earth, and that God accepted His shed blood in remission of my sins and yours.

I don't buy the reasoning that argues God created other beings elsewhere "in His image", meaning they are free to choose, to reason, to know right from wrong, without making a way for them to be saved from error in their ways, sin and perdition. I don't pretend to be able to conceive any way this could be done except the way God did it for you and me---through His only Son, Jesus Christ.

AMERICA, BLESSED IN ALL GOD'S UNIVERSE!

A lone in the vast universe, my home on Planet Earth is of all places, America, land of the free, home of the brave!

And especially if you believe as I do that we are alone in the cosmos, unique, there is nothing out there like us, then you have to appreciate God's blessings all the more because you live in this amazing country.

Just think about it.....you might just as well have found yourself in someplace like Rwanda, or Cuba, or almost anyplace else. But you didn't. You are blessed to live here, in America!

So, if you believe as I do that we are alone in the cosmos, and of all the places on this planet you might have been, I fall to my knees thanking God for letting me be part of a land where still, more than anywhere else, you can become whatever your skill, physicality, intelligence, and the breaks let you become. You can actually become the person God had in mind when you were made.

If I'm satisfied being a bum, I can be a bum...and I probably won't starve to death in America. If I want to work hard, change my station in life, I can.

In fact, as long as I'm not harming others, I can do and become almost anything I want in America. In fact, it's the only place in the whole universe like this! I don't have to worry about being broken in on in the middle of the night and hauled off to a dungeon or gulag. I'm free, the way God made me. I'm free to seek and find God's highest purposes for my life. In fact, unless I am free, I cannot reach for the stars or any other quest I may want to.

I don't believe any other place like America can be found in the whole universe. And to think I'm an American, living in this one of a kind jewel of a dot in the universe, humbles me and makes me thankful.

GOD REVEALED

T he ancients like Abraham and Moses didn't even have Bibles. They hardly had access to scrolls, parchments or any other written revelations about God. God revealed Himself to them in other ways.

He made Himself known to Abraham in a burning bush on Mount Moriah. He appeared to Moses, Aaron and their multitude as fire in the night sky and a cloud during the day. He revealed Himself in a whirlwind, and to others He was revealed in dreams. He outright spoke to some men and women, and came to others as a still, small voice.

The ancients had no churches they could attend, sharing the Word of God with others. Or congregations mixing and mingling after church over coffee and donuts.

They had to come into relationship with God through faith, believing. It's interesting that it's the same now as it was then......by simple faith, believing.

Now I have something magnificent they didn't have to help show me the way....the Holy Bible, relating more than 4,000 years of relationships between man and God!

No amount of ceremony, catechism or sacrament will save my soul to eternity. Nor would it long ago. Faith and belief have always been the stuff of salvation.

I love the amazing story in Genesis 30 thru Genesis 50 about the life and fortunes of Abraham's great grandson, the son of Jacob, Joseph. Sold into slavery by jealous brothers, just a boy, he grew up in pagan Egypt. But he did right in the eyes of God and was faithful. Genesis 39 describes an episode in which Joseph wouldn't give in to the adulterous demands of his prominent master's wife because he knew it was wrong. He got thrown into prison because the spurned wife lied, claiming that Joseph violated her. He eventually came out on top anyway because he honored God, and ended up running the country!

Who taught Joseph right from wrong? He grew up in that strange land without father or mother, and I doubt he had any mentors who believed in Jehovah God. How did he know what to do? Right from wrong?

There can be only one answer....God revealed Himself directly to Joseph just as He did to Abraham, Moses and the other ancients....He wrote His will and His way on their hearts....and He has written His way on my heart and yours too. Jeremiah the prophet writes, "I will put my law within them, and I will write it on their hearts; and I will be their God and they shall be my people."(Jer: 33-35).

RIGHTFUL PRAYERS

M ost of all, I want to pray rightfully. What is "rightful praying"? It is prayer that is pleasing to the Lord God. Aren't all prayers pleasing to God? No. Therefore the purpose of this Essay is to share what's on my heart about praying and pleasing our Father in Heaven.

I used to pray a lot for myself, asking God for things like taking a special trip, or some material thing I could touch and feel.

Maturing as a Believer, I believe God wants to fellowship with me. He wants me to know Him better. Prayer time for me has evolved. More and more, it's a time of fellowship with God. Sometime ago, I stopped flooding the Lord with request after request, loading up my time of prayer with petitions.

God wants me to let up a little, giving Him space to respond. "Yes Lord, I'm listening." Punctuate my sentences with pauses here and there. Just feel the Lord's presence. Let Him wrap you in His love. Listen to the thoughts flowing through your mind. They may carry God's message.

James, the brother of Christ Jesus, said "You want something and do not have it; so you commit murder. And you covet something and cannot obtain it; so you engage in disputes and conflicts. You do not have, because you do not ask. You ask and do not receive, because you ask wrongly, in order to spend what you get on your pleasures." (James 4:2-3). Am I asking amiss in my prayers? Is my heart right when I come before the Lord? Or is my prayer time loaded with asking God to gimme this and gimme that?

Jesus taught us to pray boldly, not irreverently, but boldly. I will place my petitions completely within the realm of God's will for me....not my will, Lord, but Thine. I will ask God to help me pray according to His will....to come before Him with a right heart, not self-seeking or with malice. I'll ask the Lord to prepare me for my time of prayer, removing all obstacles from my heart that stand in the way of getting through to Him.

Then I have the great privilege and honor of coming before the Lord, Master of my soul, Master of all there is, with a heart that is open and trusting.

Christ Jesus dropped the clue to finding happiness, quoted in John 14:27---"Peace I leave with you—my peace I give unto you---not as the world gives...." It's vital to note that even the "Lord's Prayer" doesn't seek "outcomes". We are always busy asking God to give us particular "outcomes"...Jesus' model prayer does not seek an outcome.

Jesus brother, James, again hits us between the eyes, telling us that we don't receive because we ask wrongly, greedily, selfishly...we ask amiss. (Jas 4:1-3). Then James gives us deeper insights (Jas 4:13-15), instructing us to stop always asking God for specific outcomes...the particular outcome is within God's sovereignty to grant, according to His will. We can most certainly ask, BUT...don't just harp on the outcome...and, ask humbly, according to His will in the matter.

Instead of dwelling on outcomes, dwell instead on getting to know God better... fellowshipping with Him...living closer to God in everything we do...finding joy in Bible study and in our time of fellowship with Him. Do these things in your own still, quiet, secret place of the day. Live close to Him, and eventually you, yourself, will literally become His will!

God will grant you and me "peace that passes all understanding..." and maybe even some gangbuster surprise outcomes we didn't expect, all within His sovereign grace!

BARNEY AND RUFUS WON'T BE IN HEAVEN

I couldn't have loved any animals more than my son's two Short-Haired German Pointer dogs, Rufus and Barney. They were whirling dervishes, full of life, always on the move, and could run more than thirty miles per hour. They brought many hours of joy to our family!

While these two were really special, I've loved all my pets....Skippy, my little Fox Terrier when I was a kid; Tincup, the chattering canary; Lou, the red rooster that sat on my chair back during meals when I was little; and Maudy, the horse I used to ride all over my Aunt and Uncle's farm at Omen.

Wonderful as they've all been, I won't see them in Heaven because they don't have souls! You and I do have souls, and they live eternally. Animals don't!   When they die, they die, that's it....it's all over...sayonara!

Do we not understand God's hierarchy? Making man "a little lower than the angels", God put everything on earth "under man's feet", for all things on earth are "in subjection to man." God even made Jesus a little lower than the angels for His earthly sojourn. (Heb 2:7-9).

But in Heaven "we are to judge the angels." I take this to mean in Heaven, we will be above the angels in God's hierarchy.(1 Cor 6:2-4). I see no place in God's hierarchy for animals beyond their life on earth.

The soul God breathed into you and me differentiates us from animals. God made you and me intelligent beings, "in His own image". My soul is the omnipotent control center that harnesses and integrates all my capacities for "good or for evil".

Much as I loved Barney, bless his heart, he didn't have a soul! This means he can't live forever!

This in no way means God doesn't love and care for birds in the air, deer, bears, moose and all other creatures roaming the earth and swimming in earth's waters. The Bible teaches that God so cares for His creatures that "not even a falling sparrow" escapes God's attention (Matt 10:29-31).

As much as God cares, it doesn't even come close to His love and care for you and me. Jesus said, "Even the hairs of your head are all counted. So don't be afraid; you are of more value than many sparrows." (Matt 10:30, Luke 12:7).

From the beginning, God gave mankind dominion over all His creation, to use for our well-being, including fish, fowl, animals and vegetation for our consumption or other use to sustain ourselves! Praise God for His great and abundant gifts!

SAP AND BLOOD

I 've heard and read the story about Cain and Abel all my life. Just about everybody can tell you the story about these two brothers, sons of Adam and Eve, and how in a rage Cain killed his brother, Abel (Gen 4:1-16) committing the first "murder".

Each man had prepared his own unique offering to God, obviously seeking to please God and receive His blessings. Cain offered produce from his fields, the fruit of the earth, maybe grains and other produce. Brother Abel chose a meaty portion of the first born of his flock of sheep to offer. Each man hoped his offering would be acceptable to God. It turns out that God had no regard for Cain and his grain offering, while Abel and his meaty offering found favor with God.

Cain was angry, and even God's consolation didn't calm him down. Cain, still jealous and angry, invited his brother to join him in the field. There he premeditatedly killed his brother Abel!

Accompanying footnotes in my Harper's Study Bible explain that Abel's blood offering simply was more acceptable to God than Cain's fruit of the soil. Still another interpretation is that it had less to do with the nature of the offerings than the attitude of each man. While both may be valid interpretations, I wanted to know more about those interpretations, somehow feeling I was investigating a mystery....turning over in my mind, what's the difference between sap and blood ?

It came to me that God gave Adam and Eve a pretty strong signal when he removed their makeshift leaf clothing, dressing them instead in garments made from animal skins. He did this after they disobediently ate from the "tree of the knowledge of good and evil" in Eden and suddenly became aware of their nakedness. To cover themselves, they sewed fig leaves together in the form of loincloths. God stripped them of their leaf coverings. I might think He then would substitute some other kind of leafy material, things like corn shucks, palm leaves or flowers...maybe finding these more to His liking...But no! That's not what happened! He covered them with the skins of animals!

For certain, the blood of animals had to be shed by God in the process of taking their skins. These skins didn't just grow on trees. Nor did the animals they came from have tree sap or vegetable juices flowing in their veins! They were filled with red corpuscular blood which was shed in the process of taking their skins.

I've removed the skins of many game animals, and I can promise you it's a bloody affair, and the animal isn't alive to tell about it!

Mind you, this was not just any old blood---it was the blood of innocent animals! The skins God used to cover Adam and Eve were the hides of sinless, innocent animals. Animals are innocent and sinless because, not being made in the image of God, they have no soul...they are ruled by instinct...eat when you are hungry, attack when you feel threatened, scratch when you itch and so on. Animals are without sin and they are innocent. Don't confuse an animal's disobedience or his bad behavior with sin and innocence. They aren't the same thing.

So far as I know, plants are neither innocent, sinless or sinful, or guilty. Plants may weep sap when their fruit is harvested or their skin or bark is cut. But this is a far cry from the shedding of blood. And as far as I know, animals of the field and woods are just like plant life in regards to sin, guilt and innocence. They are innocent. The only offering acceptable to God, wiping out sin, is the blood of the sinless, innocent animal. The ancients were so commanded by God.

Then came Jesus the Christ, as innocent and sinless as any animal roaming the earth! Because of his sinlessness and innocence, Jesus was and is the perfect propitiation for my sin and yours. His innocent, sinless blood was shed at the crucifixion. Believing as I do that earthly mankind is the only creature in all creation capable of sinning against God, it took an absolutely awesome sacrifice to wash us clean. Jesus, God's only begotten sinless Son, was that sacrifice. There could be no other.

By claiming Jesus as my Lord and Savior, I am saved from my sins and will have eternal life with Him in God's Heavenly Kingdom!

WHAT TO SEEK FIRST

"But seek first his Kingdom and his righteousness, and all these things will be given to you as well"(Matthew 6:33).

I've come to believe this means Everything! No exceptions! God wants to be my very first thought---not my second, third or fourth.

God wants the first of my time. He wants to have fellowship with me, and me with Him....before my morning coffee....before I have breakfast....before I get caught up in the cares of the day.

He wants me to spend a little time in the Bible before the press of the day takes over.

In an emergency, God wants my prayers first---not when I determine "prayer is the only thing left for me to do", after I've tried everything else.

God asks for my first and best, not what's left over!

SOLITUDE

I go to bed late at night, warm and cozy beneath the covers with Margery near me. Gazing out our windows into the black sky of night, our own galaxy, the Milky Way, is smeared across the blackness like a blob of milk smeared across a black kitchen counter top. It consists of an almost unimaginable number of objects swirling around in the cosmos.

And to think, our own home galaxy is just one of billions! The immensity of it all is too magnificent to get my mind around!

Yet I'm here alone with God in my thoughts. My silent thoughts turn into prayers and petitions, lifted up before His Throne of Grace. He hears and knows each and every word and thought even though I don't make an audible sound. And I listen to Him quietly, as God laden thoughts and ideas cross my mind.

I'm awed by His presence, knowing that He who created it all knows me, hears my every thought, and loves me.

The immensity of God's love is beyond my comprehension when I remember there aren't any other creatures like you and me in the vastness of His universe! God made the here and now. God made all that is rational. God made the billions of stars. But only one galaxy is inhabited by souls who know the righteous world of faith. I am wrapped in God's love and attentive care. Just as I lie in my physical bed, so do I lie in my bed of thoughts. In righteous faith, I am humbled that He is here, with me.

Wrapped in this starry blanket of space, time and infinity, it's almost too wonderful realizing I am loved by the One who made it all!

If I could travel to the very edge of space, time and eternity, I would find no greater love than He has for you and me. And I'm warmed believing that I'd not run across any little green men, any Extraterrestrials, Shreck's, flying saucers or other UFOs, or any dog like, cat like, horse like or bird like critters.

He who created everything shed all His love on you and me! He didn't water down our indescribable value to Him by doing it elsewhere.

"For God so loved the world that He gave His only begotten Son, that whoever believes in Him has eternal life". (John 3:16).

I NEEDED THE QUIET

This poem spoke words of encouragement to me every day many years ago, as I was going through the long, occasionally frustrating process of recovery after having major orthopedic surgery---pretty well laid up for weeks at a time---three different times. I hope it means as much to you as it did me.

I needed the quiet, so He drew me aside,

Into the shadows where we could confide.

Away from the bustle where all the day long

I hurried and worried when active and strong.

I needed the quiet though at first I rebelled.

But gently, so gently, my cross He upheld,

And whispered so sweetly of spiritual things.

Though weakened in body, my spirit took wings,

To heights never dreamed of when happy and gay.

He loved me so greatly He drew me away.

I needed the quiet. No prison my bed, But a beautiful

Valley of blessings instead----

A place to grow richer in Jesus to hide.

I needed the quiet, so He drew me aside.

- By Alice Hansche Mortenson

HE WILL BE WAITING THERE TO RECEIVE ME

P art of me is afraid to die....another part of me looks forward to going home to Heaven, living forever with Christ Jesus in the presence of God.

I need to buck myself up and get over any fears, because fear reflects a lack of faith. Let me share with you a little about the basis of these fears, in the interest of strengthening my faith, and yours.

God's cosmos is vast....larger than we can comprehend. Now here's the silly part---I don't want God to lose track of me. In my heart I know there's no reason whatever to be concerned about this happening, because He made everything there is and He loves you and me. We can't even think of God in our terms. We aren't equipped for this, but I expect we will be when we get to Heaven.

Think with me about the immensity of it all.

God's universe contains something in the order of 10 followed by 21 zeroes objects---stars, suns, planets, units of mass, etc. That's a billion trillion objects! And at the moment of conception, generally called the "Big Bang", an almost unimaginable condition existed....just imagine the entire universe crunched down to maybe the size of a pea. Yet it contained virtually an infinite amount of energy! Its temperature was virtually infinite as well.

In an instant, everything expanded, releasing the energy of the universe, accelerating outward at unimaginable speeds. As the new universe expanded to a higher and higher volume, the temperature decreased, like Boyle's Law says it would.

This cataclysmic instant occurred some 14 to 15 billion years ago, give or take a few million years. Depending on the velocity of its expansion, you can reckon its size now to be on the order of 10 followed by 24 zeroes miles across....that's a trillion trillion miles! Light, the fastest commodity in all the universe, would need billions of years to travel from end to end!

These are frightfully large numbers if you think about being alone somewhere in its distant midst....but for the presence of Christ Jesus to greet me.

It's like when my children were ten and twelve, and I'd put them on a plane for a long nonstop ride to see grandma and granddad. What joy and relief for the children when they saw their grandparents, waiting to pick them up. You see them standing at the gate, waiting to pick you up! But during the flight, my children might have worried a couple of moments what to do if no one was there to meet them. If you have been let down time and again in your young life by parents or others, I could certainly understand your worry….you'd more or less come to expect disappointment. But if they had been faithful and true, you learned to trust them and to believe their word. I doubt you'd have apprehensions like a few less secure youngsters on the plane.

My experience with God is that He is faithful and true. He takes care of me when I'm too weak to take care of myself. He loves me more than I can comprehend, and wants what is good and right for me. Even when He allows things to come into my life that are difficult, this is His way of preparing me and making me a better person.

All of my experience with God proves to me He will be there to receive me. "There " may be trillions of miles away, or it could be just around the corner. I've no concept of where "there" may be, if it is anyplace at all…maybe Heaven is another dimension of time and space, that can't be marked by location. But I'm certain of one thing….He won't let me get lost!

I'll end by telling you a reality I've come to. It would be vastly more difficult for me to imagine a universe without God. I don't know how atheists do it.

Everything I see or experience shouts out God's love and faithfulness for you and me. He will be there to welcome me home. Time and space pale by comparison….

I'm reminded of Genesis 18:3, in which Abraham invited three strangers to pause and rest from their journey along the dusty road that ran by his home. Abraham had no idea that these three were angels, on a mission from God to destroy the wicked cities of Sodom and Gomorrah. Abraham said, "My Lord, if I find favor with you, do not pass by your servant"…let me give you water and food to eat… Thus was the inspiration for that wonderful old Hymn, "Pass Me Not, O Gentle Savior" by Fanny Crosby, 1868 and Howard Doane,1870. "Pass me not, O gentle Savior, Hear my humble cry; While on others Thou art calling, Do not pass me by"

209

THOUGHTS ON THE RAPTURE AND EVERLASTING LIFE

N othing is too hard for God!

He can reassemble the atoms and molecules of my body to create a new body, fit for eternal life in Heaven. Burning my corpse in cremation and scattering my ashes in the wind won't keep Him from "rapturing" all my parts back together. He will do this! He will do this if I'm buried beneath the sea. He will do this if I'm embalmed and entombed in a casket. I am certain that God will reintegrate my being just as He said He would, no matter how my remains are handled!

You must understand that my soul and yours are different entities from our earthly bodies. We are the only creatures who have souls as well as bodies...animals are without souls. I know this may sound crass, but it is true nonetheless. Sometimes we confuse the issue, saying this is a spirited horse, or my dog has great spirit. It might be well for you to reread my Essay, "Barney and Rufus Won't Be In Heaven", if you have questions about this.

The very instant my earthly body dies, my eternal soul goes to be with God. There's no delay, no waiting around. It happens in a flash! Some speak about "soul sleep" following death of the body....this is rubbish....there is nothing scriptural about soul sleep. The Bible teaches that our souls will remain with God until the return of Jesus Christ to earth, which is described clearly by the Apostle Paul in 1 Thessalonians 4 and 5.

Jesus Christ will be accompanied by the souls of all who've died and gone to be with Him. It will happen in a cataclysmic atmospheric spectacle, above the earth in the clouds with trumpets blasting for all to see and hear. No matter where my body's constituents lie, the Bible teaches they will be raptured into a new imperishable body, fit for all eternity, and mated up with my soul, all in the presence of Christ Jesus!

I believe my new body will be similar in many respects to Jesus' resurrected body, described in all four New Testament Gospels, and my soul will inhabit my new body.

You and I will recognize one another, although our new appearance may be a little different from our earthly forms. Like the resurrected Jesus, we will eat, drink, speak, and enjoy fellowship with others. We will know our loved ones who preceded us, and we will need no introductions. We won't procreate, so I doubt our new bodies will be shaped by genetic codes. And it seems we'll be able to move around instantaneously, without restriction, if Jesus' resurrected body points the way.

Only God Himself knows when all this will take place. I'm happy, knowing I'll be there when it happens!

HE GOT MY ATTENTION

Three different times I have been trapped like a prisoner in my own physical body. Each one was of my own doing and perhaps the doing of the Lord. Three different surgeries required my right foot and leg to be in plaster casts for a total of five months. I was severely incapacitated during these periods, unable to drive a car or get around much for the first time in my seven decades of living. Specifically, if we wanted the bones and tendons to knit together so the operations would be successes, it was essential for me to avoid putting any weight at all on my cast bound right foot and leg. This meant I was basically dependent on Marge for everything.....bathing and cleaning me; preparing all our meals, which troubled me no end as I've always enjoyed being the grocery shopper and meal preparer in our family; loading and unloading a heavy, cumbersome wheelchair in the car trunk for occasional outings; and doing everything else I normally did for us. She, in addition, continued to carry her usual load....keeping up with and paying all our bills, managing our budget and planning ahead.

Never once did she complain. Her quiet, tender patience spoke volumes to me! I'm sure I'd have found much to complain about if I'd been in her shoes.

Initially I was anxious, not wanting to accept my limitations. I hated the plaster cast, feeling like an animal in chains, having to ask for everything. Barry, the surgeon, lifted my spirits, making the cast Aggie Maroon with an aTm logo at the top. I looked forward to bi-weekly visits with him to check my healing progress, getting those all-important x-rays, and getting needed fixes for the cast. Each visit was like passing a gate on a slalom course! Marge always made it a special occasion, and we'd go out for lunch afterward and take in a movie. She was my cheerleader!

I prayed a lot about our circumstances, surprised at the length of time healing required. I'm ashamed to say most of my prayers were asking God for "speedy healing". Asking God to help me accept my circumstances for what they were hadn't occurred to me! And it hadn't struck me that I should be asking God to help me be a blessing to Margery, my surgeon and his staff and all others with whom I came in contact.

Eventually, I realized healing wouldn't be quick. Having lived much of my life by the credo, "I want what I want, and I want it now not later," the very idea of a long period of impairment and healing was jolting.

I decided to begin thanking God for my circumstances, praising Him for "getting my attention". I asked Him to help me grow as a husband, father, human being and as His child through Christ Jesus. I asked God to help me order my life each day to come up with a program of prayer, writing, study, exercise within my limitations, and interactions with others, that would be pleasing to Him and satisfying to me. And above all, to fellowship with me and through the Holy Spirit to guide my prayers.

God answered my humble requests and even gave me more abundantly than I asked! The weeks seemed to start flying by. Each visit to the doctor was a celebration. And I settled into a routine that captured my interests every day. Many years later I still follow this daily program! This helped me set up a "routine", a program for my life.

Like my healing, He didn't get my attention "quick". Only after the third operation did I look forward to the comfort of this routine and began to realize new values in my daily life....even after I was let out of "prison".

And above all else, God gave me peace that exceeded my ability to understand it!

HOW TO BE HAPPY!

E veryone wants to be happy! It's a strange bird indeed who doesn't desire Happiness, though I'm sorry to say there are those who appear not to want it.

I'd like to let you in on a little secret told me by a wise old man twenty five years ago. Unfortunately I heard this after blowing chance after chance for what I thought would bring me Happiness.

He said I should think of Happiness as a stool with three legs. All three legs are required for the stool to be stable. Remove any one of the three and it will topple over. Remove two, and don't even try to make it stand. But you can sit on it with reasonable confidence if all three legs are attached. What are the three essential legs ?

- Someplace to go

- Something to do

- Someone to love

I guarantee Happiness will not prevail in your life if you have only one of these. You might find marginal Happiness from time to time with two. But I've found that maintaining all three affords more or less lasting Happiness!

"Someplace to go" doesn't have to be a fine executive suite high up in a skyscraper…it can be a mechanic's garage, or a little farm. My Happy Place to go these days is to my small, cozy studio where I write and study.

"Something to do" doesn't have to be running a company. It should be something that brings you enjoyment. In my case it's studying, writing and making dinner.

"Someone to love" gets a little more complicated. For me, it's easily the Love of My Life, Margery. Without her, I'd be lost. A pet fills this gap at least temporarily for some. But don't give up…you can find that third leg of the stool!

The concept of the three legged stool is deceptively simple---yet it can be amazingly complex in reality. It's such a fun concept to run with in your mind. Every day, remind yourself of the three legs of your stool. Turn them over in your mind. Be thankful!

If you hold onto the three legs of your stool, in time you'll come to an even more wonderful state....Joy!

GOLDEN RULE PEOPLE

A re you a "Golden Rule Person"?

Do you know any of these "Golden Rule People"?

I try really hard each day to be a "Golden Rule Person". You know, one of the many principles to live by Jesus Christ gave us in his Sermon on the Mount (Matt 7:12): "In everything, do to others as you would have them do to you; for this is the law of the prophets." In a nutshell, this sums up the teachings of Moses.

But, what happens if I continue to deal with others the way I'd like them to treat me, and they treat me shabbily or disrespectfully over and over?

Do I reach a point finally when I decide they themselves want to be treated shabbily because this is the way they always treat me? Sort of the Golden Rule in reverse? Am I to assume that person, like me, is a Golden Rule Person and is simply showing how he wants to be treated?

How does this comport with Jesus' admonition to turn the other cheek when you are slapped (Matt 5:39); or to forgive my brother not just seventy times, but seventy times seven (Matt 18:21)?

I do believe at some point the obverse of the Golden Rule gets the upper hand, and we decide indeed they expect to be treated shabbily!

But prepare yourself for an eruption if you indeed reverse the tables this way, especially if it's with one of your grown children or another close member of your family or friends that are supposedly close. You may be excoriated for treating the other person in a shabby manner, even though that's the sort of treatment they've shown you. You may hear something like, "How dare you treat me that way"!

You could then try to explain you're just a Golden Rule Person. Maybe it'll work, maybe it won't. But both sides will be wiser.

216

KNOWING AND DOING GOD'S WILL

How many times have I said to myself, "I sure wish I knew the will of God in this matter or that." For to know His will in a matter then do it is the ultimate we could ask for.

If you believe as I believe that God has a specific plan for the life of each and every person, all things in my life fit together better if I can know and act in accord with that divine plan.

But I have to be in tune, on the same page, with God to discern His will. I must remember that God wants good things for me, just as my earthly father did...but even more!

He makes His will known to me in many different ways....some are so surprising I least expect them. Sometimes it comes through the words of another person...sometimes through a particular passage of Scripture...maybe once in a while through an idea that gets into my mind...and sometimes when I am praying through a particular matter.

If I am trusting the Lord to guide me, I've got to be sensitive to everything and everyone I pass along the way. My "spiritual ears" have to be trained to listen. I have to tell myself to stop babbling and listen!

Sometimes the Lord has to hit me over the head with a two by four to get my attention...but hopefully not too often!

It just seems like things usually work out when they are supposed to, and they don't when they aren't supposed to.

I usually end up in trouble when I'm so determined to achieve a certain outcome that I force it...sort of like trying to squeeze a round peg into a square hole.

This observation seems to hold true in every aspect of my life, especially in human relationships, work and where and how to live.

Knowing and doing God's will requires all of my senses (sight, sound, smell, taste, touch) in every corner of my life. With each passing day, I am more or less conscious of these aspects as I strive to stay in tune.

Here is my special prayer:

"Lord Jesus, please help me to sense your guidance, every day. Please give me a mind that is clear and discerning of Your leanings, even if they are subtle. Lord please protect me from myself, from my own hard driving hardheadedness, and keep me from straying from Your will. Please help me to know who or what to listen to, and who or what not to. And Lord, I gratefully thank You for that one You have so often used to help me see Your will, Margery."

You may want to develop your own special prayer....

ETERNITY

E verything about Jehovah God absolutely amazes me...I'm at a loss for words to even remotely characterize His magnificence!

Sometimes I think about how time means nothing to God, yet our earthly clocks are at the center of everything in my life and yours. I'm reminded of His timelessness throughout the Bible, from Genesis through Revelation. Moses' prayer in Psalms 90 declares that, "A thousand days to man is but a single day to God." Moses is simply saying that God is timeless! Time means nothing to the Lord!

Moses begins Genesis telling us "In the beginning was God, and the Word was with God...." This means just what it says, that indeed there was a Beginning. And I believe that before this Beginning there was no time, and that God and the Word (i.e. The Lord Jesus) was and is eternal! The "Beginning" was at "time zero".

I don't mean to confuse this important issue by splitting hairs---I realize that "timelessness" and the "non-existence of time" are two entirely different matters. God's "clock" either goes on and on and on ad infinitum, throughout all the past and into all the future; or, there is no such thing as God's "clock"...meaning that "time doesn't exist" to God. Just try to imagine what the absence of time means---God would look at me and instantaneously see all my past and all my future before Him in one fell swoop! It's admittedly easier for me to get my hands around the concept of an eternal, everlasting "time clock of God" than it is the idea of the "non-existence" of time. I readily admit this could be because of my limitations as a human being.

Still, I am promised "life eternal" by trusting in Jesus as my Lord and Savior, by John 3:16. My soul is "eternal" and through my soul I expect to live eternally with God in whatever system of "time" He has chosen. If there is no time in God's Heaven, that's just the way it is, and I expect to rejoice in it and be glad!

God in His wisdom used a non-Christian Jew, Albert Einstein, to show us a glimpse of timelessness, which is a profound mystery. His remarkable work revealed, among other things, that time stands still if one could move at the speed of light, 186,000 miles every second. Yet at this velocity, Einstein showed that your body mass would be infinite and would be infinitesimally tiny! Hard to imagine, is it not!

Yet it's no harder to imagine than why God set the inviolable speed of light throughout all creation at a remarkable 186,000 miles per second, no matter if the light source is moving with or against the current! This speed would whizz you completely around the earth at the equator an amazing $7^1/_2$ times in only a single second! In just one minute, you'd travel 11 million miles! To reach our sun at this speed takes about $8^1/_2$ minutes. Beginning now to get the idea that God's universe is an awfully large place?

Imagine yourself with a watch on your wrist, speeding along on a rocket ship at, say, $^6/_{10}$ths the velocity of light, while your earthbound brother, wearing his watch, observes you in the distance. Both watches were set at the same identical time at your departure. You and your brother compare your watches upon your return to earth, and to both your amazement your watch showed you were away on your trip much less time than your brother's watch shows. This leads to a ridiculous argument over how long you were away…ridiculous because both of you are correct! You simply obeyed Einstein's Laws of Relativity.

Taken to its limit, we see that Energy and Mass are interchangeable, expressed by Einstein's familiar $E = mc^2$.

So that in the very "beginning" all mass of God's universe was crammed into a tiny bundle, think of it as the size of a pea, and it contained virtually an infinite quantity of energy….and time did not exist. Yet God and the Word (Jesus) were there!

When my soul and yours go to be with God, our souls will be eternal, whether time exists with Him or not. Our souls will then live in God's dimension, in His space. Hard to understand? The most complex things to the mind of man are but foolishness to God.

PRAYER

Matt 6: 6-8 (pray in private).....

Matt 6:9-13 (the model Lord's Prayer)....

Rom 8: 26-27 (we don't know what to pray for)....

Matt 6:33 + (seek first the Kingdom of God and His righteousness)....

Have you ever just got down on your knees, asking God to let you get to know Him better? Or to just enrich your relationship with Him? Or to ask Him to help you trust and love Him more to the point of loving the Lord your God with all your heart and all your might? I call this a "process prayer".

Or, are you too busy asking God for certain outcomes in particular circumstances in your life?....Oh Lord, please let this or that thing happen....a new job, a pay raise, a new car, a new wife, a new house, and on and on. This is what I call "outcomes prayer".

Compare "outcomes praying" to what I call "process prayer". You have to admit, these are two very different kind of prayer....one, asking for deeper relationship with God, through Christ our Savior....the second is praying for outcomes, to let something turn out in a particular way.

I believe most prayer by far is of the "outcomes" type. I have to admit I have spent much of my born again life praying for "outcomes". Eventually I came to realize that God wants me to "get to know Him" better. He wants to have a deeper, richer fellowship with me. He wants me to trust Him with the "outcome"....I'm certainly in no position to demand what I want, though God honors my right to humbly request, as I recognize His sovereignty.

It brings me peace, in fact, to trust the outcome to God. My part is to love God, to be faithful to His Word, to fellowship with Him and to be open for Him to fellowship with little me!

Scripture makes it crystal clear He wants to give me "good gifts". Romans 8:28 tells me, for example, that... "All things work together for the good of those that love the Lord..."

I've too often behaved like a spoiled brat, wanting what I want, sulking, maybe even angry when the outcome was not what I wanted and expected! I would have been more content if I had truly trusted Him with the outcome.

But trusting God this way tests my faith. Is my faith such that I'm able and willing to let go and trust Him to give the outcome that's best for me? Remember, faith is so powerful that God reckons it the same as righteousness!

The Word of God says that I receive not, because I ask amiss…I pray for the wrong things and in the wrong way. Is this a reminder I should be praying more process-wise, less outcomes-wise?

My world would undoubtedly be a happier more satisfying place if I could let up on so much outcome-orientation with God while growing in my love of Him, our fellowship together and my willing to trust the outcomes to His loving hands. God's "outcomes" many times are hard for me to swallow, because they went against the grain in terms of my particular wants and desires…I didn't get that job I wanted…someone just got sicker and sicker and didn't recover…my family problems didn't go away, maybe they even got worse…etc. As I ask God to grant me a certain "outcome", I need to ask Him for the strength, grace and gratitude to accept, live with, handle whatever outcome He gives me. I need to ask God to help me this way each and every day!

TRILLIONS OF SOULS!

I was struck with an almost unholy thought when I recently saw pictures on the evening TV Newscast of throngs of impoverished, hungry men, women and children in barrios and slum infested hillsides, crowded into several large cities in Latin America. My unholy thought was:

"Doesn't God care about those poor people? Does He love me more than these? I certainly seem to be enjoying more of His mercies and largess than those impoverished unfortunates".

After catching myself thinking this way, it came to me that God loves each and every one of us the same...and that each and every one of us has a soul, precious to God....that Christ Jesus died and rose from the tomb for all of us.

Then I thought, "I wonder how many have lived and died since the beginning". All must have had souls, and all were precious to the Lord....if my soul and the souls of all the living are precious to Him, it follows that the souls of all who've gone before are just as precious. It must be an almost staggeringly large number!

I decided to make an estimate, integrating under a notional graph of population versus time, say since the time of Adam and Eve maybe 7000 or so years ago. (Please don't hold me to a scale of absolute accuracy, lest you miss the point I'm trying to make).

Can you imagine I came up with an estimate of at least One Trillion, and maybe more! I'm talking about human beings like you and me. Each had a soul which was precious to God! Just try to visualize that immense number of souls...it's one thousand billion....and it could even be greater, depending on the accuracy of my assumptions....maybe Ten Trillion or more! It may be safe to say that a range of 1-10 trillion souls have lived and walked the face of this planet. That's a multiple of the Six Billion or so souls now populating planet Earth! The Bible tells us that God had a plan in mind for each and every life.

Our Lord keeps track of them all, even down to the details of our genetic codes, and the numbers of hairs on each of our heads. Nothing I can imagine is too hard for Him.

CONSTANTS AND VARIABLES

"God, grant me the serenity to accept the things I cannot change, courage to change the things I can, and wisdom to know the difference."

Alcoholics Anonymous, "The Serenity Prayer"

This short, magnificent prayer asks the Lord to help us wisely divine between the "things I cannot change" (i.e. life's Constants, more or less); and the " things I can" (think of these as life's Variables, more or less).

Often lacking in discernment, you and I tend to get the "Constants "and "Variables" confused, mixed up. We too often mount an all-out drive to change things or situations we can't change. Then we may pitch a fit in our disappointment!

Mathematicians understand well the inscrutable search for "universal constants", like Pi or C. In turn, one must always be cognizant of the variables which must be separated to solve equations.

I for one have wasted much valuable time trying to convert some human "Constant" into a copacetic "Variable" who would be more to my liking, seeing things my way. The result is usually like trying to make a stream flow uphill instead of down; or like pushing the end of a wet noodle.

I'll forever more be praying the old tried and true Serenity Prayer, working to become more skilled at discerning the difference between Constants and Variables....the things I can reasonably expect to change, and the things I cannot.

SATAN AND EVIL HAD TO BE....

W hy, in the beautiful world God created, must Satan and evil run rampant? Wouldn't it be an absolutely wonderful world if the Devil, his Angels and all their evil didn't exist? Has our loving God, all knowing and all powerful, allowed Satan to run rampant in the lives of men and women wreaking havoc, causing bad things to happen to them----"bad things sometimes happen to good people".

Wrestling with this philosophical conundrum for a long time, I eventually copped out by telling myself, "That's just God's way".

Then one morning, God opened my mind while I studied through Genesis for the umpty umpth time. I hadn't seen it in this light before---

By creating man "in God's own image" (Gen 1:27), He made us with the capacity to choose, empowering you and me with enormous powers of reasoning. This power of analysis undergirds and enhances our ability to choose.... "And let them rule over the fish of the sea, birds of the air, livestock, over all the earth, and over all the creatures that move along the ground".

"So God created man in His own image, in the very image of Himself He created him---male and female He made them, and set them up to have dominion over, i.e. to rule, the world and everything in it"! Wow and double Wow!

No other creature or being of any kind bears the Image of God--- not dogs, cats, horses, fish, birds or any other living thing, on earth or anywhere else in God's vast cosmos.

It follows then that men and women are the only creatures with the capacity to discern between "Right" and "Wrong", intelligently choosing between them. Goats, deer, sheep, dogs and cats do not have mine and your ability to discern. Animals can be induced, coaxed, trained or even beaten to make them behave a certain way---even so, he will always be driven by instinct to satisfy his immediate needs (i.e. hunger, sex, fear etc.). He has no sense of right and wrong --- he doesn't naturally know right from wrong.

If this is true, the animal is Sinless --- He simply cannot commit Sin! The Old Testament teaches us that animals were sacrificed at the Temple as an offering to the Lord. The animals were without the stain of sin—they were sinless, and as such were acceptable as sacrifices to the Lord.

If God created you and me in His image, given the faculty to choose, to divine between good and bad, right and wrong, we absolutely MUST be able to choose between Good and Evil. It would not be consistent with God's image if I could ONLY choose between or among the Good....If I were constitutionally incapable of choosing Bad or Evil.

So it was ESSENTIAL for us to be able to opt for the Bad, Evil option. Else we wouldn't be "in God's own image", free to choose.

God underscored this aspect of creation, placing the "Tree of the Knowledge of Good and Evil" in the Garden of Eden, along with the "Tree of Life" (Gen 2:9). But He admonished the man NOT to eat from the perverse Tree of Knowledge, even BEFORE woman appeared, because "if you do, you will surely die (Gen 2:16-17).

So from the beginning, God made it possible for you and me to choose to obey Him or not, to choose between good and evil. Otherwise mankind wouldn't have borne God's own image!

Now this brings us to another philosophical dilemma...could God in fact choose to do evil? I believe the answer is a resounding YES! Jesus told us that He and God are ONE... "you've seen Me, you've seen the Father". We are told that Christ Jesus was tempted in every way like we are tempted, but HE DIDN'T YIELD TO SIN. Being pure, free of the stain of sin, Jesus Christ was the acceptable sacrifice for my sin and yours, for all time. Sinless Christ did at one time what generations and generations of animal sacrifices could never do, to be the perfect propitiation for my sin, once for all time!

He could have chosen to sin, but He did not! Matthew 4 provides a remarkably lucid discussion of Satan's attempts to trip Jesus up, causing him to stumble. If Jesus is indeed a third of the Triune God, then God also HIMSELF resisted Satan's beguiling attempts. That Jesus remained sinless enabled HIM to become the perfect human sacrifice, once, for all people and all time, taking upon Himself all the sins ever committed by mankind! He wouldn't have been the perfectly acceptable sacrifice for you, me and all mankind if he had succumbed to the wiles of the Devil.

If I was truly made in the image of God, I have to be able to choose---- to opt between Right and Wrong, good and bad, obedience and evil.

MANAGING EXPECTATIONS

I never even thought about this idea before being introduced to it by my mentor at BDM Corporation, Dr. Dan McDonald, during the 1980's. Dr. Dan, BDM's co- founder, was a superb practitioner of the art of "managing expectations", a vital skill in the technical support contracting and engineering consulting world in which BDM was a major player.

Clients inevitably expect the contractor to deliver more than promised, even faster. So the not-so-skilled program manager finds himself sometimes in great difficulty with an unhappy customer. Construction contractors and even Medical Doctors often encounter the very same dilemma. Sometimes we promise more than we can actually deliver to win the contract or get a piece of business in the first place. Unless steps are taken in the beginning to shape and begin to realistically manage what the customer is expecting, you may soon find yourself at an uncomfortable loggerhead!

While learning to practice this art under Dr. Dan's watchful eye, I'm still learning to "manage expectations" well beyond the business realm where I was schooled. I'm discovering, for example, that "managing my own expectations" usually is as important as managing the expectations of others!

Let's face it---disappointment nearly always results from falling short of what's expected, either because someone didn't measure up to what you expected, or you didn't measure up yourself.

In most business dealings, expectations are spelled out in contract language. Still it's amazing how often customer/provider relationships sour because something wasn't spelled out clearly or was somehow misinterpreted by one party or the other. In everyday dealings, expectations are simply verbalized, or sometimes just assumed based on an unspoken standard.

This applies to our everyday dealings with our wives, husbands, boy or girlfriends, our children, bosses, peers, friends and co-workers.

I've learned that it's always better to confirm, verbally, joint understandings of expected outcomes---take the time up front to say "Do we both agree that the result will be X, Y and Z"?

Just taking a few minutes to clear up and be sure of expectations at the very beginning of any relationship or situation pays huge dividends! Then be upfront enough to deal with things anytime they start to get off track. Bring it up to the other side without delay---don't just sweep it under the rug, or think it will go away. Go to the effort to be clear---don't let things sour.

Managing my own expectations is vitally important, and is often the lynchpin in my own happiness or unhappiness, my own joy or disappointment.

CHARACTER

C haracter is what I do when nobody is looking!

Even my secret thoughts go into building or tearing down my Character. My secret actions certainly are aspects of my Character, good or bad. Yes, the littlest things you and I do count one way or the other.

Did the clerk give me back too much change after checking me out? Did I pocket the overage, or did I point out the mistake?

Did I wrongfully make use of "stolen" data or information in a transaction of some kind?

Have I misused personal information I came into about another person? Have I broken a trust? Did I snoop into someone's personal data or information, maybe their cell phone or their personal files, when I had the chance?

Did I steal something that seemed trivial at the time? Did I take something that didn't belong to me when I thought nobody was looking?

Did I lie to cover up my wrong-doing? Did I pass the blame onto others to hide my mistake?

Did I cheat on that exam when I thought I could get away with it?

Have I made ill-gotten gains on a business deal by cheating somebody?

Did I turn a blind eye, and by doing so, condone bad (un-Christ like) behavior? I've learned to say: "I see what you are doing, and to me it's not right. I do not respect your right to make that decision".

Have I come to the point of realizing that God's Holy Spirit is with me 24/7 and never, never leaves me? Can I possibly realize that I can never think, say or do anything absent God's Holy Spirit? Or does that even matter to me?

We tend to judge politicians by "How they say what they say and how they look saying it". But shouldn't I be much more concerned about the true Character of the man or woman I'm about to vote for? What

229

"secret things" does that man or woman harbor? What's the candidate's true Character? "I'd like you to give me some examples of your good character".

I want to be represented by people of good Character---not just a correct vision, or a charismatic style, or a powerful appearance. How often have you ever heard "Character" mentioned in political campaigns? Or in hiring? Or is Character just old fashioned, passé, out of date?

My dad was an honest man. Unashamedly, he said he'd rather be honest, poor and of good Character than a rich liar or cheat. He was willing to sacrifice money to maintain character. He was an unusual man!

RESURRECTION

S uppose you and I were two flies on a celestial wall, looking down on a world in which everybody believes "When you die, you die, that's it, it's all over---you're gone, there's no life ever after"! The people in this awful world obviously don't believe each of us has an indestructible, eternal soul---that eternal component of our being.

Why would these people have any reason to be caring, decent, considerate beings? Why would the needs and feelings of others matter at all? Wouldn't it just be a dog eat dog world, each person for himself, getting anything and everything by any and every possible means?

Kind of beginning to sound like it's an "animal world", doesn't it. Actually it's a soulless world.

All my waking hours would be spent giving myself all the ease and luxury I could amass while fending off the onslaughts of others, wanting what I have amassed. Everybody would be busy trying to take it from me. And I'd probably stay awake at night, scheming about who I could take what from to add to my stash!

How could I ever get any rest, any sleep? I couldn't trust anyone, even my own flesh and blood!

Who could possibly want to live in a world like this? Certainly not I!

But our amazing world is inhabited by both kinds of people---those who believe "It's over when it's over"; and those who believe in eternal life. Admittedly there are many, many "lukewarmists" out there, seemingly content to say "I just don't know".

I submit that those non-believers, if you could dig deeply into their psyche, would not like living in a world of like-minded beings. They want to live in a world where there are "enough of us who believe". They want to live in an orderly society where there aren't "too many of them" compared to us. That way they can do wrong and maybe get away with it without having to fend off attackers every minute of every day.

Just ask one of them if he'd like to live in a world where everybody believes as he does. If he can think about your question even superficially, the answer is NO!

This Easter Season, I've declared with every fiber of my being that the DEATH and RESURRECTION of JESUS the CHRIST is the most important event in all history!

Jesus gives us unquestionable proof that ETERNAL LIFE FOLLOWS OUR BODILY DEATH! I expect my resurrected being to possess the kind of properties Jesus manifested in his resurrected state. Read the exciting 24th Chapter of Luke, which describes Jesus' eleven appearances as the resurrected Christ.

RESURRECTION 2

I want to tell you up front that the purpose of this Essay is to strengthen your faith that Jesus Christ, after suffering humiliation, torture, then death on the cross, arose from the tomb and returned to life.

Please refer to the passages of Scripture in Luke 22:47-71, and the entirety of Luke Chapters 23 and 24. The sweeping events described in these passages, and His resurrection, i.e. His return from death to life, is absolutely central to Christian faith. Refer to the Book of Acts of the Apostles, especially the first three Chapters to see for yourself how men and women were literally propelled into fearless action, spreading the Gospel message across Judea and eventually the world after they experienced the resurrected Christ.

The bottom line of this Essay is that His resurrection was the impetus, the spark needed to impel ordinary men and women to go forth, spreading the news about Jesus the Messiah.... that Jesus truly was the promised Christ, that He was whom He said He was, the Son of God, empowered to heal and forgive sins, the Savior of the world. Without Jesus' resurrection, why would anyone have risked his life and the lives of his family? This fact, more than any other, proves that Jesus returned to life after His death on the cross. Because of this, Christianity and the church have survived, expanded and thrived for almost twenty centuries throughout the world, just as Jesus commanded in   Matt 28:19-20.

Think with me about the events that took place during the Passover celebration in Jerusalem almost 2,000 years ago, beginning on Friday, the 15th of Nisan (April 6, 30 C.E.). Jesus was arrested late at night at a garden partway up the Mount of Olives, opposite the city of Jerusalem. He went there with his disciples to pray after their Passover Supper in the city. It was a bit of a hike to get there late at night, in the darkness, on a full stomach. I suspect that someone in their group carried a torch, else the moon must have been bright enough to light their way. They trudged down a fairly steep trail from the Eastern wall of the city, across the Kidron Brook on the valley floor, then continued up a path on the lower part of the Mount of Olives to reach a Garden called Gethsemane. This is where they often met. Torch lights and lanterns flickered here and there in the sleeping city across the Kidron half a mile away. His followers were tired, their eyelids were heavy, and they had trouble staying awake while Jesus prayed.

Finally a mob carrying torches and weapons showed up to arrest Jesus, with none other than one of His own, the traitor Judas Iscariot pointing the way. After a brief discussion, Jesus was led away for a highly uncustomary night time trial for His alleged "crimes".

Peter, as far as we know, after an altercation with one of the mob, was the only disciple with enough "courage" to follow to see where they were taking Jesus. Everybody else scattered in fear for their lives. Even Peter's arguable "courage" disappeared as he denied knowing Jesus three times when onlookers, warming by a fire outside the trial, pointed fingers at him. Jesus' other followers hid out then sought safety in the hinterlands. A few including John, "the disciple He loved" and Mary Magdalene, laid low around the city---we know this because they showed up after He was nailed to the cross. Some of the others went north to Galilee, returning to their families and livelihoods.

It wasn't even His own followers who, with permission from Pilate, took His body before nightfall on the 15th of Nisan and prepared it for the tomb. This was done by Joseph, a closet believing member of the powerful ruling council; and another wealthy believer, Nicodemus. After washing the body, they wrapped it with strips of linen with fragrant spices tucked into the folds. He was laid in a freshly hewn tomb belonging to Joseph. A large stone was rolled into place to secure the crypt. I doubt these two men ever witnessed firsthand the miracles He performed.

His disciples had lived with Him day and night for three years and had been privy to one miracle after another. Still, they doubted! They may have thought it was all over, after His death. All must have feared for their lives, knowing that Jesus had been tortured during the farcical hearing; beaten to a bloody pulp within an inch of His life by a professional Roman lictor in the wee hours of the morning; then put to death in the most humiliating and painful way imaginable. Who among His followers would choose to suffer such a diabolical fate? Reasonable people might believe they could be in for the same kind of treatment Jesus got!

None of them was "guilty" of "committing crimes against the established Synagogical order and the State." They fled out of fear for their lives! Who is to say the Roman Legions wouldn't come looking for them next? Jesus was the one who "forgave sin", claiming to be so empowered; they didn't. He was the one who claimed to be God's own Son. It was He who claimed to be a King whose Kingdom was not of this world. After all, this claim posed a threat to the Emperor, his Rome based Empire and his lackeys in Judea. It was He who called the Temple Rulers all kinds of names, like vipers and "white washed walls", and turned over the tables of money changers in the Temple courts. Why did His disciples run for cover when it was Jesus who committed these "egregious crimes", not they? They must feared being accused of aiding and abetting Jesus, which could make them "guilty by association". They were accomplices as Jesus committed these "crimes". Now their leader and champion had been put to death, and they were alone.

The truth of the matter is: they didn't really understand or believe the vision He gave them about precisely what was going to happen to Him and His promises to return from the grave after three days (see Mark 10:33-34). They thought their three year adventure with Jesus was all over and done with. And what an exciting three years it had been!

The city was crowded with hundreds of thousands of visitors that 15th of Nisan afternoon to celebrate the Passover. Every available room in Jerusalem was taken, and others overflowed to camp out on the Mount of Olives and other areas around the city. Many knew about the three public crucifixions that took place that day. Many were afraid, some were appalled, and many were indifferent. All must have experienced the widespread physical upheavals that day---the sky blackened like night for three hours; the earth shook with a quake; the large hanging tapestry dividing the "Holy Place" from the "Holy of Holies" in the Temple ripped from top to bottom; and some claimed to have seen ghosts — spirits of the dead — in and around the city! Many that day must have been gripped by awe and fear!

Then the miracle of all miracles happened in the early morning hours of the 17th of Nisan! Mary Magdalene and other women brought fresh spices to the tomb to clean and freshen Jesus' body. Somehow they learned where His body had been laid. Approaching the tomb, they were shocked to find the large sealing stone rolled away from the crypt and Jesus' body was not there. Two angelic figures in gleaming clothing announced that He was risen and good naturedly chided the women for "looking for the living among the dead". Then it struck them that Jesus had told them exactly what was going to happen, including His promise to return from the grave after three days (see Matt 26:31-32, Mark 14:27-28).

They hurried back and announced their amazing discovery to a group of His followers. Peter and others hurried to the tomb, confirming what the women had seen. One by one, the eleven became convinced that they were truly experiencing the resurrected Jesus Christ! Even Thomas Dydimus, "the doubter" got convinced.

For the next forty days, He appeared to His disciples many times, and again performed amazing miracles in their presence. During one visitation, He breathed the Holy Spirit, the Great Comforter, out over and upon His followers.

He was seen by at least 5,000 before leaving earth for His home in Heaven at the Throne of God.

Now here's the clincher for all time and all Christendom! His followers feared for their lives during Christ's trial and crucifixion. But after experiencing His resurrection, these same men and women threw caution to the wind and went public, aggressively proclaiming the good news about Christ. They knew their actions were tantamount to committing suicide! Their message was that Jesus was whom He said He was---the Risen Lord, the Son of God! They were risking their lives, and they knew it.

These were men and women who could reason and analyze. They certainly weren't going to foolishly throw their lives away, and they certainly didn't want to become victims suffering the kinds of nightmarish treatment Jesus got. Yet they went everywhere, proclaiming the message of Salvation through Jesus Christ. And they knew torture and death could come to them, but they went ahead anyway. They carried the Gospel of Jesus Christ throughout Judea and the region.

Some were martyred because they proclaimed the Gospel of Jesus Christ. Peter's price was to suffer crucifixion in Rome, tradition says upside down. Paul was beheaded. Young Stephen was stoned to death in Jerusalem. Some were fed to wild animals. John died in isolation on Patmos. Countless numbers of Saints have paid the supreme price over the centuries for one reason only--- they proclaimed that Jesus Christ was and is Lord and Savior.

Today's church of Jesus Christ, now worldwide, is rooted in those men and women 2,000 years ago who saw Him resurrected from death's tomb. They saw living proof that He was all He claimed to be. And they staked their own lives on His everlasting message of Salvation!

How can I doubt, as one of more than a trillion souls to have lived on this earth, that Jesus Christ was resurrected and that He offers me that peace, which goes beyond earthly comprehension, now and forever more. It is a joy of vision that is greater than the beauty of any and all colors and shapes; a joy of sound that transcends all melodies or the spoken word; a joy that encompasses my very being.

CAN I LOSE MY SALVATION?

"It is by the prince of demons (Satan) that he drives out demons" (Matt 9:34).

"...the Pharisees said, "It is only by Beelzebub, the prince of demons, that this fellow drives out demons" (Matt 12:24).

"And so I tell you, every sin and blasphemy will be forgiven men, but the blasphemy against the Spirit will not be forgiven. Anyone who speaks a word against the Son of Man (Jesus himself) will be forgiven, but anyone who speaks against the Holy Spirit will not be forgiven, either in this age or the age to come (Matt 12:31,32).

Jesus was endlessly harassed and lambasted by Pharisees and "religious officials". After healing a blind, mute demon possessed man, the event described by Jesus' Disciple Matthew tells us a group of Pharisees witnessing this miracle had the temerity to confront Jesus, telling the other witnesses that it was only by calling on Satan's powers to cast out demons that the man was made whole!

Aware of their derision, Jesus basically said, you may call me what you want, but ascribing works of the Holy Spirit of God to the Devil is unforgiveable now and in all eternity.

Central to the entire Bible is a deep-seated truth---God hates sin. This means THERE WILL BE NO SIN OR UNFORGIVEN SINNERS IN HEAVEN! Jesus tells you and me very clearly in Matthew that all sins are forgivable EXCEPT--- the sin of crediting Satan with works that are accomplished by the Hand of God!

Once I profess my faith in Christ Jesus, trusting Him to save me, now and forevermore, can I fall away and be lost to perdition?

I admit that this question sometimes troubled me as I progressed through some of life's Dark Valleys after I had yielded to temptation. Would the Lord still love me? Could He possibly forgive me? Have I lost my home in Heaven?

That I was born again, a new creature in Christ, on that April 14th day in 1974 has never, never been a question in my mind.

Then for about twenty years, I lived, worked and walked in the world, believing and trusting my salvation, yet still struggling with some of the old aspects of my life.... lust, greed, and alcohol. I remained undoubtedly cut-throat in business, determined to win at all costs.

Ashamed, I admit that more than once I wondered if the salvation I'd experienced in 1974 was still there for me. How could I have experienced the new birth in Christ Jesus if I sometimes lived like the devil? Inevitably, I'd return to a realization that I had truly been reborn, a new creature in Christ. If you insist on proof, I'm sorry, I can't give it to you--- I just knew it in my heart. Still at times, I was tormented! When I found myself struggling, I found reassurance reading the Apostle Paul's account of his personal struggles (Rom 7:14-28).

The fact was, I was saved but hadn't fully yielded to the Master----I continued to hold out for myself. I mightn't have been so conflicted if I'd never heard the Word of God and His Message of Salvation in the first place! I knew when I did wrong because I came under conviction, just as Paul explains. Alas, I was a double-minded man, saved yet holding out for myself!

The long and short of it is I WILL NOT AND CANNOT LOSE MY SALVATION! I will not attribute the works of God to Satan. I will avoid sorcery, sorceresses, fortune tellers, so-called Black Magic and Ouija Boards! I will not worship the "starry hosts" scattered by the hands of God across the heavens! And I will assiduously avoid worshipping the creation instead of the Creator, the Lord God!

Yielding to Him sure makes the walk with the Lord easier, with greater peace than I can sometimes understand... and vastly richer!

THOUGHTS ABOUT FAMILY

I always wanted to have a picture perfect "All American Family"....you know Mom, Dad and a couple of scrubbed, cotton topped smiling kids....families like you see around tables in a breakfast shop, each with a pile of pancakes, on Saturday morning.

I tried and tried and tried some more to make this a reality. But divorce, family breakup and often acrimonious circumstances aren't much help. In fact, it puts everybody in the family, and close friends as well, through Post Matrimonial Hell. Little wonder, GOD HATES DIVORCE (Mark10:1-12)! Divorce is an unkind and terribly messy thing that damages children and usually everyone involved...I know this first hand!

As the years passed and my fortunes improved, I continued to pursue my dreams for that united All American Family, complete with Grandma and Grandpa the proud patriarchs; adult children; and wonderful, obedient, respectful grandchildren, all nearby, sharing joys, sorrows, and celebrating Holidays together....You know, like all good families do!

Margery and I love each of them and are so proud of them all. Yet, in spite of all our best efforts, we are scattered over considerable distances from one another, like ever so many modern families. We are thankful every day for the miracle of cell phones, computers, reliable automobiles and great highways for long distance travel, and sometimes airplanes when bad weather makes driving too hazardous for two oldsters!

I continued to plead with the Lord to somehow bring my disparate family together, still dreaming of that All American Unity. And so I continued my "outcome" type of prayer: "Please Lord, give me a perfect family..." Never mind what His will is. Never mind the imperfect definition of a "Perfect Family". Never mind the absurdity of such "perfection". Certainly this seems like a noble, upstanding thing to pray about....I'm sure the Lord will honor my prayer and eventually grant my wishes. Not once did I ask Him His will in this matter!

Suddenly it was Mother's Day Sunday. Margery and I sat in our usual spot at morning church service. Stair-stepped All American Families filled the pews ahead of us...we were in the rear of the sanctuary. Practically every pew ahead of us was occupied by three, sometimes four generations of families. Marge and I were "odd men out" that morning. The two of us sat sans familia in a sanctuary that was chock-a- block with families I'd always envied. They would enjoy the church service together, they would obviously go to Grandma's and Grandpa's for a three or more generational meal, brothers, sisters, aunts, uncles, cousins....everybody!

Then it struck me Holidays were like that too! The food would be prepared to perfection. Smiles on all the faces would dazzle a toothpaste commercial. Not a single family member would be in trouble, in some kind of disagreement with other family members, or unable to "pitch in" for family activities.

We'd been invited many times to join other family gatherings like this, since our own family was so far away. And we were happy to be included. This was really nice when, sometimes, we weren't able to be nearer our own for the occasion.

Then it hit me like a ton of bricks! So help me, I heard God say to me, "Martin, stop envying all these families and being jealous of them. For now, I want you right where you are"!

Tears welled up in my eyes, and I heard that old Hymn, "Just as I am without one plea, but that Thy blood was shed for me. Fightings within, fightings without, O Lamb of God, I come. I come."

I remembered that every day in my prayers, all those on my list are seniors our ages, patriarchal and matriarchal in their families, and each family spans multiple generations, filling those pews on special Sunday mornings.

The Lord showed me that I was jealous, even to the point of envy, of these blessed hierarchical families, maybe even angry that they'd been blessed with something I hadn't in spite of all my efforts. Then I felt ashamed because of my envy and jealousy. I silently confessed these feelings to the Lord as Margery and I sat quietly at the back of the church. I thanked God for all those families and for just letting me be there at that moment. And I thanked the Lord for all of our family, in all of their circumstances, whether near or far away.

My spirits were lifted, and I shared my experience with Margery on the drive home. Together, we recognized that none of these families is "perfect". They just suck it up and pull together through their differences. And like our family, they celebrate special occasions together several times a year.

A MORNING PRAYER

O Lord, please forgive me for going off the deep end in despair when I've asked you for something, time and time again, and it doesn't go my way.

It's obvious that I haven't yet learned that You, in Your Sovereignty, have the final say in all things.

Please forgive me because I've tried time and again to make You into some kind of "Spiritual Santa Claus". Please help me to grow up as a Follower of Your Son, Jesus.

Teach me, O Lord, to trust You in all things as You lead me down Life's Highway. I know, Lord, there are rapturous joys and deep calamities along this road. Help me to hold onto You as I experience both.

Please help me, Lord, as I struggle to internalize in my heart and being the testimony of your servant, Paul, who said in his Letter to the Romans, Chapter 8 verse 28: "All things work together for the good of those that love the Lord and are called according to His purposes". I struggle to manifest these words in my being, Lord, when I am disappointed.

Too often, Lord, I've gotten upset and angry when things didn't work out the way I wanted. I've sometimes behaved like a spoiled, petulant child, and I ask You to forgive me.

Lord, I confess that some disappointments are hard for me to bear, especially when the lives of those I love are affected. Please help me, Father, as I struggle with even the deepest calamities. Help me to remember, Lord, that You are with me whatever comes my way. You, Father, are with me, giving me strength and life even as tears of sorrow flow down my cheeks.

Thank you, Father, for giving me this day and all the tomorrows, to live life with You through its ups and downs, its joys and sorrows.

Amen

THE MIRACLE OF COMPOUND INTEREST

P hysicist Albert Einstein said, "Compound Interest is a universal miracle" ...because compound interest creates something from virtually nothing! Not even the well-known First Law of Thermodynamics can achieve the likes of Compound Interest!

Dear Reader, I don't want you to get lost in the mathematics of Compound Interest, so I promise to be straightforward in explaining it...so, please bear with me. I deliberately belabor several key points to be sure we have communicated properly.

Everything about Compound Interest flows to and from the following equation:

(1) $A_n = A_0 (1+r)^n$

This simply relates how an amount invested "now" at time zero, A_0, grows over time — years, months, etc. —to become and amount, A_n, when compounded at some interest rate r.

Equation (1) is a simple algebraic expression whose beauty is that it can be manipulated in many ways...by specifying any three variables, you can solve for the fourth. For example, if we know A_0, the initial amount to be invested; r, the rate of the interest it will earn; and n, the time period the investment will be compounded, we can calculate A_n, to determine what the amount invested will be worth at the end of the time period n.

Another extremely useful manipulation is to calculate r, the rate of interest, which would be required to satisfy a given investment growth over a specific period of time. Say for example I have an amount A_0 to invest and I want to grow to A_n after n years of compounding. Wouldn't it be useful to know the interest rate, r, that would cause this to happen. (We call this the "internal interest rate" — much more on this later).

Another example: just think of the value of being able to calculate how long, n, an investment. A_0, must be held to double in value at a particular rate of interest.

Modern hand held calculators such as the HP or TI BA II (which I prefer) can be used to greatly simplify these calculations. Or for those diehards intent on doing things the old fashioned way, logarithmic functions and tables can be used in solving the following equation in logarithmic form:

(1A) $$\text{Log } A_n = \text{Log } A_0 + n\text{Log } (1+r)$$

Note that this is the same as Equation (1) shown earlier...it's just expressed logarithmically. I strongly suggest using a hand held calculator with financial functions!

———

Now I want to show you the derivation of the all-important Equation (1). By getting familiar with these basics, you will understand how Equation (1) comes about, so you'll become more proficient in its use. Specifically, I want you to grow comfortable with the whole cabal of "the time value of money"...present value, future value, internal rate of return, etc.

Let A_0 be the amount to be invested at time zero. Let A_1 be the amount that A_0 has grown to after just one compounding period (say one year). Let r be the rate of interest earned by A_0 over the compounding period. So, after one compounding period we get the following,

$$A_1 = A_0 + rA_0 = A_0 (1+r)$$

Now let's see what A_2 would be like, starting with A_0 initially and compounding for two periods (years):

$A_2 = A_1 + rA_1$

But $\qquad\qquad\qquad\qquad$ $A_1 = A_0 + rA_0$

So, $\qquad\qquad\qquad\qquad$ $A_2 = (A_0 + rA_0) + r(A_0 + rA_0)$

Then, $\qquad\qquad\qquad\qquad$ $A_2 = A_0 + rA_0 + rA_0 + r^2A_0$

$A_2 = A_0 + 2rA_0 + r^2A_0$

$A_2 = A_0 (1+2r+r^2)$

Then simplifying $\qquad\qquad$ $A_2 = A_0 (1+r)(1+r)$

So, $\qquad\qquad\qquad\qquad$ $A_2 = A_0 (1+r)^2$

It follows that after three compounding periods,

$A_3 = A_0 (1+r)^3$

So this means in general, $\qquad$ $A_n = A_0 (1+r)^n$

Which is our old friend, Equation (1).

Equation (1) is a phenomenally important relationship. It is used extensively in real world business and investment analysis, and its philosophical implications are profound. For example, how true it is of many things that "glory now/rewards now" trumps "glory and rewards delayed". Think about it... giving me something now instead of say two years from now gives me a two year jump on what I can do with it. It - whatever "it" is — is worth more to me right now than "it" will be when you give the same "it" to me sometime in the future.

We can begin to see this more clearly if we do a simple transposition of Equation (1):

(2) $$\frac{A_0}{A_n} = \frac{1}{(1+r)^n} \quad , \quad A_0 = \frac{A_n}{(1+r)^n}$$

Clearly, the Equation (2) transposition demonstrates that for a given r, the ratio $1/(1+r)^n$ decreases as r increases — i.e., the future value is greater than the present value by compounding; and if you don't compound, your investment withers away at a rate expressed by this ratio. This is the essence of the time value of money.

Understanding this concept is very important, so that we can build on it and go forward with more real world applications.

Fundamental Equation (1) treats the specific case of how an initial amount to be invested, A_0, grows over time to become A_n. But a more general case occurs when an initial amount (investment), made at time zero, in a venture is followed by incomes and/or losses during each subsequent time period. Finally, at the end, the asset might be sold off. Even if it's not sold because you decide to keep it, the asset has a value, S, which is folded back into the year, i, cash flow. This so-called "salvage value" could be less than the original amount invested — maybe even zero or a loss — or it could be greater.

Therefore we are dealing with a series of negative and positive "cash flows" over time — that is CF_0, CF_1, CF_3, etc. Schematically, it looks like this:

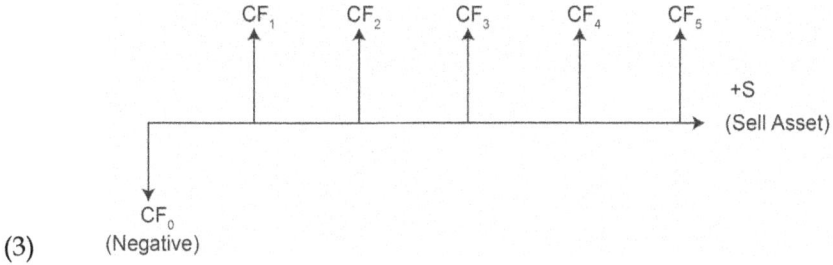

CF_1 CF_2 CF_3 CF_4 CF_5

+S
(Sell Asset)

CF_0
(3)   (Negative)

Our convention is for all outflows of funds to carry a negative (minus) sign, including the initial investment outlay, CF_0, and all inflows such as income and the final "salvage value", **S**, to be positive (plus). The CF_i are shorthand for cash flows in the ith period, positive or negative, at each time period.

The real world objective of the investor is to recover his initial outlay CF_0, as quickly as possible. After that, everything he earns is gravy! Obviously, the quicker the recovery, the higher the resultant "internal rate of return", IRR, assuming continuing earnings hold up and don't wipe out the value of a quick recovery of the initial outlay.

It's very important to understand the construct of (3), because this is how you can analyze all sorts of investments in terms of initial outlays, subsequent outlays for expansion or product improvement, and positive as well as negative cash flows. You simply have to strictly adhere to the plus and minus sign convention discussed above.

A note of clarification — — Cash Flow is the Net After Tax income in a given time period for an operating entity, plus Depreciation (and any other related items such as a mineral depletion allowance) charged in the Net After Tax income calculation. Secondly, any investments made at future time periods (for business expansion, product improvement, etc.) carry the negative sign convention, just like the initial investment, and are simply additive to that period's Cash Flow.

Now this is all well and good, but aren't earlier cash flows more valuable than later ones, on down the line? Absolutely!! That's what the "time value of money" is all about! So, how do we get all these future cash flows on an apples to apples basis with the earlier ones? Glad you asked!

Equation (2) clearly shows that early cash flows, CF_i, are worth more dollar for dollar than cash flows later on.

(2)
$$A_0 = \frac{A_n}{(1+r)^n}$$

So, a cash flow in the nth year is discountable back to its equivalent "present value" by the ratio, $1/(1 + r)^n$. That is to say that if you invest an amount, A_0, at time zero, at interest rate, r, A_0 becomes A_n in n compounding periods. Vice versa, A_n, discounts back to A_0, given r and n periods. This is called "discounting back to present value", an extremely important concept. This is how we can put all present and future cash flows on the same footing. And since the name of the game for the investor is to recover his outlays as quickly as possible, we now have a way to compute the value of IRR, the "internal rate of return" that would achieve the recovery, regardless of the pluses and minuses of future cash flows!

We can actually create a table/chart of the value of the ratio, $1/(1 + r)^n$, for a range of values for n and r.

Applying these to construct (3) of the investment problem, you can discount all future cash flows back to present value, then sum them up and compare the sum to the initial outlay. Keep trying using a different value for the "internal rate of return", r, until you finally find a value for r that lets the sum of all discounted future cash flows exactly equal the initial outlay. Then you can pat yourself on the back, because, by laborious trial and error, you have found the highly sought after "internal rate of return"...the IRR...for your particular problem!

So-called iterative trial and error calculations like this, done by hand, are tedious and time-consuming. Still, I recommend that you do it this way until you have mastered the underlying concepts. This way, you will better understand and appreciate the calculations made by your hand held when you get to that point.

The essential Equations which capture all this are as follows:

$$(4) \qquad 0= \frac{CF_0}{(negative)} + \frac{CF_1}{(1+r)} + \frac{CF_2}{(1+r)^2} + \frac{CF_3}{(1+r)^3} + \cdots$$

Then we can write the generalized Equation,

$$(5) \qquad 0 = \frac{CF_0}{(negative)} + \sum_{i=1}^{i=n} \frac{CF_i}{(1+r)^i}$$

This Equation must be satisfied in order to exactly recover the initial outlay, CF_0. Note that the initial value of the outlay, CF_0, is a negative number. Simply, summing the net inflows at future periods, discounted to their present values, must exactly square off with the initial outlay in order to zero out. The rate of return that causes this to happen is the so-called "internal rate of return", IRR. This value has many practical uses in financial and investment analysis. It is a convenient yardstick by which alternate investments can be compared.

Some analysts create what is called a "hurdle rate" against which any proposed investment must be compared. Hurdle rates may be expressed as a function of the level of risk associated with an investment — riskier investments would of necessity require higher hurdle rates to justify them.

The format of Equation (5) readily permits you to conduct "sensitivity analyses", another extremely useful and practical application. For example, you can calculate how increases or decreases of future cash flow streams impact the IRR. It's useful to understand, for example, the possible future conditions under which the IRR falls below the required hurdle rate.

I don't mean to muddy the water, but by introducing probability analysis into the mix, even greater sophistication is possible. I won't elaborate on these so-called "stochastic" methods here, because you will be very well situated indeed if you can master the basic approaches to "present value", cash flow, IRR and sensitivity analysis we've already discussed. I can't resist tempting you with just a clue to the application of stochastic methods. Just ask yourself the question, "What is the probability of achieving my cash flow projections in Year 1? Year 2? Year 3? And so on. By multiplying each probability by its respective projected cash flow, you create what is called "Expected Cash Flows". Then, following the routine of Equation (5) by discounting these Expected values back to their present values and summing them up, you end up with the "Expected IRR".

Fortunately, modern hand held calculators are able to greatly simplify all the time consuming and tedious trial and error calculations required in investment analysis. I mentioned two of these earlier, the Hewlett-Packard business calculator; and the one I prefer, the Texas Instruments BA II Plus. Learning to use the calculators adeptly takes practice, but it's definitely worth the effort and can pay you big dividends.

Just a final philosophical note...Compound interest is strictly a phenomena of our earthbound existence...God's Kingdom of Heaven is timeless!

www.ingramcontent.com/pod-product-compliance
Lightning Source LLC
Chambersburg PA
CBHW021502090426
42739CB00007B/432